The **Essential** Guide TO

Overcoming Obsessive Love

by Monique Belton, Ph.D., and Eileen Bailey

ALPHA

A member of Penguin Group (USA) Inc.

ALPHA BOOKS

Published by the Penguin Group

Penguin Group (USA) Inc., 375 Hudson Street, New York, NY 10014, USA

Penguin Group (Canada), 90 Eglinton Avenue East, Suite 700, Toronto, Ontario M4P 2Y3, Canada (a division of Pearson Penguin Canada Inc.)

Penguin Books Ltd., 80 Strand, London WC2R 0RL, England

Penguin Ireland, 25 St. Stephen's Green, Dublin 2, Ireland (a division of Penguin Books Ltd.)

Penguin Group (Australia), 250 Camberwell Road, Camberwell, Victoria 3124, Australia (a division of Pearson Australia Group Pty. Ltd.)

Penguin Books India Pvt. Ltd., 11 Community Centre, Panchsheel Park, New Delhi—110 017, India

Penguin Group (NZ), 67 Apollo Drive, Rosedale, North Shore, Auckland 1311, New Zealand (a division of Pearson New Zealand Ltd.)

Penguin Books (South Africa) (Pty.) Ltd., 24 Sturdee Avenue, Rosebank, Johannesburg 2196, South Africa

Penguin Books Ltd., Registered Offices: 80 Strand, London WC2R 0RL, England

Copyright © 2011 by Eileen Bailey

International Standard Book Number: 978-1-61564-0-904
Library of Congress Catalog Card Number: 2010917069

13   12   11   8   7   6   5   4   3   2   1

Interpretation of the printing code: The rightmost number of the first series of numbers is the year of the book's printing; the rightmost number of the second series of numbers is the number of the book's printing. For example, a printing code of 11-1 shows that the first printing occurred in 2011.

Printed in the United States of America

Note: This publication contains the opinions and ideas of its authors. It is intended to provide helpful and informative material on the subject matter covered. It is sold with the understanding that the authors and publisher are not engaged in rendering professional services in the book. If the reader requires personal assistance or advice, a competent professional should be consulted.

The authors and publisher specifically disclaim any responsibility for any liability, loss, or risk, personal or otherwise, which is incurred as a consequence, directly or indirectly, of the use and application of any of the contents of this book.

Most Alpha books are available at special quantity discounts for bulk purchases for sales promotions, premiums, fund-raising, or educational use. Special books, or book excerpts, can also be created to fit specific needs.

For details, write: Special Markets, Alpha Books, 375 Hudson Street, New York, NY 10014.

Publisher: *Marie Butler-Knight*

Associate Publisher: *Mike Sanders*

Executive Managing Editor: *Billy Fields*

Senior Acquisitions Editor: *Paul Dinas*

Senior Development Editor: *Phil Kitchel*

Senior Production Editor: *Janette Lynn*

Copy Editor: *Monica Stone*

Cover Designer: *Rebecca Batchelor*

Book Designers: *William Thomas, Rebecca Batchelor*

Indexer: *Julie Bess*

Layout: *Ayanna Lacey*

Proofreader: *Laura Caddell*

Dedication

Monique Belton: My deepest gratitude goes to my beloved parents, Mildred and York, for sharing their struggles and triumphs over obsessive love.

Eileen Bailey: This is dedicated to my husband, who is my strength, my inspiration, my lover, and my best friend.

Contents

Introduction

The phrase "obsessive love" is deceiving. It isn't love at all. Love—healthy love—is built on trust and mutual respect. In healthy love relationships, both partners want the other to be happy and secure; each wants their partner to reach for their dreams. They work together. Obsessive love, on the other hand, is built on fear and insecurity. An obsessive lover is afraid. He is afraid of losing his partner, afraid of being rejected, afraid of being abandoned. And it is this fear that drives the relationship. It is this fear that creates jealousy and possessiveness.

Most obsessive relationships don't last. The partner of the obsessive lover frequently becomes tired of her partner's overwhelming needs. She feels smothered, unable to go out without a barrage of questioning—or worse. She feels stifled because her own needs are also placed behind the needs of her partner. Most of the time, the partner of the obsessive lover ends the relationship.

This book addresses both sides of an obsessive relationship. For those who are obsessive and don't want to be—because you've seen how it consistently damages your relationships—we talk about events in your past that may have led to your fears. You may have been abandoned as a child or your early years were spent in a dysfunctional family. We discuss how to go about overcoming your fear of rejection so you can enjoy and embrace real love.

For the partners of obsessive lovers, we discuss what emotional needs this relationship might fill for you. It may be that you grew up in a house without love so, in the early stages of the relationship, the intensity of your partner's feelings makes you feel secure. But as the relationship goes on, you instead feel smothered. This book will help you find ways to make your present relationship better or help you not make the same mistakes in future relationships.

As you read through this book you'll find many case studies and examples. These are based on discussions of personal histories but are not exact histories. All of the names are fictitious. In addition, we have used "he" to describe the obsessive lover and "she" to refer to the partner of an obsessive lover. This was done for ease of writing only. It is not meant to suggest that obsessive lovers are all male and their partners are all female. Obsessive lovers can be male or female, young or old. They can be in heterosexual or same-sex relationships.

What's in This Book

We have tried to keep this book basic, giving you the information you need to understand how you ended up either as an obsessive lover or the partner of an obsessive lover. We have provided some broad concepts of love and the differences between healthy relationships and obsessive relationships. If we needed to use some technical words, we've provided definitions to help you; and there is a glossary at the end of the book with definitions of many terms used in the book.

This book is divided into five parts. Some sections are addressed to the obsessive lover, some to the partners, and some are written for both partners.

Part 1, Obsessive Love, covers all the basic information. It explains what obsessive love is, what it looks like, and some of the warning signs. We explain how an obsessive love relationship develops, from the initial romantic stage to what happens when the relationship ends. We compare a healthy love relationship to an obsessive love relationship and separate the facts from the myths.

Part 2, The Obsessive Lover, is geared to understanding what causes someone to become obsessive in their relationship. It explains how feelings of security, acceptance, and physical attraction can be confused with love, and why this can develop into obsession. We talk about some of the common obsessive behaviors and provide tips to changing these behaviors. We cover how your fear of rejection can result in self-destructive behaviors, like substance abuse or self-punishment, and what you can do to work on overcoming these behaviors.

Part 3, The Partner of an Obsessive Lover, is for the partners. We cover the fear of confrontation, the emotional ups and downs of living in a controlling relationship, and steps you can take to improve your relationships. We also cover how some of your behaviors can actually contribute to your partner's obsessiveness and how changing your actions can improve your relationship.

Part 4, Freedom from Obsessive Love, discusses how events from your past influence your self-image and how to change your attitude so you have a healthier self-image. We also cover what role counseling and therapy play in overcoming obsessive love and what to expect during counseling sessions. In the last two chapters we address developing healthy relationships, both for the obsessive lovers and their partners. We offer plenty of self-help exercises to help you form a positive self-image.

Part 5, When Obsessive Love Becomes Dangerous, addresses the instances when obsessiveness includes stalking or violence. We explain stalking and domestic violence and the warning signs of danger. We offer advice on how to protect yourself and guide you through some of the basics of using the law to obtain an order of protection.

Extras

We have provided a lot of information on understanding and overcoming obsessive love. Our sidebars offer even more information:

These help you understand terms related to obsessive love.

These offer tips and ideas to help you change your behaviors and develop a healthy outlook on love.

These provide warnings on behaviors that signal an unhealthy lover or the characteristics of obsessive love, as well as strategies to help overcome obsessive love.

Case Studies

These are examples of individuals or couples struggling with many of the issues surrounding obsessive love.

Did You Know?

These offer facts, figures and statistics about obsessive love.

You'll also see a fourth, name-changing sidebar that presents anecdotes, interesting facts, case histories, or other extended background information you should know.

Acknowledgments

Monique Belton: My deepest gratitude goes to my beloved parents, Mildred and York, who were a constant source of support and belief in me. Thanks, Mom, for being my best friend. I also thank my brother, Marc, for his savvy wisdom and for always reminding me of the bigger picture. I am thankful also for the help of Alyssa McDonald, for her friendship and listening ear. I am also grateful to Larry Julian, author of *God Is My CEO* for sharing his insights as a writer. Thanks to Bob Sandy who brought last minute support and humor. I am also deeply indebted to my clients who, by sharing their hearts and emotions with me, were a constant source of inspiration. I also appreciate all of the help countless others gave me along the way.

Eileen Bailey: Many thanks to my husband and children, who stepped up and managed the household while I took time to write this book. My deepest appreciation and respect for all those professionals who dedicate their lives to help individuals struggling to overcome unhealthy, obsessive relationships, especially those working with victims of domestic violence. Thank you to all those who shared their personal stories with me and allowed me to create examples of obsessive love throughout this book based on their experiences. I would also like to thank my agent, Marilyn Allen, for all of her hard work in making this book a reality; and Paul Dinas, Phil Kitchel, and the many other professionals at Alpha Books for their patience and invaluable input as we brought this book from an initial concept to completion.

Trademarks

All terms mentioned in this book that are known to be or are suspected of being trademarks or service marks have been appropriately capitalized. Alpha Books and Penguin Group (USA) Inc. cannot attest to the accuracy of this information. Use of a term in this book should not be regarded as affecting the validity of any trademark or service mark.

Part 1

Obsessive Love

Whether you are an obsessive lover or the partner of one, you probably want to understand what obsessive love is, and why you or your partner is so jealous or just can't stop trying to control the relationship. Or maybe you aren't sure whether your relationship is obsessive; you're wondering whether your or your partner's behaviors are normal or obsessive. Part 1 answers many of these questions.

From understanding how an obsessive relationship develops to the differences between obsessive and healthy love, we help you separate facts from myths and better understand exactly what an obsessive relationship is.

chapter 1

Understanding Obsessive Love

The differences between healthy and obsessive love

Defining acceptable social behavior vs. obsessive behavior

Clues that your relationship isn't right

We all want to find that special person—the one we can spend the rest of our life with. We want to feel special, know that our love is thinking of us and wants to spend time with us. A relationship built on love brings joy into each day. But sometimes it is not love, it is obsession.

Obsessive love is, in reality, not love at all. It is an all-consuming preoccupation with another person. Obsessive lovers believe the person they are obsessed with is the only person who can make them happy.

What Is Obsessive Love?

Some obsessive love relationships are just mildly annoying. For example, Danny met Melissa at work. He was immediately infatuated and asked her out to dinner. Melissa turned Danny down, but week after week, Danny tried again. He couldn't stop thinking about her and couldn't seem to let go of the notion that, if he kept trying, one of these weeks Melissa would say yes. Melissa was amused at times, flattered at times, and annoyed at times, but Danny's obsession seemed harmless—and it never interfered with her job—so she mostly ignored his advances.

At the other end of the spectrum are the obsessive lovers whose behaviors are more extreme. Most obsessive love relationships fall somewhere in between. Obsessive behaviors can interfere with developing healthy relationships and hurt both partners. With help and support, both obsessive lovers and their partners can learn to find healthy love relationships.

> **True Love**
>
> Relationships based on love offer mutual support and compassion. Both partners understand and appreciate the need for each partner to have outside interests. Obsessive lovers often stop a partner from going out in order to keep them in the relationship. Even if your partner is possessive, continue to pursue your own interests.

Each obsessive lover is different: you might be overcome with jealousy, while another may focus so intently on the relationship, he ignores his job and friends. Despite the differences, the majority of obsessive love relationships share some similarities:

- The obsessive lover develops an all-consuming preoccupation with another person.

- Obsessive lovers believe the other person is the one and only love of his life, and only this person can make him happy.

- Obsessive love behaviors are triggered by rejection or abandonment, or the fear of being rejected or abandoned.

- The obsessive lover is convinced his partner cannot be happy without him, and he cannot live without his partner.

Throughout this book, we use the pronouns *he* or *him* to describe the obsessive lover, and *she* or *her* to describe the partner of the obsessive lover. This doesn't mean all obsessive lovers are male and the partners are female. Obsessive lovers can be male or female; they can be young or old. Obsessive love is defined by behaviors, not gender or age.

>
> **obsession Alert**
>
> In obsessive love relationships, there is an immediate and intense physical attraction. Obsessive lovers often rush into a sexual relationship before developing an emotional bond with their partner. Because of the intensity of their attraction, they think there is an emotional bond.

Social Norms vs. Obsessive Love Behaviors

There are a number of unspoken, unwritten socially acceptable behaviors. We may not know all the rules, but we know when these rules have been broken or overstepped. For example, Penny and Jack are attracted to one another and decide to go out on a date. Penny meets Jack at a local restaurant, and during dinner they find they share many of the same interests. The evening passes quickly as they discover they both like thriller movies, the beach, and gardening.

At the end of the evening, Penny returns home and tells her roommate she liked Jack; he was nice, he was polite, and he was attentive. If he asks, she would go out with him again. Penny goes to bed, wondering if he will call but looking forward to the plans she has made with friends for the following day.

Jack, meanwhile, is exuberant. He is thrilled he and Penny had so much in common and he can't stop thinking about her. As soon as he arrives home, he texts her, "Had a wonderful time, hope you did, too." Penny is already asleep and doesn't respond. Jack gets worried, thinking Penny doesn't feel the same way. He texts again, an hour later, "Thinking of you," and again the next hour, "Can't wait to see you again." By the time Penny wakes up, she has 10 unanswered texts on her phone. She thinks Jack is sweet, but she's overwhelmed and decides it's a bit much.

True Love	Set boundaries and limitations in the early stages of a relationship if you think it is moving too quickly. By slowing down and spending less time together you can see the relationship more clearly and decide whether you want it to continue.

There are no hard and fast rules that say when or how often you should call after a first date, and, in today's world of texting and instant communication, an obsessive lover can easily become carried away. Penny just instinctively knows Jack has crossed the line. She might have been flattered receiving one text on her phone, accepting of two, but ten was way too much.

But even though Penny found Jack's behavior overwhelming, someone else might find it flattering and enjoy the attention, at least in the beginning. You might be lonely, living in a new city; or you might have grown up in a strict household, where displays of love and affection were rare. Unlike

Penny, you quickly respond to the texts, reveling in the feeling of "being wanted." You might enjoy the rapid texting and the excitement of getting to know someone quickly. The next day, you make plans to meet again. Without realizing it, you could be stepping into an obsessive relationship. It might bring out some obsessive tendencies in you!

Questions about *social norms* will continue throughout your relationship life. A new lover might wonder about your level of commitment, or whether you are ready to make a commitment at all. How much questioning is too much? When does behavior move from acceptable to unacceptable? The answer is different for each relationship and changes at each level of a relationship, but a general rule is if you are uncomfortable, feel threatened, or long for your freedom, your partner has probably overstepped your boundaries. And if you spend all your time worrying about the relationship, where your partner is, and what she is doing, you may be obsessive.

Definition

Social norms are rules within a society or group that determine acceptable and unacceptable behaviors. These rules may be unwritten, but are understood within the group and are different depending on the group's individual culture. Social norms define appropriate social interactions.

Romantic Love and Obsessive Love Similarities

The early stage of a relationship is known as the romantic stage, when love is easy and carefree. Partners tend to ignore differences and focus on similarities or shared interests. There is suddenly a "we" instead of "me and you," and it feels wonderful and exhilarating.

Expectations during the romantic stage are high. You begin to envision the future and how the other person fits into it. You believe that most of your needs and wants will be met by the other person. You idealize them. As the relationship continues, you feel ready to make a commitment that says, "I am going to share being in love with you. I will not pursue being in love with anyone else."

Whether it's a romantic or obsessive relationship, you feel an intense physical attraction in the early stage. You might express your feelings by holding hands, touching your partner's arm while talking, or making eye contact from across the room. Gifts, love notes, and other expressions of love are common during this stage. As a new couple, you usually spend as much time as possible together, making time to see each other, even missing other social events. When you can't be together, you stay in touch via the phone, texting, and/or e-mail. In healthy relationships, this communication is mutual; in obsessive relationships, it is often one-sided.

The following examples compare two new relationships, one healthy and the other showing signs of obsessiveness.

Tom met Marsha through a mutual friend. They began dating and for the next few weeks spent as much time together as possible. One day at work, Marsha was surprised by a dozen roses and a note that said, "Thinking of you." They talked every day and looked forward to their dates on weekends. When Marsha was out with friends and they asked about Tom, she smiled, and her happiness was evident to everyone. Tom was the same way. After dating for a year, Tom proposed and Marsha accepted.

Around the same time, Alex met Sandy. They also began dating. Alex was head over heels in love. Sandy also received flowers at work, every week. They spoke every day, usually three or four times. Sandy was excited and talked about Alex to all her friends. Alex couldn't stop thinking about Sandy. They began to spend weekends together almost immediately. Within a few months, however, Sandy was feeling smothered. Alex didn't want her to do anything by herself and tagged along when she met friends after work, saying he couldn't bear to be without her. After six months, Sandy broke up with Alex.

Both of these relationships started out the same; the romance, the intense feelings, and the passion were similar. Both couples wanted to be together, both couples thought about each other all the time. But while Tom and Marsha were developing an emotional bond, Alex was holding Sandy too tightly, afraid of losing her. His possessiveness drove her away.

In the beginning of a relationship, obsessive love and healthy romantic love look a whole lot alike. Both are characterized by both partners …

- Feeling strong physical attraction.
- Having constant thoughts of one another.

- Looking at the relationship through rose-colored glasses, seeing only the good in their partner.

- Feeling insecure about the relationship, not sure whether it will end up as long term.

Even in the beginning, you may have doubts or see the warning signs of an obsessive relationship, but ignore them or make excuses. After all, most early relationships look and feel similar to obsessive relationships. Even if the warning signs are blatantly obvious, other issues, such as recently getting over a neglectful lover, can cause you to ignore the signs and suddenly you are dealing with someone who is obsessed with you.

obsession Alert

In the early stages of a relationship, the nonobsessive partner is considering the possibility of a shared future, but the obsessive partner has already determined that this is his one and only love who will be his partner for life and begins to make plans for the future. There is no room for doubt.

Warning Signs

You might have nagging doubts about the relationship you are in. Maybe previous partners have called you controlling or accused you of smothering them and you are trying not to ruin this relationship. Or maybe you, as the partner, see some behaviors that are sending up warning flags, but you aren't sure if you are being too sensitive.

Misc.

Case Study: Ronnie and Patricia

Obsessive love sometimes begins within hours or days of a new relationship. Ronnie and Patricia met online. After corresponding via e-mail, they agreed to meet, even though they lived far apart. Ronnie flew in from Pennsylvania to Arizona for the weekend. A few weeks later, Patricia flew to Pennsylvania. She began talking about marriage and planning their future—even discussing selling her belongings to move in with Ronnie.

Patricia went home and Ronnie tried to slow things down. Instead of backing away, Patricia showed up again, unannounced, intending to spend a week with Ronnie. He finally broke it off and she returned to Arizona. Ronnie stopped accepting her calls, but she called his friends every few days to find out what he was doing. Not until months later did she finally stop calling.

Read each of the following questions. For each one that describes your relationship, read the short description following for more information, ideas on making the relationship work, or deciding to leave.

Is the relationship moving quickly?

If after a few weeks you think you have found the love of your life, or your partner is already professing undying love, it may be a sign of obsessiveness. You might want to set some boundaries, slow down a bit, or put limits on how much time you spend together.

Do you want to spend every moment with someone? Do you worry about the relationship when you are not together? Does your partner want to go everywhere with you or stay in constant contact when you're not together?

The insecurities and uncertainties that accompany any new love often bring out some obsessive qualities, but there is a difference between wanting to be with someone and needing to be with her to feel secure. If you feel like you need this relationship to survive, the information and self-help exercises throughout this book will help you determine why you can't get past your insecurities in your relationships.

Do you panic at the thought of losing this person? Or does your partner want constant reassurance that you are committed to the relationship?

Obsessive lovers often make "deals" saying they will change something or do something in order to make their partner stay in a relationship; others use guilt. If you remain in a relationship not because you want to, but because staying is easier than leaving, it's probably a sign of problems to come. If someone needs constant reassurance—no matter how much you try—it isn't going to be enough to make him feel secure. You need to decide if this is the type of relationship you want.

Do you want to "fix" your partner? Or does your partner continuously find little things you do wrong or criticize you because he wants you to be better?

An obsessive lover holds on to their relationship by making their partner believe that no one else could ever care more about her. He cares enough to make sure you are the best person possible—and to do that, he finds everything you do wrong and lets you know what to do to improve yourself. Constant criticism kills your self-confidence, leaving you to believe no one else would want you because you are "too fat," "too lazy," or "too stupid." Chapter 16 provides suggestions and exercises to improve your self-image.

Are you concerned every time your partner gets together with friends or relatives because they may try to persuade her not to be with you? Or does your partner complain every time you make plans to see friends or attend a family function? Does he put your friends and family down or tell you they are not good for you or are taking advantage of you?

Obsessive lovers need you to themselves. They see every other person in your life as competition for your time and a threat to your relationship. You should never need to give up your friends or your interests for another person. Continue to pursue activities outside the relationship, while offering reassurance to your partner.

Does your relationship go in cycles, from fights to making up or from turbulence to peace, on a regular basis? Does your partner act mean and hurtful one day and sweet the next day?

The obsessive lover knows when he has gone too far and is in danger of losing the relationship. He then covers his back, being extra attentive and extra nice, to show how sorry he is. The obsessed partner is drawn back in, hoping this is finally the last time—the turning point. This behavior might not be conscious; it can be a learned behavior. The obsessive lover goes too far, then as his partner reacts to his concern and apologies, he learns what will work to bring his partner back.

obsession Alert

Be careful if your partner won't respect your privacy. Obsessive lovers frequently don't respect boundaries; they may snoop into your personal life or even contact friends and relatives to find out information. This behavior can begin within days or weeks of the start of a relationship or may not show up until some event, such as becoming engaged or going away to school, triggers the obsessive feelings.

Usually relationships that begin this way continue this way. When you are in an obsessive relationship, it is hard to see the behaviors as wrong or abnormal, and the longer you stay the more normal the obsessive behaviors and your reactions become. Your thoughts are focused on making sure your partner knows how much you care, rather than on your own self-growth and happiness. You might avoid social situations with friends or co-workers, or become more and more frantic about making sure your house is perfectly cleaned or dinner is just right.

As the obsessive lover, you justify your behaviors because keeping and controlling your relationship is the most important thing in your life. It is all that matters, and the end justifies the means. You will do whatever it takes to make sure the relationship continues.

Fantasy Obsessions

Obsessive love often forms inside of a relationship, when the fear of rejection overcomes all sense of security and an obsessive lover acts in irrational ways to hold on to a partner, even when both are unhappy. But sometimes obsessive love develops in other situations, when the obsessive lover is infatuated with someone he barely knows or may have never even met.

I Want You, So You Want Me

You meet someone at the coffee shop, maybe even have one or two dates, but no relationship develops. Still, you feel a deep physical attraction. As an obsessive lover, you feel drawn to this person and begin to mistake these feelings for love. You can't stop thinking of her and visiting the place you met again and again, hoping to see her again. You put emphasis on little things. She might have given you a compliment or touched your arm when talking to you. These, to you, are signs of interest.

Marian is an example of this type of obsessive love. Marian met John at the laundromat on a Thursday evening. Marian had seen him there before and thought he was cute, but had never spoken to him. But that evening they stood side by side, loading clothes into the washers, and began talking. While they both waited for their clothes to finish, they laughed and joked. By the time they were done, she had given him her phone number. But John never called. Marian was sure something was wrong, that he meant to call but lost her number, or maybe he had misunderstood. In Marian's mind, John had felt the same spark she did. Over and over she told herself,

"He must have felt it, too." She couldn't understand why he didn't call; it made no sense.

Marian could barely think of anything else—seeing John again was all that mattered. She drove by the laundromat every night. She turned down invitations from friends to do anything on Thursdays because she "needed" to do her wash every week at the same time, just in case John was there.

Marian's situation is not uncommon. Any one of us can meet someone and instantly wonder about the possibilities; the issue is whether we become obsessive. It's not the feeling but how much, how often, and what actions we take that determines whether we are infatuated or obsessed.

Imaginary Relationships

Although less common, some people become infatuated with someone they've never met. Picture the teenage girl, "in love" with the latest heart-throb. She imagines herself meeting him and falling in love. She might write letters to him, research him on the Internet, write his name over and over, and fantasize about their future together. We have all heard stories about obsessed fans who go to great lengths to get the attention of their fantasy lover.

Fantasy relationships don't have to involve a superstar. It could be your neighbor down the street or a co-worker, someone you don't know and have never shared a relationship with. But as time goes on, the fantasy grows. You create an entire relationship in your mind, imagining places you would go together and conversations you would have.

obsession Alert

If you are not able to function or complete regular daily activities such as caring for yourself, going to work, or completing normal chores because of continuous thoughts about someone else, you may be obsessed. Even if you continue to go to work and care for yourself, but your free time is spent thinking about or doing something related to the object of your affection, you might be obsessed.

Even though this sounds similar to the harmless infatuation of the teenage girl, this type of obsession can still cause problems. Ignoring other responsibilities or ignoring friends can result just as much from a fantasy obsession as an obsession with a person you know.

Essential Takeaways

- Obsessive lovers believe the person with whom they are obsessed is the only person who can make them happy or bring meaning to their life.
- An obsessive lover has a tremendous fear of being rejected.
- The early stages of a relationship, called romantic love, often resemble obsessive love.
- Panic at the thought of losing a partner is one warning sign of obsessive love.

chapter 2

The Anatomy of Obsessive Love Relationships

The four stages of obsessive relationships

Giving up being an individual for being part of a couple

How the ending of the relationship impacts the obsessive lover

From romance to emotional bonds in healthy relationships

This chapter looks at how obsessive love develops. You probably want to improve your relationship or get help so you won't repeat the same mistakes in your next relationship. It is important to know how you progressed from flirting to controlling, or being controlled.

Keep in mind that each relationship is different and your relationship may never develop to some of the extremes listed in this chapter or in this book—even after years of being together.

How Obsessive Love Develops

This chapter follows an imaginary couple, Tony and Jenna, as their relationship changes and follows the struggles each partner goes through. Again, many individuals involved in obsessive love relationships will never experience the extreme behaviors outlined in the later stages.

Romance

In Chapter 1, we talked about how obsessive love relationships resemble the romantic love of new relationships. Partners are often infatuated, ignoring differences and looking forward to a future full of possibilities. However, the obsessive partner may jump into the relationship too quickly, wanting to "get serious" or move the relationship to the next level almost immediately.

Tony and Jenna had only been dating for a few weeks when Tony declared his love. He had never met anyone like Jenna, he told his friends, "It was love at first sight." They saw or spoke to each other every day. To Tony, it was amazing how much they had in common. Both enjoyed taking long walks, shopping for antiques, and visiting historical sites. This coming weekend they had plans to go to the art museum. Tony was ready to move to the next level and discuss having an exclusive relationship. He was sure Jenna felt the same way.

Jenna was enjoying the time she spent with Tony and thought the relationship might grow into something serious. She thought Tony was funny, and liked that he could always make her laugh. It had been an enjoyable two weeks, but Jenna wasn't ready to make any commitments. She wanted to take her time and see where the relationship led. She was concerned that Tony was upset because she had plans to go out with friends on Friday night and she'd had to promise Tony they would still be going to the museum the following day. She understood Tony's feelings—he had a rough childhood and he had said several times he grew up in a house without love. Jenna knew he was just excited about the relationship. After all, they did have a lot of fun together. Jenna assumed that Tony would not need these reassurances as the relationship matured.

Jenna was willing to look past the warning flag Tony sent up when, after just two weeks, he didn't seem to want to share Jenna, even with her friends. The thrill and excitement of the relationship overshadowed any doubt Jenna had. Jenna had an underlying insecurity and her ego was boosted by his intense need for her.

True Love	When deciding if you want to move forward in your relationship, judge your partner as you would a friend. Does he show integrity? Do your personalities match? Are his values similar to yours? Do his words and actions match? How does he get along with others? Your partner should also be your friend. Make sure you get along together. Frequent arguments and disagreements in the early stages of a relationship should be a warning sign.

In a healthy love relationship, couples take time to get to know one another, discover what they have in common, learn to appreciate their differences, and share opinions and viewpoints on the world. The obsessive lover, on the other hand, usually begins fantasizing about lifelong love before a truly deep emotional connection has even had a chance to develop. The connection that does develop is based on physical attraction, for example, appearance, physical type, or a resemblance to someone you once loved. The connection is so strong the obsessive lover, or both partners, believe it is love, even though they may not know each other well.

If you or your partner have the feeling that you don't need time to get to know the other person because, "I feel as if I have known you all my life," it can be an illusion brought on by intense sexual attraction—and a warning sign of obsessive love. Jenna got caught up in the whirlwind of new romance and, like many of us, was willing to look past any negative qualities Tony had. Instead, she only focused on the romantic feelings of new love and ignored any doubts she felt.

You might be wondering if your new relationship is obsessive. You might be seeing signs of possessiveness or jealousy, or something doesn't feel right to you. The warning signs in Chapter 1 and the checklist at the end of this chapter can help you distinguish healthy love from obsessive love.

I'm Still an Individual

As a relationship develops, the initial infatuation usually gives way to wanting to be part of a couple, yet retain—or reclaim—your individuality. As an obsessive lover, this time in the relationship is extremely difficult. You don't want to be an individual—you only want to be part of a couple and you want your partner to feel the same. When she pulls away, to explore her own interests or join friends, you become anxious. You begin to question her, wanting to know what she has been doing, with whom, and where. You begin to question her loyalty and commitment. You may call throughout the day, send text messages or e-mails, and accuse her of cheating if you don't get an immediate reply; or stop by to see her, unannounced, to check up on her. Your partner begins to feel smothered.

Imagine that Tony and Jenna continue dating. Jenna still makes plans to spend time with her friends, but Tony is becoming more anxious about these evenings away from him. He doesn't understand why she doesn't want to spend all of her time with him. He worries about Jenna meeting someone else when she is out with her friends. The few times he has met her friends, they didn't seem to like him much, and he worries they will try to talk Jenna out of the relationship. On Saturday, he questions Jenna incessantly about the previous evening. What did she do? Where did they go? Who was there? Did any other guy speak to her? What did he say?

obsession Alert

It is not advisable to choose your partners based on whether friends and family approve. However, if all your friends have objections to a relationship, you might want to at least listen to their concerns and try to look at your relationship objectively.

Jenna likes Tony and likes spending time with him, but she is getting increasingly annoyed and frustrated with the questioning, the accusations, and the mistrust. She believes she is a trustworthy person and doesn't understand why Tony doesn't believe her. She doesn't have as much fun when she is with him as she did earlier in the relationship. Jenna is starting to feel smothered, and is thinking about breaking off the relationship.

At this point, as the partner of an obsessive lover, you think that maybe, given enough time, you will be able to make your partner see that you love him and that you can be trusted. "It isn't his fault," you tell yourself. "His parents didn't care; he never learned to trust anyone." You may believe your love will make the difference in his life; you will love him enough to soothe his jealousy and insecurities. You bounce between wanting to pursue your interests and wanting to have your partner believe in you. You are torn.

Total Obsession

Some relationships end at this time. If not, the obsession probably continues to escalate. As the obsessive lover, you need constant attention and reassurance from your partner. Some thoughts and behaviors that may occur at this point of the relationship are ...

- You think of nothing else besides the relationship, sometimes ignoring other responsibilities.

- You continually worry about your partner cheating.

- You sometimes accuse her of infidelity, even without any evidence.

- You may check up on her throughout the day, driving by her workplace or calling her continuously.

- You persistently question her commitment to the relationship.

- You resent any time she spends with other people and may manipulate her so she only spends time with you.

These behaviors can change as the relationship changes. When an obsessive lover feels secure, the behaviors may disappear completely. At other times, the behaviors may be overwhelming for the partner of the obsessive lover. Because of this, the partner can believe the behaviors have disappeared completely, only to be more confused when they resurface.

Case Study: Dawn and Todd

MISC.

Dawn and Todd were celebrating their fifth anniversary by going away for the weekend. Dawn wasn't sure why she was still in the relationship. She knew she should leave. Every day was a struggle—the accusations kept coming. Even this weekend, while they were supposed to be enjoying a romantic getaway, her husband was watching her every move. He even began a fight in the restaurant, saying she was flirting with the waiter. It was as if she couldn't look at someone without being accused of flirting or having a "secret boyfriend." In the beginning, she relished the attention, believing it showed how much he loved her, but instead of becoming more sure of her love, he seemed to trust her less with each passing day.

Tony and Jenna, by this time, are *dysfunctional* in their relationship. Tony has come close to losing his job. He works as a computer operator but lately has made some costly mistakes. His concentration is off; his thoughts are more focused on what Jenna is doing. He worries she is going to leave him for another man. Sometimes he worries so much he leaves work to check on her. He hasn't caught her with someone else yet, but he's sure he will.

Definition

Dysfunctional is impairment in the ability to function. Obsessive relationships can be dysfunctional if conflict occurs regularly and one partner acts in a way that is accommodating to the controlling partner.

Tony monitors everything Jenna does; even when she goes to the grocery store, he times how long she is gone and questions her if it takes longer than expected. She has given up her Friday nights with her friends because it isn't worth the argument that will undoubtedly occur before or after. Jenna spends her days trying to do everything right, trying not to upset Tony. She is unhappy and unsatisfied, but she isn't sure how to get back her freedom. She worries about what Tony will do if she leaves—and even if he *will* let her leave. But Jenna has to take that chance. She leaves him.

This is where this relationship ends. Some end before it comes to this, and some end at an even more drastic place—you have finally had enough. You cannot take the constant barrage of accusations, the controlling behavior, and the neediness of your obsessive lover. You are ready to reclaim control of your life. You may still love your partner, but you love yourself more. You want to be happy again.

If you are the obsessive lover, you are in pain; there is fear, anxiety, sadness, rage, a roller coaster of intense emotions. All you want is for the relationship to continue. It's all you think about, all you care about. Your job, your family—none of it means anything if you can't have the relationship.

After It's Over

Once the relationship ends, as the obsessive lover, you may become depressed and despondent, or you may become aggressive. You might try to reenter the romantic stage, sending gifts, apologizing, and working to win back your partner. You don't see any future without her.

Tony couldn't believe Jenna had left. At first he told himself she just needed a break; that she would be back. When she didn't return his calls and refused to see him, he began to panic. She wasn't just rejecting the relationship, she was rejecting *him*. He called, he texted, he did everything he could think of, but Jenna ignored his efforts. Tony was sure there was another man involved, someone telling Jenna what to do.

obsession Alert

In obsessive relationships, both partners can end up feeling isolated from friends and family. Obsessive lovers often manipulate situations to keep their partner to themselves. If your relationship is ending, try to reconnect with friends to find emotional support.

Jenna went back and forth. She was sure leaving was the right thing to do, but she felt guilty. Maybe if she went back he would change. But she knew going back wouldn't change anything; Tony wasn't going to stop being obsessive and controlling.

The ending of an obsessive relationship is difficult for everyone. As the obsessive lover, you feel as if your life is falling apart, that nothing will ever be right again. As the target of an obsession, you are emotionally exhausted and sometimes frightened. Moreover, despite all the pain, both partners are still emotionally attached to each other.

As we saw with Jenna, when you have invested so much into a relationship this is never an easy decision. You may have doubts, wonder if you are doing the right thing, or waver between going back and staying away. The partner of an obsessive lover often leaves many times, only to come back again—sometimes because of guilt, sometimes because once you leave, you focus on the good times in the relationship and want to try again.

As the partner of an obsessive lover, leaving a relationship doesn't make the pain go away. You may continue to wonder ...

- What you did to provoke the behaviors.

- Why you didn't see the warning signs.

- If your actions somehow contributed to the obsession.

- Why he didn't take you seriously, or listen to you when you said, "No."

- Why you can't help him.

As the obsessive lover, you may blame your partner, feeling betrayed. You may wonder why your partner left, feeling as if your only fault was loving your partner too much. Or it may seem as if you are the party at fault. But your pain is real as well. You feel the intense pain of a failed relationship. Ghosts from your past become jumbled, making you feel unlovable.

When two people begin dating, there are many different possible endings. During the romantic stage, both visualize and dream of the future. They envision happy endings, undying love, and the furor of passion lasting a lifetime. No one pictures the relationship ending with the pain associated with obsessive love.

Healthy Love vs. Obsessive Love

In the beginning, there is some blurring of the differences between healthy love and obsessive love. As the relationship develops, however, these differences become more obvious.

The Stages of Healthy Relationships

Just as an obsessive relationship progresses through different stages, so do healthy relationships. Most relationships go through the following stages:

- Romantic love

- Learning about each other

- Acceptance of positive and negative qualities in the partner

- Commitment

- Stability

There is normally a physical attraction in the beginning of a healthy love relationship. During this, the romantic love stage, each person puts forth their best self, working hard to impress the other person. Conflict is avoided because it threatens the relationship.

In the stage that follows, partners learn to communicate with one another and accept each other's differences. You learn to expand your horizons and learn about your new partner's interests. Maybe you've never been interested in football, but your new partner enjoys watching football every Sunday. You might take time to learn about the game so you can spend Sunday afternoons together, or at least understand when he talks about football. You also expect your partner to take an interest in your hobbies. At the same time, you don't need to be together every minute. You have "together" interests and you have "individual" interests.

True Love	No matter what stage of a relationship you may be in, communication is important. When couples begin to experience problems, communication is one of the first areas to disintegrate. Any efforts to work on improving a relationship need to start with communication. Set aside a specific time to talk with one another and agree this time will be free of yelling, screaming, or insulting one another. Each partner should feel free to express their opinions.

Imagine Tony and Jenna's relationship taking a different path. Rather than being controlling, possessive, and jealous, Tony could have embraced Jenna's desire to spend Friday nights with her friends—and made plans to get together with his friends as well. Then when they saw one another on Saturday, they could share lively conversation about their evenings out and share stories about what they did. The time away would actually bring them closer.

In the third stage, you accept both the positive and negative qualities of one another, while focusing on shared interests and beliefs. During this stage, your emotional bond deepens. You are learning to communicate honestly with one another while accepting that you don't always need to agree. When the relationship reaches a certain point, you are ready to make a commitment. In healthy relationships, this commitment is mutual. Both partners are ready to take the next step.

If we imagine Tony and Jenna in a healthy, rather than an obsessive, relationship, we can envision them celebrating their one year anniversary. Tony would be thrilled with the relationship, excited that he found a compassionate, caring person like Jenna. Even though her job requires her to travel once in a while and he would miss her when she's gone, he would enjoy listening to stories about her trips when she returns. He would be proud of her accomplishments at work and admire her determination. Tony would be thinking about proposing.

Jenna would find it hard to believe an entire year went by. She would like that Tony still makes her laugh and when they're together life is good. She would be thrilled that Tony's job is going well. Sometimes they might find that work is busy and they don't get to spend as much time together as they would like, but it makes being together that much better. Jenna would be sure they can spend the rest of their lives together.

obsession Alert

In obsessive, unhealthy relationships, trust usually doesn't develop. The obsessive partner remains untrusting, accusing the other person of cheating no matter how much time has passed. Many times jealousy gets worse as time goes on. Sometimes it only appears when the relationship becomes more committed. As the partner of an obsessive lover, you might be flattered by the jealousy at first, "It shows how much he cares."

As time goes on in a healthy relationship, trust grows. The partners become more comfortable with each other and develop a deep respect for one another. Although the exhilaration of romance doesn't usually last forever, an emotional bond grows in its place. The feelings of romance—the high energy, giddiness, and euphoria common in new relationships—still bloom from time to time, such as on a vacation, when working toward a shared goal, or when you spend quality time together. These moments are important and renew your sense of togetherness and love.

Relationship Quiz

The following compares some of the typical behaviors of obsessive love with those found in healthy love relationships. In each pair, check which description best fits your relationship.

❏ Open, honest communication is important to both partners.

❏ I hold back my opinions because I'm scared of making my partner angry; *or* I am not willing to listen to my partner's opinion.

❏ Both of us share and are open about our commitment to the relationship. Our level of commitment is balanced and we are not worried our partner is going to leave.

❏ The relationship is unbalanced; my partner wants the relationship more than I do; *or* I always worry my partner is going to leave.

❑ Neither of us feels the need to test the other's loyalty.

❑ Despite my partner telling me she loves me, I still constantly ask for reassurance; *or* my partner continually questions my commitment to the relationship.

❑ Both my partner and I enjoy activities outside the relationship.

❑ My partner gets upset and jealous when I want to spend time with other friends; *or* I get anxious when she wants to go out with friends or do something without me.

❑ My partner and I encourage each other to continue relationships with friends and family.

❑ My partner has asked me to choose between my family and him; *or* my partner's family doesn't like me and I don't want her spending time with them.

❑ We respect each other's opinions and beliefs, even if they are different. We can disagree without being disagreeable.

❑ I usually shy away from expressing opinions that differ from my partner's. It may be more a matter of avoidance of possible conflict; *or* I feel threatened if my partner doesn't share my opinions.

❑ We are concerned about each other's happiness.

❑ My partner tells me he cares but acts as if he only cares about his own needs; *or,* I do care, but I need her to understand what I need.

❑ If I need space, my partner respects my wishes, as I do for him.

❑ My partner gets angry if I ask for space; *or* I don't see why she needs space when being together should make her feel better.

If you have checked even a few of the second choices in each set, you may be in an obsessive relationship. Support groups and therapy can help. Part 4 discusses different ways to cope with an obsessive relationship and work toward a healthy relationship. If you don't want to stay together, the strategies in that part can help you to not repeat the same mistakes in your next relationship.

Essential Takeaways

- During the romantic stage of a relationship, obsessive partners frequently rush to move to the next level, wanting to get serious quickly.
- The obsessive lover resists the partner in maintaining friendships and other interests outside the relationship.
- In healthy relationships, partners learn to accept both positive and negative traits in the other person.
- Communication is stilted in obsessive love relationships because the nonobsessive partner may be afraid to speak her opinion.

chapter 3

Myths About Obsessive Love

Romantic love vs. obsessive love

Differences between obsessive compulsive disorder and obsessive love

Possible outcomes of obsessive love relationships

Love as a tool to fix your partner

Do you believe love must be intense and all-consuming to be "real"? Do you believe if someone is jealous it's a sign of how much he loves you? Do you think there is no hope for a relationship with someone who is obsessed?

These questions represent just some of the many myths surrounding obsessive love. In this chapter, we will address some common myths, misunderstandings, and misconceptions about obsessive love.

Obsessive Love Is Passionate Love

Myth: *Obsessive love is no more than an intense passion, much like what we see in the movies.*

We want romance. We want to be swept off our feet. We want to feel the exhilaration and excitement of new love. And we want it to last forever, just like in the movies.

From the time you were little, you heard stories of intense, romantic relationships. Cinderella and

Snow White found true, everlasting love at first sight. Of course, Prince Charming was rather obsessive. After meeting Cinderella for just one hour, he used all his resources (and he had many resources) to go door to door throughout the kingdom, searching for her. By today's standards, this is excessive and obsessive. But as you watch the movie, you see romance and passion, not obsession.

And so it goes with many movies, books, and stories that have fascinated us for years—such as *The Phantom of the Opera* and *Romeo and Juliet*. As an intelligent adult, you know these stories are unrealistic. Even so, you crave the powerful feelings that come with passionate, romantic love.

True Love	Although we think of Romeo and Juliet as adults, making adult decisions about life and love, Juliet was 13 years old in the play. We are never given Romeo's age, but it is assumed he was no more than a few years older. In movies and in plays around the world, Romeo and Juliet are attributed with mature love, when in fact, this is a story of young love.

Rose was ready for a relationship. She was 24 and hadn't yet had a serious love affair. She had dated off and on, but nothing ever developed into something long term. The longest relationship had been for six months with Harry. Usually, Rose got bored. She loved how she would feel when she first met someone. It was intense and exciting. She would wake up thinking about her new boyfriend and couldn't wait to talk to him. She thought about him all day. But each time, as the relationship became more practical—both partners getting up early to go to work and going to the same old family commitments on weekends—Rose got bored. Everyday love wasn't good enough for Rose. She wanted fireworks.

When love does come along, you might feel the excitement, the thrill of new love. But as love matures, the exhilaration gives way to a deep emotional bond, and the excitement mellows to being comfortable with one another. Is this enough? Are you satisfied with the feelings of mature love? You might not be. You might constantly seek the intensity of new love. Jealousy, possessiveness, and the intensity of obsessive love might draw you in, giving you the feeling of the passion you see on the movie screen. Anything less feels boring.

Healthy love relationships go through stages. In the beginning it is characterized by intensity and passion. But as love grows, a different type of relationship develops, one with trust and respect for one another. Passion doesn't disappear, but will be toned down.

As you begin a new relationship, think about what you want and what is realistic. Are you reaching for a relationship based on what you see in the movies? Or are you searching for true love, love that isn't measured by fireworks and intensity but by a deep feeling for one another?

Communication is essential to any good relationship. Both partners need to feel comfortable and secure expressing opinions and sharing feelings. Trust and respect are built through talking honestly about your wants, desires, and wishes.

Be involved in each other's lives, but be aware of the difference between being involved and being obsessed. You want to show your interest in what your partner is doing. Ask questions about his job and hobbies, expressing genuine interest. Find interests and hobbies you both share.

As much as you want to share interests with your partner and spend time with him, don't give up your own life to do so. Keep in touch with friends and explore your own interests. These experiences help you bring outside interests into the relationship, and keep you stimulated and interesting to your partner.

Your relationship doesn't have to be a fairy tale to be successful. Base your relationship on good communication, mutual respect, and trust. If you can accomplish that, the intensity of your love will continue to grow.

> **True Love**
>
> Don't be afraid of conflict. Learning to resolve conflicts strengthens relationships. If both partners respect the other's opinion and actively listen, conflicts can bring you closer. Here are some tips for resolving conflicts with respect:
>
> - Use "I" statements to express how you feel instead of starting with "you" which can sound like an accusation.
> - Stick to discussing the current issue. Don't rehash old arguments.
> - Avoid calling names or insulting each other.
> - Look at your partner when talking to him.
> - Set up a time to talk when both partners are prepared to work on finding a solution to the problem.

Obsessive Love vs. Obsessive Compulsive Disorder

Myth: *Obsessive love is a form of obsessive compulsive disorder.*

Obsessive love is not a type of obsessive compulsive disorder (OCD). OCD is a mental disorder. An obsession as it relates to OCD is an idea or thought that continually preoccupies or intrudes on a person's mind. A compulsion is a repeated action or ritual that is done in order to alleviate the obsessive thought. Here's a common example of OCD behavior:

Jed was ready to go to bed. He checked the front door; it was locked. He checked the stove; it was off. He made sure all the lights were turned off. He did this every night just before bedtime. As he was brushing his teeth, he began to wonder if the front door was locked. He knew he had checked it, but couldn't stop worrying. He went through his ritual again, checking the door, the stove, the lights. Everything was as it should be. He still couldn't stop the thoughts and before he finally got into bed, he had checked everything 10 additional times. Jed knew his thoughts were irrational. He knew, logically, that he had checked everything and everything was okay. Even so, his obsessions still haunted him. Each night he checked everything a minimum of 10 times—sometimes more than 20. His obsessions robbed him of a good night's sleep, and made him tired the next day at work.

With OCD, you know the thoughts are irrational but feel helpless to stop them. Besides thoughts or ideas, obsessions can be images or inappropriate impulses or behaviors. They probably interfere with your life and cause you additional anxiety.

When you are obsessed with a person, you have an insatiable need to know what the person is doing and with whom they are doing it. You need constant reassurance of their love. True, these obsessions can be intrusive and can affect your job or other relationships. But one major difference between the obsessions of OCD and the obsessions of obsessive love is that the obsessive lover is not always aware that these thoughts are irrational. Usually, he doesn't realize how his behaviors, as a result of his obsession, might be alarming to the other person. He justifies his behavior because he believes it's perfectly rational.

Another difference is that there are no compulsions or rituals the obsessive lover completes in order to rid himself of the obsession. Many obsessive lovers do engage in certain behaviors, such as constant texting or phoning their partner, but these are not rituals or compulsive actions like those who suffer from OCD.

obsession Alert

Someone with OCD can have the same thought over and over, and it may seem to come from insecurity within a relationship. For example, you might wonder, "Do I make her happy?" and not be able to shake the thought. Your partner might repeatedly ask, "Do you love me?" This type of behavior is caused by obsessive compulsive disorder but could be easily confused with obsessive love.

Someone with obsessive love is not obsessed with a thought, but with a *person*. It is not an inability to overcome an obsessive *thought*, but the fear of rejection, that drives obsessive love.

Obsessive Love Relationships and Danger

Myth: *Obsessive love relationships are never dangerous. They can be smothering but there is no physical danger.*

Most obsessive love relationships are not dangerous. The partner of the obsessive lover might feel trapped or isolated, but most of the time, there is no threat of physical danger. Sometimes, however, obsessive lovers cross the line.

There have been plenty of stories about obsessive love that turned dangerous. For example, *The Denver Post*, on February 20, 2009, reported the murder of Amber Cremeens, who was stalked by a previous boyfriend, Tyler James Martin. According to the paper, Amber had been stalked for several years, moving to Kansas City then Denver to get away from Martin, who continued to follow her. While Amber was moving to a secret residence with the help of her new boyfriend, Martin was in Colorado, talking to friends about reuniting with the love of his life. On a Tuesday night in February, Amber's new boyfriend received a frantic phone call. Amber told him that Martin was trying to run her off the road as she drove home from a local gym. She told him the license plate of the car chasing her, which matched Martin's car. Her boyfriend immediately called 911, but by the time police arrived, Amber had been shot and killed. Several days later, according to *The Rocky Mountain News*, Tyler James Martin barricaded himself in a relative's home in Chicago and shot himself.

We often hear on the news about someone's current- or ex-partner attacking or killing her. These types of news stories are scary and paint a bleak picture of obsessive love. And indeed, sometimes there is a reason to leave—and leave quickly. Some studies have shown a correlation between jealousy and the potential for violence in a relationship. If you feel you are in danger in your relationship, you should seek help immediately.

Obsessive Love and Violence

Myth: *All obsessive love relationships include physical violence.*

On the flip side is the mistaken belief that all obsessive love relationships become violent. Just as it is not true that there is *never* any danger, it is also not true that *all* obsessive relationships end in violence. Most obsessive love relationships are difficult. One partner feels he loves more intensely than the other, and needs to hold on to the relationship despite the consequences.

misc.

Case Study: Marissa and Brandon

Marissa and Brandon dated for several months before moving in together. Marissa hadn't been sure if she was ready, but Brandon had seemed so sure—and she did love him—so, in the end, she agreed. Brandon had always been jealous. Marissa thought this would go away when she moved in, but he became even more possessive. He wanted her to quit her job so he could take care of her. He complained when she went to see her family. He talked about her friends negatively. Additionally, Brandon found fault in everything she did, so she tried harder to make him happy.

After two years of living with Brandon, Marissa felt alone and lonely. She was sure she had made a mistake moving in with him. She wanted to leave but was worried about how Brandon would react. She finally got up the nerve and, one day while he was at work, Marissa packed up and left. Brandon spent months trying to get her back. He called, he followed her, he sent her flowers. At first Marissa would talk to Brandon, trying to explain why she left, but after a few times she stopped answering his calls and refused delivery of the flowers. It took months but Brandon finally stopped calling. The last Marissa heard, Brandon had begun a new relationship. She felt sorry for the next girl, but hoped Brandon had learned from his experience and would be different this time. Still, she's glad it isn't her and that the relationship is over.

These relationships are usually dysfunctional. Many end because, as the partner of an obsessive lover, you become tired of possessive, controlling behavior. You eventually want out of the relationship so you may regain your freedom and life. Sometimes the obsessive lover becomes more frantic when the relationship ends and might harass or follow you, trying to revive your love.

An obsessive lover sees his behaviors as justified, not as criminal or hurtful. He is sure that, if he could just talk to you again, you would see that you were meant to be together. The constant calling, the texting, showing up at your job, sending gifts—it's all meant to woo you back. Many obsessive lovers might be shocked to realize that their behavior could be considered stalking. He's sure all of this is part of the relationship and his actions never reach a level of physical violence.

Love Addiction

Myth: *Love addiction is the same as obsessive love.*

Love addiction refers to being addicted to the feeling of being in love. There are some similarities between love addiction and obsessive love. In both, you may …

- Fantasize about spending the rest of your life with someone you just met.
- Have a hard time letting go of relationships.
- Behave in ways that smother your partner.
- Experience an intense initial physical attraction.
- Have a fear of abandonment or rejection.

However, even though there are some similar behaviors, the love addict feels incomplete when not in a relationship. As soon as one relationship ends or is nearing the end, the love addict seeks out a new relationship. She may begin a series of affairs, moving quickly in and out of relationships, or become addicted to sex. As someone with a love addiction, your sense of self becomes stifled. Your measure of self-worth is based on whether you are in a relationship, which makes you dependent on your partner. Without him, you feel useless. Who the partner is does not matter as much as having a partner.

Definition

Love addiction is a progressive illness characterized by being addicted to romantic relationships. Love is used as a way to fill an emotional need and provide stability, much as a drug addict uses drugs and an alcoholic uses alcohol. As with other addicts, the love addict will use manipulative methods to attract a partner and will often move from relationship to relationship or from sexual encounter to sexual encounter. Twelve-step programs, such as Sex and Love Addicts Anonymous, can help someone overcome love addiction.

Becky felt hopeless in between relationships. Her last relationship, with Jim, ended badly. She had felt the relationship was going nowhere—that Jim was getting ready to leave her—so she started an affair with a co-worker, David. Once Jim found out, he left. Becky immediately became obsessed with David, but he didn't want more than a casual fling. Becky was lost. Jim was gone and David only wanted to get together once in a while—and just for sex. Out of a desperate need to be part of a couple, Becky began hanging out at singles bars. She had a succession of one-night stands, quickly becoming infatuated with each one, but most of the men didn't want anything more than sex from her. She would tightly cling to anyone who showed her some attention.

Becky, like many people addicted to love, wanted acceptance and the safety and security a relationship brings. But her fear of being alone made her hold on to any hope of a relationship, and her neediness often drove away potential partners.

The fear of rejection and abandonment drives the behaviors of both obsessive lovers and love addicts. Those behaviors, however, are different. In an obsessive love relationship the rejected partner holds on and is not able to let go, sometimes going to the extreme of stalking someone once the relationship has ended. In love addiction, the addict quickly seeks out a new relationship to fill the void.

Fixing Your Partner

Myth: *With enough love, you can fix your partner's jealousy and possessiveness, and drive away his insecurities.*

When you fall in love, you fall in love with the whole person—good, bad, and otherwise. In the beginning you are sure that, together, you can overcome any adversity. You can help him through anything. When you learn about his troubled childhood, you feel badly for him. It helps explain his insecurity and his jealousy. You want to help him and you know, if you love him enough, you can fix him. You can love him enough so he won't be jealous. You can love him enough that he can overcome his past.

In healthy relationships, both partners help and support one another. This is different than wanting to "fix" someone with your love. If you want to help your partner, think about your motives. Are you trying to solve your partner's problems or are you offering him support as he works to solve his own problems?

A good example of this is to imagine your partner is looking for a job. You offer your support by editing his resumé, dropping inquiries in the mailbox, taking messages from prospective employers, and staying positive and supportive; but you don't fill out applications or attend the interviews. You offer your support, but you can't do it for him. It's the same in other aspects of your lives: offer your support without enabling him.

Wendy met Charlie through a friend. They were instantly attracted to each other and started dating. Charlie told Wendy that his parents had divorced when he was three and he never saw his father again. His mother worked two jobs to pay the bills and he rarely saw her. From the time he was in elementary school, Charlie came home from school to an empty house. Dinner was usually waiting for him in the refrigerator. He ate, did his homework sometimes, and then watched television and played video games. By the time his mother got home, he was asleep. On weekends, she stayed in bed, trying to catch up on sleep. She never attended any school functions or even asked about his schoolwork. He knew she was working to help him, but the reality was, he had no adult in his life from an early age. He was left on his own; what's more, he never had the chance to see how a married couple acted together.

Wendy felt bad for Charlie: he never understood why his father left and never returned. He never understood why his mother couldn't make some time for him. He felt abandoned by both his parents. Wendy knew Charlie hurt, and that made him jealous and possessive. He was afraid of losing her like he had lost his parents. She was sure, if she loved him enough, he would get over the pain of his childhood.

<table>
<tr><td>True Love</td><td>As children, we form our identities based on the people most important to us, usually Mom and Dad. When those people reject us, we feel we are unlovable, of little value to anyone. We create this as our identity and it influences all our future relationships. In healthy love, both partners have self-respect and self-love, as well as respect and love for the other person. If you have a fear of rejection or are dealing with an unhealthy self-image, you may want to work with a therapist on finding ways to improve your self-esteem. It isn't until you are able to love yourself that you can love your partner.</td></tr>
</table>

Unfortunately, it doesn't work that way. You, as the partner of an obsessive lover, cannot make up for the past and make everything better with love. Because the jealousy, possessiveness, and obsessiveness are caused by events and situations dating to his childhood, your obsessive partner will need to face his past and understand that rejection and abandonment issues are controlling his adult life. You can't love him enough, because love is not the solution. Your obsessive lover needs to face the situations that caused his fears and learn that he is lovable and deserves love. You cannot teach him that, no matter how much you love him.

Obsessive Love Treatment

Myth: *There is no treatment for obsessive love and obsessive love relationships are hopeless.*

It is true there is no pill to take, no diet to follow, and no medical intervention that will cure obsessive love. As an obsessive lover, you need to hold on to your relationship, but your partner keeps telling you that you are smothering her. You might feel your life is out of control. The pain and fear of rejection is driving every decision you make and, most of the time, you feel as if your life is falling apart. You want help, but help for what? For being jealous? For not wanting to let go of love?

There is help. Obsessive lovers can overcome their fear of rejection and abandonment. They can learn how to develop healthy love relationships. It isn't easy, but it can be done. In Part 4, we'll talk about different types of therapy and counseling as well as what types of issues you can work on during your therapy sessions. We'll also talk about ways you can help yourself.

There is help for both partners in an obsessive love relationship. It is a long process, not a quick fix. It is a journey into finding yourself, facing your past and your pain, and learning how to love. Some obsessive love relationships probably aren't worth fixing, but the right one will flourish with some guidance and help. Not all obsessive love relationships are doomed. Whether your relationship is hopeless, or able to be helped, is up to you and your partner.

Essential Takeaways

- Society and culture confuse passionate, romantic love with obsessive love.
- Even though both share the word obsessive, obsessive compulsive disorder is much different than obsessive love.
- Most obsessive love relationships end without violence.
- Obsessive lovers can be helped through therapy and can learn to develop healthy love relationships.

Part 2

The Obsessive Lover

Obsessive love and new love share many of the same characteristics. When you first fall in love, there are feelings of euphoria, uncertainty, intense passion, and a need to be with your new lover as much as possible. But how do you know if these feelings are normal or if they have crossed the line to obsessive? In this part we'll have questions to ask yourself to help you see problem areas in your relationship. We'll also talk about what types of situations trigger obsessiveness.

Since each person is different and each person shows love in their own way, it can be hard to know which behaviors are obsessive and which are not. We'll go over some of the most common relationship problems and behaviors that result from obsessive love—such as jealousy or not respecting your partner's personal boundaries—and we'll offer tips on how to overcome these behaviors.

Sometimes obsessive lovers use other behaviors, such as self-punishment or drinking, to compensate for feelings of loneliness or rejection. Even though they aren't focused on your partner, these behaviors are still destructive to you and your relationship. We'll talk about how you can identify self-destructive patterns and work to overcome them.

chapter 4

Are You Obsessive?

How to know if you are an obsessive lover

Security and acceptance can be mistaken for love

Imaginary or fantasy relationships may combat loneliness

Sexual relationships can create a false feeling of emotional bonding

Obsessive love is often triggered by rejection or fear of it

Love makes our lives worthwhile. How, then, could anything done in the name of love be wrong? How could being obsessive about love, doing whatever you have to do to preserve your relationship, or wanting to stay together no matter what, be a bad thing?

Being passionate or excited about your relationship doesn't necessarily make you obsessive. But if you are wondering if you are obsessive, this chapter will help you decide if you are. If so, it will help you see where these behaviors came from so you can develop healthy relationships in your future.

10 Questions to Ask Yourself

You might already know you are obsessive, or have the tendency to be, when you fall in love. Or you may know that some of your behaviors are borderline but not be quite sure whether you have crossed into obsessiveness.

The following checklist can help you determine whether you need to overcome your overwhelming feelings of possessiveness.

❏ Do you spend a lot of time wanting someone who is not available, either physically or emotionally? Do you consistently fantasize about someone?

❏ Do you believe that, if you try hard enough, the other person will "come around" or learn to love you?

❏ Do you think your love for this person is so great that it will be able to overcome her not wanting you, that she will eventually love you?

❏ Do you think you are the victim because someone has rejected you or won't agree to what you want?

❏ Do you constantly think about the other person so that you lose sleep, don't eat, or miss time at work?

❏ Do you believe your life is worthless without this person?

❏ Do you think this person is the only person who can make you happy?

❏ Do you call this person over and over, or spend hours waiting for her to call? Do you go to her place of employment or home without being invited? Do you send gifts even though she has asked you not to?

❏ Do you spend your days wondering what she is doing? Who she is with? Do you check up on her to make sure she is where she says she is?

❏ Have you followed her to find out where she is going?

If you have answered "yes" to even two or three of the above questions, you may be obsessive. Obsessive love, its thought processes and behaviors, is often learned from past experiences. Because it is learned, it can be unlearned. Part 4 offers some strategies to help you overcome obsessiveness and create healthy relationships in your life.

True love involves trust. If you are struggling to control jealousy, keep a log of when you feel jealous. Write down what is going on in your relationship, what situation made you jealous, what you said and did. Include what you could have done differently. Discuss your log with your partner, letting her know you are sincere in your efforts to put your jealousy behind you.

Confusing Other Emotions with Love

A romantic relationship is supposed to be a part of your life. In an obsessive relationship, it becomes your lifeline. You think you can't live without it.

Security

As an obsessive lover, your relationships fill an emptiness in your life. As a child, your parents may not have given you the love and attention you needed. As an adult, you search for the acceptance and security you didn't receive as a child. In most homes, children know their parents will be there to help, guide, and support them. But if you didn't have this, you seek it out as an adult. And once you find security, you hang on. Even one day without your partner seems unbearable.

Even when the relationship is over, you can't bear to let it go. You would have to face being rejected and you don't think you can. A bad relationship is better than no relationship, so you hold onto it. Even the illusion of a relationship is better than being alone.

A relationship doesn't need to end for you to feel rejected. When your partner chooses to spend the afternoon on her own instead of with you, it can feel like rejection. Imagine waking up on a Saturday morning, expecting to spend the day with your girlfriend. As you lay in bed, you plan out your day. You envision sharing your morning coffee, an afternoon matinee, and an intimate dinner afterward. Before you even get out of bed or discuss your plans with your partner, your day comes alive in your mind.

True Love

You might have abandonment issues—even if your parents tried to give you love and attention. Here are some ways children can feel rejected or abandoned:

- Feeling ignored after the birth of a sibling.

- Having a sibling with physical or mental difficulties that require the parents to pay more attention to him.

- Being left alone in a hospital when ill.

- The death of a parent or grandparent.

- Having a parent (or parents) with an addiction or dependency.

- Frequent arguing or chaos in the household.

Sometimes, these result in difficulties in adult relationships unless you work to resolve the issues and understand their source.

But once you get up, your partner tells you her cousin is in town and she will be spending the day with her. "I'll be back sometime tonight," she says as she gives you a kiss and heads out the door. You are devastated. Your plans are ruined. Your day looks bleak. A healthy person in a healthy relationship could adjust by finding something else to do or calling a friend, but you can't. You spend your day sulking, feeling angry. Your thoughts keep returning to your spoiled plans. You can't get over that she chose her cousin over you. You feel dejected and alone, and these feelings intensify throughout the afternoon. You can't think of anything else. By the time she comes home, you either ignore her, still brooding; or start an argument, angry that she abandoned you.

Your obsession with your girlfriend took over your entire day. You weren't able to enjoy yourself or accomplish anything. Your obsession probably ruined your evening as well. Once your girlfriend returned home, you were angry and could not enjoy spending time with her. Even though your girlfriend had not rejected or abandoned you, it felt like she had. She didn't say, and didn't think, "I don't want to be with him today." She simply made plans with her cousin. Your girlfriend didn't cause your anger and despair; it was your own insecurities.

Acceptance

Besides security, we want to be accepted. Maybe you grew up with overly critical parents. No matter what you did, your parents told you it wasn't good enough. You grew up feeling that you can't do anything right and no one is ever going to love you. You grew up trying to find someone to accept you.

It's easy enough when you first start a relationship. You either don't see or minimize your new partner's faults, and she doesn't see yours. You're both focusing on everything that's right, and you want to hold onto these feelings.

Inevitably, though, reality and your human imperfections will start to assert themselves. You see every difference as an attack on your relationship. If she has a different opinion than you, your insecurities grow. If she makes dinner differently, you see it as an attack on your way of doing things. Each difference is blown out of proportion and, to you, is a dent in your perfect life. If there are too many dents, she might leave you.

Your partner can begin holding back opinions, saying she agrees with you even when she doesn't. She might spend extra effort making sure your dinner is cooked right, your house just so. On the surface this sounds ideal for you, but it isn't. In healthy relationships, both partners should feel free to express their opinions and a home should combine both ways of doing things. The relationship becomes smothering for your partner. She worries more about what you need and want than what she does. The relationship becomes one sided. These types of relationships rarely go the distance.

If these examples sound like you, it is time to work on increasing your feelings of self-worth. It is time to move beyond how your parents treated you and begin to treat yourself well. A relationship based on fear is never good. Take the time to complete the self-help exercises in Chapter 16 to raise your self-esteem.

Loneliness

You are lonely. You crave love and companionship but it seems out of reach. Every relationhip ends badly or doesn't even get started. You can't stand to be alone, but you can't seem to find someone to love.

Todd's mother was an alcoholic. Sometimes she was attentive but most times she was drunk from early afternoon on. From the time he was six, she would go to the bar at night, leaving him home alone. Todd didn't have any close friends. The other kids at school made fun of his dirty clothes and unkempt appearance. He was used to being alone, but that didn't lessen the pain of loneliness that he lived with.

As an adult, Todd's social life was nonexistant. When a co-worker, Mary, started talking to Todd, he was surprised. Wanting a relationship more than anything, Todd quickly became infatuated with Mary. They shared an interest in local sports and photography. Mary liked Todd. She thought he was sweet.

He started bringing her small gifts almost daily, a cup of coffee, flowers, candy. He wanted to show her how much he cared, even though they had only shared a few conversations and had lunch together once. Mary eventually agreed to go out with Todd and they went out on a few dates. Todd began immediately assuming they would be together forever. He talked as if they were already a couple and discussed their future. Todd's intensity scared Mary and she began avoiding him.

Todd thought Mary was the answer to his loneliness. He latched onto the relationship, or the idea of having a relationship. He couldn't let go. He couldn't deal with the possibility of Mary ending the relationship. It meant he would once again be alone and lonely. Todd continued to pursue Mary, leaving gifts on her desk, calling her, following her when she went out to lunch, hoping she would ask him to join her. Mary eventually found a different job, one away from Todd.

After years of intense loneliness, once a relationship begins, you are afraid it will end. You cling to it, holding tightly because you can't stand the thought of being alone again. Even thinking about the relationship being over can send you into a state of panic. Your thoughts, from the time you wake up until the time you go to sleep revolve around keeping the relationship alive. When the relationship does end, you may not believe it.

Believing Attraction Is Love

Love at first sight. Is it real? Can you love someone you don't know? Most obsessive relationships begin with an intense physical attraction. You want her. You need her. The feelings are so strong, you believe it must be love.

All romantic relationships, both healthy ones and obsessive ones, include physical attraction. Because sex is part of most romantic relationships, physical attraction is important. We don't want to date someone we don't have at least some attraction to. In healthy relationships, attraction is just the first step. It helps us decide whom we want to date. From there, we learn about the other person and develop an emotional bond—or not.

obsession Alert

A survey completed for the dating website Parship indicated that more than 75 percent of people believe it takes at least five dates to decide whether to become serious. If you are deciding on a relationship within minutes of meeting someone, you are probably rushing in and may have obsessive tendencies in your relationships.

In obsessive relationships, the initial attraction is confused with love. When you are infatuated based on appearances alone, internal personality traits are usually attached to looks. For example, suppose a man meets a beautiful woman, he may think, "She is so beautiful and has a great personality," even if he hasn't been with her long enough to know whether she's always that pleasant or patient. It's impossible to be "in love" with someone you don't know!

Joe did exactly that when he met Claire at a mutual friend's barbecue. As soon as Joe saw Claire sitting across the yard, he fell in love, or at least he thought he was in love. He could tell she was everything he wanted in a woman: she had long brown hair, was not so skinny she looked ill, and had a wide smile. She was perfect. Just watching her, he knew she had a great personality. He wanted—no, he *needed*—to meet her.

Joe began asking around, looking for an introduction. Finally, he met her and they talked for a few minutes before she moved on to socialize with other guests. Joe couldn't let her get away. He appeared at her side throughout the day, offering to get her a drink or something to eat. He found excuses to sit near her.

After the picnic, even though Joe had actually spent very little time speaking to Claire, he told his friend, "She's the woman of my dreams. I am going to marry her!"

Joe and Claire actually dated for a few weeks, and he continued moving quickly, declaring his love and his intention to get married within days of their first meeting. His intensity so early in the relationship drove Claire away.

Too often, we believe that love is a magical feeling that will come upon us when we meet the right person. We buy into the fairy tale mentality we learned from watching Cinderella or Snow White. An initial attraction can make us feel like we've known someone our entire life, even if, in reality, we've just met.

Attraction is a good place to start; it isn't the end. When you're attracted to someone, begin slowly, learn about the other person's interests, values, likes, and dislikes. Find out if these match your view of the world. This will help you decide if you want to move ahead with the relationship or if you should look for someone more compatible.

Sex and Love

Lust can be confused with love. But lust is driven by a physical need, while love is driven by an emotional need. Women are more apt to confuse lust with love. This may be because society doesn't approve of women being lustful, so they may be more apt to associate sexual desire with love. Women instead "fall in love" with partners they are attracted to.

Lust is an intense, highly charged physical attraction, combined with longing for an intimate sexual relationship.

In addition to lust, the act of sex itself may make us feel as if there is an emotional bond—even if none is there. There is a desire to be cuddled or held after sex. These feelings are driven by chemical changes in the brain caused by sex but disguise themselves as feelings of love. Sexual encounters, for men, often create feelings of possessiveness toward their partners.

Sometimes, the pleasure of sex drives our relationships. When the sex is good, you may ignore other factors, such as: whether your partner shares the same morals or values, you have shared interests, and you enjoy other activities together—you know, besides sex. Relationships built entirely on lust or sex rarely last for long, and rarely provide the emotional satisfaction you are craving.

True Love	Bonding after sexual encounters can be frequently seen in women who are obsessive, possibly because the hormone oxytocin is released during orgasm. Some experts speculate that the release of this hormone makes women prone to bonding with their partner during sex. Men, though perhaps less often, can also mistake sex for an emotional connection.

But what does all this have to do with obsessive love? Since obsessive love is not really love at all but an obsession (an intense attachment) based on the illusion or fantasy of love, these types of relationships feel like they fill the emptiness inside you. These types of relationships feed your need for connection to another person. Once the connection is made, you can't let go.

Dana was in just such a relationship. Dana met Greg at a bar. She was immediately attracted to his good looks and muscular body. They had a great time and Dana ended up inviting Greg home with her. The sex was great—"better," Dana said, "than with any other man." Greg left the next morning, promising to call her the following week since he was going out of town for a few days. Greg did call and they got together the following week for a repeat. Soon, their relationship developed into having steamy sex one or two nights a week. The rest of the time, Dana rarely heard from Greg. All her friends told her he was just using her, but Dana didn't believe them. "He has an important job; he's busy."

When Greg reduced the time he spent with Dana, calling once a week, or even once every other week, Dana started getting nervous. She started calling Greg, even driving by his home to see if she could see him. Sometimes, she parked down the street, watching his house. Dana was sure Greg loved her like she did him, and that it was just a matter of time before they got married. Even being confronted with Greg being home when he told her he was out of town didn't bother her too much. "He must not feel well and doesn't want to worry me."

Dana's relationship with Greg was built entirely around sex. They didn't go out to dinner or the movies, they didn't socialize with her friends or his. They didn't talk about their dreams or interests. Their time together was one or two nights a week, in bed. Even so, Dana became obsessed with the illusion there was a real relationship. In her mind, there would be candlelit dinners at the finest restaurants in town and afternoons wandering through museums when Greg wasn't so busy with work. She had even begun planning her wedding, researching where to hold the reception and what type of wedding dress she would wear.

When Greg finally broke off the relationship because he met someone else, Dana went into a full-blown depression, refusing to go to work or see friends. Even though there was no deep, emotional relationship, the final rejection was just as humiliating and devastating as if it had been a long-term relationship.

Obsessive lovers who deny reality process information differently because your denial becomes your reality. When faced with the truth that your partner doesn't want to be in a relationship, you filter information to make it fit the situation because the other option is too painful. Dana was confronted with Greg lying to her about being out of town, but changed the information to fit her reality. You may have done the same thing in relationships. Continuing the relationship is all that matters to you. You twist facts and view the relationship through your own needs.

Triggers to Obsessive Love Behaviors

As you have seen in the different examples throughout this chapter, obsessive love can happen inside an existing relationship or through an imaginary relationship. The common thread is fear of rejection or abandonment.

Experts believe the roots of this fear first develop in childhood, with many obsessive lovers having a troubled early life. You may have experienced …

- An alcoholic parent who gave love inconsistently.

- A parent who abused or neglected you.

- A parent who abandoned you.

- A parent who had depression or another mental illness that made it impossible for her to properly care for you.

Other factors, such as the death of a parent or close relative, can also form a deep fear of abandonment.

Most obsessive lovers don't put together (connect) their childhood experiences with their fear as adults. For example, as an obsessive lover, you probably aren't going to say, "Because my mother didn't offer me the love I needed, I am afraid you will leave, too." It is usually an unconscious fear, buried deep within your memories, but still, this fear drives your adult relationships. Simply put, it's part of your reality, and your obsessive actions seem perfectly rational, because the fear is real. What's more, you assume everyone has it, so you believe your behavior is not only rational, but normal. Just as when you were a child, crying for mom to come and care for you, you feel the same desperation waiting for your partner to arrive home or waiting to talk to her. You might not understand why you panic at the thought of losing someone, but you do panic.

MISC.

Case Study: Donna

Donna's father worked long hours and was hardly ever home. Her mother suffered from severe depression and, from the time Donna was young, she needed to take care of herself. Some days her mother never got out of bed. Donna believed she had done something wrong or that her mother didn't like being a mother. As an adult, Donna searched for the love she had never been shown. Whenever she was in a relationship, she was worried her partner would figure out there was "something wrong with her" or she was "unlovable" and leave. She clung to each relationship as if her life depended on it. She became anxious every time her partner left the house, even to go to work. She normally called him several times every day, just to be reassured he was coming home in the evening. Her possessiveness would eventually drive her partners away; even so, in the next relationship, she would do the same thing again. The calling was a way to reduce anxiety by reconnecting.

As an obsessive lover, when faced with a relationship ending, your first thought is, "I can't live without her" or "Without him I will never be happy." You don't see an end to the suffering from the breakup. Your focus on the end of the relationship stops any recovery. Your focus is on the pain of now. Your behaviors are driven by doing whatever is necessary to avoid this pain and this means doing whatever is necessary to make sure the relationship continues.

Even though many obsessive thoughts and behaviors are triggered by a breakup, you can have the same reactions while still in a relationship. Even the thought of a possible rejection brings fear. You show this fear through jealousy and possessiveness. As your fear grows, your actions become more intense. There might be constant texts, e-mails, or calls. You might be afraid to let your partner out of your sight, fearful she won't return. This is the worst-case scenario, not a certainty; more common is constant texts, e-mails, and calls. It does happen though. This possessiveness, however, usually pushes your partner away. She pulls away, resenting the lack of trust. As you sense her pulling away, your fear grows and you tighten your grip, trying to control her in an effort to keep her. Usually, your possessive actions will eventually drive your partner away—the very thing you are trying to prevent.

Essential Takeaways

- As an obsessive lover, you believe if you are persistent enough, your partner will love you.
- If you did not receive security and acceptance as a child, you may develop a dependency on relationships as an adult.
- Physical attraction is sometimes mistaken for love.
- You may believe you are in love with someone you have a sexual relationship with, even if you have not developed an emotional connection.

chapter 5

Obsessive Behaviors

Are you possessive? A quiz to find out

What does harassment include?

Self-help tips to reduce controlling behaviors

Possessive behavior can be one of the biggest problems in relationships. When you are too possessive it shows a lack of trust and usually leads to acting controlling toward your partner. Possessive behaviors are intended to maintain a relationship, but usually end up backfiring. As an obsessive lover, you probably aren't even aware of how your behaviors make your partner feel smothered. You believe possessiveness will give you what you want, an everlasting relationship, but usually, you end up with the opposite—your partner leaving.

Possessiveness Quiz

Think about how you would react to the following situations.

You're at a party and your partner is sitting across the room. Her ex sits down next to her and they start talking and laughing together. What would you do?

    a. Go over, ask your partner if she wants a drink or something to eat, and give her a kiss, making sure her ex gets the message that she is with you.

    b. Storm over and interrupt to make sure she knows you are angry, and her ex knows you don't want him speaking to her.

    c. Continue socializing and enjoying the party. Whether or not this worries you, you trust your partner to tell you what happened later if it's important.

You have a date planned but at the last minute your partner calls and says she isn't feeling well and needs to cancel. What would you do?

    a. Tell your partner you hope she feels better and that you will call tomorrow.

    b. Drive by her house to see if she is really home.

    c. Tell your partner you hope she feels better and then call some friends to make other plans.

You and your partner are attending a party at a friend's house. What would you do?

    a. Mingle with other people, but check on your partner throughout the night, making sure you know where she is most of the time.

    b. Stick close by your partner. You want to know who she's talking to and make sure everyone knows she is with you.

    c. Mingle with friends while your partner mingles with her friends. You find each other once in a while, but you know you can trust each other and that you'll leave together.

obsession Alert   As an obsessive lover, you frequently make mountains out of molehills. For example, if your partner is speaking quietly to another guest at a party, you might become enraged, thinking she is whispering secrets, rather than assuming she is just talking with a friend. You might have self-control and let your partner know how you feel later or you might barge into the conversation, telling your partner you need to talk to her alone, then letting your partner know they don't need to talk to anyone but you.

Your partner is out for the evening with friends. You weren't invited. What would you do?

   a. Follow your partner to find out where she is going and who she is with, without letting her see you.

   b. Spend the evening worrying that your partner is cheating or might meet someone when she is out.

   c. Make plans to hang out with your friends.

Your partner left her cell phone sitting on the table. It looks like she has received several text messages. What would you do?

   a. As soon as your partner returns, mention the texts and try to get her to explain who they were from.

   b. Check your partner's phone and read the texts. While you have her phone, you check recent calls as well.

   c. Do nothing; you get texts from friends and you assume she does as well.

You and your partner will be attending a family wedding. It is the first time your partner is meeting your family. What would you do?

   a. You check out the outfit your partner bought to make sure you like it before going to the wedding.

   b. You go with your partner to buy a dress. You want to make sure she looks amazing when she meets your family.

   c. You don't need to see what your partner will be wearing—she always looks amazing.

If you have answered mostly:

a. You might not be all the way to obsessive yet, but there are some definite warning signs. It is time to keep your possessiveness under control before it does serious damage to your relationship.

b. You are showing obsessiveness in your relationship. It's time to work on your own insecurities and self-esteem. Your level of possessiveness could put your relationship in danger.

c. You trust your partner and are not at all possessive.

If you are possessive, you might use your love as an excuse for your actions, saying "I just love you so much, I can't bear to be away from you." Love, however, does not include jealousy or controlling actions.

Jealousy

Jealousy is a negative reaction to losing, or the fear of losing, someone to another person. When you are jealous, it signifies insecurity and a lack of trust in your partner. Jealousy is a major problem within relationships and is the cause of many breakups.

It is hard to hide jealousy or keep it under control. Not saying how you feel, especially as your emotions grow into obsessions, can make you feel like you are going crazy. But keeping your jealousy under control is critical to creating a satisfying relationship for you and your partner. Your jealousy probably takes over your thoughts, even when you don't want it to. Your partner probably gets upset that you don't trust her.

True Love

Accept that your jealousy is your problem and is caused by your own internal conflicts, not by anything your partner has done. Improving your self-confidence can help you feel more secure with yourself and improve your relationship. Chapter 12 provides tools for improving your self-image.

Adam's jealousy would crop up for no apparent reason. Each time, he would feel guilty afterward; he wanted so much to trust Carla, but he felt nagging doubts in the back of his mind and once these thoughts took hold, he couldn't stop them. One day they were in his car, on their way to meet some friends for dinner. As usual, Adam was driving and Carla was looking out the side window as they passed some road construction. One of the workers looked up and met Carla's gaze. Adam suddenly became suspicious. He began accusing Carla of being attracted to the construction worker, "You want to be with him, don't you?" Carla didn't know where this sudden jealousy had come from or why, but she was tired of Adam constantly accusing her of having affairs with friends, co-workers, or even men she looked at.

Adam and Carla fought the rest of the way to the restaurant. Adam continued to accuse Carla of wanting other men and she kept getting angrier until she threatened to leave him if he couldn't trust her. By the time they arrived and met their friends, Adam was sorry he had acted rashly. He hopped out of the car to open Carla's door and acted especially attentive and apologetic the rest of the night. That was pretty much how their life seemed to go: they'd be calm, getting along well, then Adam's jealousy would pop up out of nowhere and he would accuse her of cheating, of wanting to cheat, or of being interested in someone she didn't even know. Carla would try to reason with him, he'd remain jealous, and then she would get mad. Finally Adam would feel guilty and act overly kind. Then they would start all over. Carla wasn't sure how much longer she could continue the cycle and how much longer she wanted to be with someone who didn't trust her.

The following provides you with some ways to begin improving your relationship by keeping your jealousy under control.

- Think about what triggers your jealous thoughts or behaviors. Do you get jealous most often when you are in a particular situation, like a party or social event? Do you become jealous if your partner speaks with someone of the opposite sex? Knowing what situations cause jealous feelings can help you be more prepared.

- Come up with coping strategies for the situations where jealousy is most likely to occur. You might want to write down some simple phrases to repeat to yourself when you notice jealous feelings beginning. You might say, "I know she loves me. Talking to someone else does not mean she is interested. I respect her and trust her."

- Lower your expectations as to how much time your partner needs to spend with you. Unrealistic expectations will not be fulfilled and will lead to negative feelings. Certainly you and your partner want to spend time together and do things together. But you don't need to spend every minute together. Time spent individually is just as important as togetherness. For example, count the number of hours per week or per day and set a lower limit for time together. Slowly wean yourself from trying to absorb every minute of your partner's life—set goals for other things to do or other people to be with.

- Stay positive. Jealousy is based on fear. Instead of focusing on negative possibilities, focus on the good in your relationship. Focusing on thoughts or feelings of jealousy may undo your relationship and you can end up with nobody. Train yourself to think of what you enjoy with your partner. Write down the reasons you should trust her so you can refer to them when you feel overwhelmed.

- Think about the person you are jealous of. Has this person done anything to deserve your suspicions? Do they deserve your trust or your lack of trust? Look for explanations that are factual.

- Talk about your jealous feelings with your partner only when you are alone and calm. If you discuss your feelings in public or when emotional, you will cause more problems. Keep your mouth closed until you can openly discuss your feelings, and be willing to listen to how your jealousy makes your partner feel.

True Love

A study published in the *CyberPsychology & Behavior Journal* showed that extensive use of Facebook actually increased feelings of jealousy. The accessibility of information, the ability to study a partner's profile, knowing each time a person of the opposite sex was added to the friends list, and misunderstandings about a posted status all contributed to feelings of jealousy.

Sometimes, jealousy occurs because of past infidelity, in either your current relationship or a previous one. If it was in your current relationship, you will need to decide whether you want to stay. If you do, it will take time to overcome the hurt, but continual accusations will not help. If you keep thinking or saying, "I can't get over this," that indicates that you need to either get help to accept what has already happened, or just end the relationship because it will be a constant source of conflict. You are programming yourself to stay stuck in that feeling. If your jealousy arises from a previous relationship, you will need to continue to remind yourself that your current partner has done nothing to cause your mistrust and not continue to take previous hurts out on your current partner. You may find that you need the help of a counselor if you want to get over this.

Control

Control is much harder to explain than jealousy. Controlling actions can vary widely and can range from subtle—where a partner doesn't realize she is being controlled—to obvious—where a partner seems to accept the control. Usually, controlling actions are somewhere in between. Often the obsessive partner denies he is controlling. "I'm only trying to help." Some examples of controlling behaviors include:

- **Time.** You continually make your partner wait for you. It might be waiting to go to bed, waiting to leave for a social event, or waiting for him to complete a task or chore. This is used as a way to say, "I am more important than you." It is meant to make the partner feel inferior.

- **Resources.** Money means freedom and if you are controlling, you need to control the money. You can't let your partner have unlimited resources that would enable her to leave. Some partners dole out an "allowance" to their partners or make them ask and explain why they need money. Others use money as a "reward," doling out financial favors when their partner does what they want.

- **Verbal or body language.** You might control your partner through actions or words, making sure she is afraid of getting you angry if she steps out of line. This might include refusing to speak to her if she goes out with friends, walking away when she wants to talk, or sulking or pouting when she does something you don't want her to do.

- **Making her responsible for your actions.** You can control someone by changing the circumstances to fit your needs. You blame your partner for your actions. For example, if you get upset when she goes out with friends, you might say, "If you didn't insist on going out without me, I wouldn't get mad." You are making her responsible for keeping you calm, keeping your emotions under control.

- **Put-downs.** You need to make sure your partner understands that you are better than her, you're the boss. In order to do so, you need to put her in her place. You might tell her she has gained weight, she is stupid, or she doesn't understand complicated things.

- **Power plays.** This type of behavior is used to make sure your partner knows you are in control. All controlling behavior is a type of power play, but some is specifically meant to create a sense of dominance, such as demanding or withholding sex.

Controlling behaviors are used to keep your partner dependent on you for money, for freedom, or for self-esteem. By controlling your partner, you feel you can keep her in the relationship. But you can't control how someone feels, no matter what you do. Controlling behaviors may work in the short term. You might get what you want—a partner who's afraid to leave or doesn't have the resources to—but in the end, you create an unhappy and unsatisfying relationship for both of you.

If you see yourself in some of the above examples, the following suggestions might help you curb your obsessive, controlling behaviors. Think about the reasons you want to be controlling. Most people are controlling because they fear losing something or someone. They fear the unknown. What is it you fear?

Keep a journal of your thoughts. Some of the questions you should answer are:

- When do you feel the need to be controlling?

- How does being controlling help you?

- How does it hurt you and the other people in your life?

- What triggers your controlling behaviors?

- Do certain situations cause you to act in controlling ways? Ask for help with this one. Friends and family will be able to point out controlling behaviors or times when you were controlling.

Once you understand why you are controlling, find alternative ways of looking at and responding to situations. For example, Ben began keeping track of his controlling behaviors. He wrote down:

> *Seeing Abby talking with another man bothers me.*
> *I start thinking that she is going to fall for him and I*
> *need to get her away. If I can't get her away, I just get*
> *more and more angry until I can't think of anything*
> *else. I usually storm over and stop Abby from talking*
> *to him and force her to include me in the conversation.*

> *Abby is smart and confident and she chooses to be*
> *with me. I'm so happy that I'm the person she loves.*
> *But that doesn't mean she cannot talk to anyone else.*
> *She can talk to another man without falling for him.*
> *I will work to remember this when I see her talking to*
> *someone else.*

True Love	Changing your controlling behavior can feel overwhelming. Take one step at a time and focus on one behavior. Making several small changes can add up to large changes.

Ben wrote down his thoughts on a separate paper and kept it with him. If he saw Abby talking to another man, he took it out and read it to himself—repeatedly, if necessary. This helped Ben remember Abby could talk to someone else and still return to him. This exercise didn't immediately make Ben less jealous or controlling, but it did help to give him something specific to do when his feelings of jealousy were taking over. Abby appreciated Ben's efforts to overcome his controlling actions.

obsession Alert

Withholding sex is a power play meant to shame and humiliate your partner. When you refuse to have sex, you are saying, "I will only give you sex if you do what I want," or "You are not desirable." It places the blame on your partner. Some obsessive partners demand sex as a "right," showing their superiority in the relationship. They may harass or nag their partner to give them sex whenever they "need" it. Their partner feels used, not loved.

Harassment

We mostly think of harassment outside of a relationship, someone who is unable to accept "no" or a breakup, but harassment is seen within relationships as well. To an obsessive partner, even a few hours away can seem unbearable. Whether in or out of a relationship, harassing behaviors cause stress and your partner can pull back, resenting the lack of privacy and trust.

Phone Calls

Cell phones have become a part of our everyday life. We have the ability to instantly get in touch with friends, family, or anyone else we need no matter where we are or what we are doing. As an obsessive partner, a cell phone turns into your lifeline, especially when you are away from your partner. But cell phones can become intrusive.

Carl and Beth had been dating for six months. Beth's job as a real estate agent required her to spend much of her time meeting potential clients out of the office. Carl accepted Beth's job but admitted it made him nervous. He didn't like the idea of Beth meeting other men throughout the day, especially at a house instead of in her office. Whenever Beth had an appointment, Carl would call. He usually told her it was because he was concerned for her safety, but Beth knew he was trying to find out what she was doing and who she was with.

When on appointments, it wasn't unusual for Beth to receive between 5 and 10 phone calls from Carl. He would call to see if she wanted to meet after work for a drink, what movie she wanted to see, what restaurant she wanted to meet at, or he'd make up some other reason to call. At first, Beth would keep her phone on because she didn't want to miss a call from a client, but after a few appointments when the phone didn't stop ringing, she started turning it off. This drove Carl crazy and he would keep calling, over and over. One time, Beth had 20 missed calls when she turned her phone back on, all from Carl.

Beth tried repeatedly, unsuccessfully, to explain to Carl that his calls were interfering with her ability to do her job. But Carl didn't listen. His insecurity about their relationship was more compelling than Beth's needs.

He couldn't stop calling. The more anxious he became, the more he called. The cycle continued until Beth couldn't take it any more and eventually broke up with Carl.

Mail and the Internet

People don't use snail mail, as it is now called, as often as e-mail anymore, but it's still a way to stay in contact with someone from afar. Receiving letters or gifts in the mail can be romantic—unless you don't want any contact with the sender. An obsessive lover uses these tactics to stay in touch, to let the receiver know he is still around and still thinking of her.

A study in *CyberPsychology & Behavior Journal* showed almost 20 percent of respondents continuously monitored their partners through Facebook and more than 10 percent of the respondents felt it was difficult to curb the amount of time they spent viewing their partner's profile.

The Internet, e-mail, instant messaging, or social networking sites give you instant and continual access to your partner. Is it access to the partner or something else? Not only can you stay in touch throughout the day, you can check online to find out what your partner is doing and with whom. You look to see who your partner is interacting with, who has tagged them, who comments on their statuses. You look for "clues" and often jump to incorrect conclusions. You use this information to make accusations.

Even though the Internet lets you find out a great deal of information or cyber-follow someone, it's still an intrusion into her privacy. A healthy relationship must balance openness with respect for privacy. As an obsessive lover, you probably have crossed the line at least once. With more open boundaries and blurred lines, you will need to be more aware of what makes your partner uncomfortable and how much contact is too much.

Drive-Bys

Your partner said she was tired and didn't feel like going out tonight. You aren't sure if she was telling the truth or whether it was an excuse. So you drive by her house to see if her car is there. You think it's harmless. She won't even know that you drove by and it will make you feel better.

Mike didn't think it would be a problem to drive by Sharon's house after she cancelled a date. She had said it had been a hard day at work and she just wanted to have a quick dinner and head off to bed. Mike wasn't so sure. He thought she might be making up an excuse. Maybe she had a date with someone else. So he drove by. Sharon's car was in the driveway. The lights were out in the house. It looked like she was asleep. So Mike left. But an hour later, he drove by again. The car was still in the driveway, the house still dark. Later that night, Mike took one more drive to check it out. Still the same.

Was Mike wrong? Did his actions really hurt Sharon if she never knew he'd driven by? Mike's actions clearly show a lack of trust. Sharon had put her needs first; she was tired, and she needed a good night's sleep. But Mike couldn't accept Sharon's explanation—and, even after driving by once and seeing for himself, he continued to go by and check. Even though Sharon didn't know about the drive-bys, Mike invaded Sharon's privacy.

True Love

When you don't trust your partner, you are giving her the responsibility of proving her love. Since love is an emotion and can't be proven, you are asking for the impossible. Trust can't come from another person; it comes from feeling secure within yourself. If there is a lack of trust in your relationship, the first place to start is improving your own self-image.

Furthermore, hiding or not admitting actions that your partner would disapprove of is fundamentally dishonest. If Sharon knew, she would probably see Mike's actions as creepy. It's unnerving to know someone is watching or spying on you. Mike may not have emotionally hurt Sharon on that night, but chances are, his possessiveness shows up in other ways. Once Mike decided to drive by Sharon's house, he may do it again and again, night after night, to help relieve his anxiety about their relationship. If Mike doesn't believe Sharon's explanation about being tired, he will question other things she does as well. After all, he is lying to her; it's not inconceivable that she would lie to him.

Drive-bys in a relationship, such as Mike and Sharon's, signal a problem. Rather than satisfying the need to know, the mistrust usually grows, despite finding evidence that nothing is going on. Drive-bys can also happen in imaginary relationships or after a relationship has ended. They are a way to be near the person or to stay aware of what she is doing. They can be part of harassment.

Unannounced Visits

As an obsessive lover, driving by your partner's house might not even be enough. You might stop by their house or their job, even when not asked or not welcome. Your overwhelming need to see, be near, or talk to your partner pushes you to keep trying, despite objections. You believe that if you are persistent she will change her mind. If she sees how much you love her, she will love you back. Other times the excuse is "I just had to explain."

Sam felt this way about Trish. They had been on a few dates, then Trish said she didn't want to see Sam again. He didn't understand; his feelings for Trish were so strong. He was sure she was "the one." Sam tried calling and texting, but she never answered her phone or texted back. Sam thought, "If I could just show her how much I care, I know she will change her mind and give us another chance."

Trish had met Sam at a restaurant on both dates and hadn't invited him to her house. But Sam had done some research on the Internet; he knew where she lived and where she worked. At first he would drive by, taking note of what time she left for work and what time she got home. It never occurred to Sam that he was stalking Trish. Instead, in his mind he was getting to know her.

After he knew Trish's schedule, he bought roses and stopped by her house one evening. Trish was surprised; she didn't recall ever telling Sam where she lived. She politely explained to Sam that she thought he was nice, but she just wasn't interested right now. Sam went home, remembering the words "nice" and "not right now." He was sure Trish just needed a little time. He waited two weeks before showing up at her job to take her to lunch. Trish again told Sam she wasn't interested, this time a little harsher. Sam still didn't get the message; he just thought she might be having a hard day at work. The following week, he again brought her flowers at her home. This time, Trish told Sam not to come to her house or job again.

Sam, like many obsessive lovers, jumped into a relationship even though it seemed one-sided. He hung onto words like "nice" and "not right now," thinking Trish had an interest in developing a relationship in the future, even though her actions indicated she did not want any relationship with Sam. He felt that he was wooing Trish and showing her why she should love him. He was doing all the things that he has seen in movies and heard in songs—he just wanted her to give him a chance.

As an obsessive lover, you focus only on your needs, sometimes projecting your feelings on to the other person and believing she feels the same way you do. Other times you think the romantic gestures will win over the object of your affection or that your feelings are so strong, she will eventually come to love you.

Even when faced with rejection, you latch on to any thread of hope, no matter how small. In your mind, your love is so strong it can overcome any obstacle, even the obstacle that the other person has no interest. In your mind, once she sees the depth of your feelings, she will open her heart to you.

Showing up at someone's home or workplace intrudes into their privacy. It steps over personal boundaries. In healthy relationships, both partners want to get to know one another. Both partners have a desire to get to know each other and share information. If your partner doesn't share information, such as her address or where she works, it is because she does not feel comfortable inviting you into her personal world. Trish made this message clear but Sam didn't want to hear it.

Respecting Personal Boundaries

We each set up *personal boundaries* to help keep us safe. Boundaries are not meant to create distance between us and our loved ones, but to bring us closer by defining what we want and need in the relationship. As an obsessive lover, you may have trouble respecting the personal boundaries set up by your partner. You believe your actions are in the best interest of your partner. You believe your actions, done in the name of love, are justifiable.

Definition

Personal boundaries are guidelines, rules, or limits you set up within your relationships with other people to keep you safe. Some examples of personal boundaries are: you may not hit me, I will not fight with you if you are going to yell, don't call me after 11:00 P.M., don't call me at work.

Your partner, however, might view your obsessive behaviors as controlling or smothering. In order to improve your relationship, you will need to learn how to respect your partner's boundaries.

The first step to respecting boundaries is to accept *no* for an answer. As a child, our parents told us no all the time. "No, you cannot cross the street by yourself" or "No, you may not have dessert before you eat your dinner." We learned, or did not learn, whether boundaries were flexible or rigid based on our parents' response to our behaviors. When our parents told us no but we did something anyway, if we were punished, we learned that no was important. If we were not reprimanded or punished, we learned no doesn't always mean no. Lack of consequences says that no could mean maybe.

In a healthy romantic relationship, partners respect this very important word. For example, Barry and Sandy have been dating for a few weeks. Barry wants to take Sandy out to lunch and calls her at work. Sandy explains to Barry that she does not want him to contact her at work. Barry, wanting to continue the relationship, apologizes and asks Sandy when a good time to call would be.

As an obsessive lover, Barry might not accept no, believing Sandy might be hiding something at work, maybe another guy. Instead of respecting her wishes to be left alone at work, he texts her, calls, and even stops by. He wants to know what's going on, he wants to test her commitment, he wants to let her know he cares enough to call. Barry isn't willing to respect the word no. For many obsessive lovers, no just means try harder. Obsessive lovers need to work on translating no as a stop sign.

The second step in respecting boundaries is simply to ask when you don't know. In our first example, Barry asked Sandy when she felt it was okay for him to call. If you aren't sure what your partner expects, ask. If you discuss and set rules about communication, you'll both know what is acceptable and what would be considered obsessive. Here are some examples of things you may need to establish:

- How many texts she considers appropriate in a day?
- How many phone calls are appropriate in a day?
- What hour is too late to call on the phone?
- Is it okay to call at work?
- How often does she want to see you? Once a week? Twice a week?

As your relationship develops, your questions will change and some answers will become apparent as you get to know one another. If you aren't sure, ask. Listen to the answer and follow it. Don't try to argue that what she is comfortable with is wrong just because you want more.

obsession Alert

Obsessive lovers often see making a mistake as a crack in the relationship and become scared the relationship will end. Keep in mind, you will make mistakes. As you are learning about each other, you will do some things wrong and do some things right. Listen to your partner. Find out what she likes and what she doesn't. Use this information to make your relationship the best it can be.

The next step in learning respect for another person's boundaries is to put yourself in your partner's shoes. Before you call your partner at work, think about what might happen. She could get in trouble; she could be busy and you are interrupting her; she could be having a bad day and won't be patient with you. If you do care about this person, you should care about her well-being. If your actions in any way hurt your partner, stop. Also think about how you would feel if she did to you what you did to her.

Essential Takeaways

- Finding alternative strategies for coping with jealous feelings can help.
- Respect your partner's requests when deciding how often and what time to call or text.
- Drive-bys may not immediately hurt someone but can still be a form of harassment, and keeping them secret is dishonest.
- Learning to accept no as an answer is the first step to learning to respect personal boundaries.

chapter 6

Self-Destructive Behaviors

Expressing anger constructively

Changing negative self-talk to positive

Overcoming problems at work

Substance abuse to numb emotional pain

It is hard to live with the fear of rejection and abandonment, or the frustration of failed or difficult relationships. Sometimes these feeling go on for years and take a steep emotional toll. You may try to numb the pain with other unhealthy behaviors.

In this chapter we'll talk about self-destructive ways obsessive lovers cope with the anguish of being obsessed with another person. We'll also provide some suggestions of more positive ways to manage specific behaviors.

Self-Punishment

Why would we want to purposely hurt or punish ourselves? Why would we want to create more pain in our lives? Even though it doesn't make sense, we all do it to some degree. We punish ourselves, internally criticizing our own behavior, beating our selves up over each perceived mistake. Left untended, this guilt and shame can boil over and appear in our lives as anger, self-recriminations, or self-harm, even as thoughts of suicide.

Anger

Anger is a normal human emotion. It is considered a natural self-defense function, a warning signal to potential threats, rivals, or foes. Anger, as an emotion, is not positive or negative. It is how we use and express our anger that makes it a destructive or constructive force in our life.

Case Study: Tom

Tom is currently in a relationship with Sally. When Tom was a child his father frequently lost his temper, yelling at Tom's mother, Tom, and Tom's brother on a daily basis. It seemed they couldn't do anything right. Tom worked hard to get good grades, but even a B would warrant his father yelling that he could do better. If Tom cut the grass, he missed a spot. His father always pointed out what Tom did wrong; he never praised him for what he did right. On the other hand, when Tom's mother got angry, she got quiet. She would give you the silent treatment. Once, when Tom got into trouble in high school, his mother didn't speak to him for three days.

As an adult, Tom varied in his expression of anger. He had learned both anger styles from his parents. Sometimes he would sulk, not speaking. Usually, the anger would eventually pass, even if it took a few days. Other times, the anger would just continue to build until he exploded. Sally never knew what to expect. Sometimes she would come home and Tom wouldn't speak to her, even if he was just angry at something that had happened at work. Other times she would come home to Tom ranting about some wrong she had unknowingly committed. Tom's anger began to control the relationship. Sally spent her days making sure everything went Tom's way just to avoid the anger.

You may have been taught as a child that expressing your anger was bad. Your parents may have punished you or sent you to your room when you talked back, got mad at a sibling, or showed your anger in other ways instead of teaching you healthy, constructive ways of coping with your anger. Your parents may have used hitting or violence as a way of coping with their anger. As a result, you might bottle-up your anger until you explode or strike out at others when your anger becomes overwhelming.

Before we talk about how to constructively use anger, it is important to understand how our anger can appear negatively and how it impacts our relationships. If you see yourself in any of the following examples, you probably need to find more positive ways of expressing your anger.

- **Silent anger:** Giving someone the silent treatment, avoiding eye contact, talking behind someone's back. You may not even know you are giving someone the silent treatment; you just can't express yourself or communicate when angry. You shut down.

- **Manipulation:** Provoking anger; pretending to be sad, hurt, or sick to cause a reaction or sympathy; withholding financial resources, evoking guilt in your partner.

- **Passive-aggression:** Ignoring people, sleeping when you are supposed to be helping around the house, or manipulating people into thinking they are at fault, when really you are doing the manipulating agreeing to do something but never doing it.

- **Dispassion:** Unresponsive, showing no feelings, treating people as objects, hiding anger through addictive behaviors such as overeating or substance abuse.

- **Obsessive behavior:** Demanding perfection, extreme cleanliness.

- **Evasiveness:** Avoiding conflict, being silent during arguments.

- **Threats:** Using words or violent behavior such as slamming doors to suggest harm to another person or another person's property.

- **Hurtfulness:** Using inappropriate or foul language, verbal abuse, blaming others, making hurtful remarks.

- **Destructiveness:** Destroying property; purposely hurting animals; other risk-taking behavior, such as driving fast or recklessly.

- **Bullying:** Threatening people, picking on people, using power to intimidate, mild violence, such as pushing or poking people.

- **Vengeance:** Punishing for real or perceived actions, unwillingness to "forgive and forget," taking revenge.

Misc.

Did You Know?

A research study completed by Dr. George Vaillant at the Harvard Laboratory for the Study of Adult Development, which tracked adult development of 824 men and women for over 45 years, showed that those who learned to use anger productively had better emotional and physical intimacy with their partners.

The first step in learning to use your anger to your benefit is to acknowledge it. You need to accept that you are angry and recognize how the anger makes you feel. Do you feel an increased energy, a quickened heartbeat, a rush of adrenaline? Instead of using your energy in a harmful way—such as blowing up or saying hurtful things—focus your energy on finding a solution to the problem.

Usually, if you react suddenly, with the force of your anger, your partner will become defensive. It is better to set up a time to talk about the issue later, when you have had time to calm down and think objectively. Use the time between realizing you're angry and having the discussion to sort through your feelings and come up with potential solutions. Write them down and have them with you when you talk to your partner; you may forget everything you planned to say if you find yourself getting angry again during the discussion. Avoid blaming your partner, using foul language, or saying things that are hurtful or mean. Express your anger in terms of how it makes you feel. Use "I" statements, such as, "I am feeling frustrated because …" instead of "You make me mad when you …." Starting with "you" makes your partner become defensive. You want to solve a problem, not create additional problems.

You may want to say to your partner, "You make me so mad"—but *you* make you mad. Your belief system and your expectations make you mad. You can change your feelings by changing your thoughts and beliefs. However it is easier said than done, anger management is a serious challenge. Don't wait until you have to go to a court-mandated group; you gain the most when it's your idea and the desire to change your behavior comes from within. Chapter 10 has some specific strategies for conflict resolution and anger management.

Make your expectations clear. Your partner cannot read your mind or know what you want. If you are vague, you are probably going to end up disappointed with the outcome. After you let your partner know how you feel, it is time to listen. Be willing to find out how she feels, even if you don't agree. Don't interrupt, and look at her when she is speaking. Pay attention to what she is saying.

When you have both calmly stated your views, you should be able to work together to find a solution. This sometimes means you and your partner will need to compromise your expectations so both of you are satisfied with the outcome. By using this method, you are showing respect and caring for your partner and it may give you a deeper emotional connection. Even when the situation doesn't involve your partner, following these steps helps you use your anger to find positive solutions to life's problems.

Self-Recriminations

Some obsessive lovers don't direct their anger at their partner but rather at themselves. This is more frequently found in relationships where both partners are obsessive. *Self-recrimination* is just as harmful to you and your relationship as anger. Every thought drives your self-esteem lower. You constantly replay every hurtful word, every destructive argument, blaming and putting yourself down each time. Your guilt and regret build until you are filled with self-loathing.

Definition

Self-recrimination is blaming and punishing yourself. It is associated with persistent blaming for current or past perceived failures.

Negative self-talk lowers your self-esteem. It makes you feel worthless, which in turn increases your fear that your partner will leave. Why would she want to stay with someone like you? At the same time, you are afraid of being alone. Your obsession increases.

It is possible to change your self-recriminations to positive self-talk. Start by becoming aware of how you talk to yourself. You might not even realize how often you tell yourself you are no good, or that you are to blame for all the bad things that happen, or even that you deserve to be unhappy. Keep a list or a journal of your thoughts, taking note of what you say to yourself. Write down every negative thought or comment. Think about your relationship and write down your feelings. How many of those thoughts are negative?

Now write down positive thoughts to correspond to all the negative ones. For example, if you wrote down, "I am so thoughtless, no wonder she's always mad at me," write down "I can be thoughtful, for example ...." Or if you wrote, "I am so stupid, I did ..." then write, "I did something wrong, but will take this opportunity to learn a better way of doing it." You can wear a rubber band around your wrist and snap it every time you realize you are having a negative thought, to snap you out of the thought pattern. In addition, when you find yourself being negative, say, "Stop," and replace the thought with the positive alternative.

This process is not going to be an immediate fix. You have probably been using self-recriminations for many years. Be patient with yourself. Keep up with the journal even if you find it difficult or don't see a difference. Your mind will believe whatever you tell it to believe. The more often you tell yourself positive things, the more you will start to believe it.

Dysfunction in Everyday Life

Obsessive love is all-consuming. It is difficult to devote the time, attention, and resources needed to guarantee that your relationship stays intact and still have time to keep up with other parts of your life. For many obsessive lovers, it is what you think about when you wake up. It is what you think about all day. It is what you think about before falling asleep. It is all you think about.

Avoiding Work

Our jobs require our time. We spend approximately 40 hours each week at work. Our jobs require our attention. As an obsessive lover, your job has probably suffered. You might miss time at work because of your need to know what your partner is doing. You might make excessive phone calls or texts to your partner, leave to check on your partner, or spend time searching social networking sites to find information about your partner. You might have lower productivity or make mistakes because you can't concentrate.

Paul has been married for almost 10 years. His wife, Cindi, has worked at an insurance company for most of their married life. Paul works swing shift, alternating every other week from day shift to second shift. Cindi is always on his mind. When he's on the day shift, Paul drives by her work on his lunch hour to make sure her car is there. After seeing her car, he is satisfied, for a few minutes; but by the time he gets back to work he begins to wonder who she is talking to at work, or whether she is having an affair with one of her co-workers. Instead of going back to work, he calls and says he will be late, then goes back to see Cindi.

When he works evenings, it's even worse. He is sure she is out with someone else. He takes his dinner break to drive by his own house to make sure she's there. Sometimes he stops in, but he doesn't stop in every night because then she would expect it and be prepared; he wants it to be a surprise. He never catches Cindi with another man, but the thought still consumes him. He has lost several jobs because of lateness or not being at his post during working hours, but it doesn't matter. Checking on Cindi, making sure she is not cheating, is all he cares about.

True Love	Worry about your relationship comes from your own insecurities. Instead of focusing on the worst that can happen, work with your partner on creating plans for your future. Find a goal you both share, such as buying a car or a home. When at work, having a reason to be there that includes your partner, can help you stay focused.

Unfortunately, this type of behavior is not unusual in obsessive love relationships and can begin a downward spiral. You might not lose your job, but you might be seen as a substandard employee, someone undependable or unable to do their job well. You are passed over for promotions and stuck in a career dead-end. Either way, your self-esteem plummets. You may be angry at yourself for giving in to the urges to leave work, but you can't help yourself. Suppose you don't have a job. This is just one more reason to fear your partner leaving. Why would she want to stay with someone who isn't working? You feel even worse and the worry you tried to avoid grows.

Ignoring Other Relationships

Having a strong circle of social relationships is good for your emotional and physical health. In a review of research on how social relationships impact health, completed at Brigham Young University and the University of North Carolina at Chapel Hill and published in the July 2010 issue of PLoS Medicine, having a strong network of friends increases your lifespan. Those with poor social connections had an average 50 percent higher chance of death within the study period, the same as the mortality difference between smokers and nonsmokers.

Other studies showed many health benefits in individuals with strong support networks from friends and relatives. A few of these studies:

- In a study completed at Carnegie Mellon University, the human immune system worked better in those individuals with a larger network of friends.

- A study published in the journal *Cancer* showed that cancer patients also showed a higher level of recovery, with more positive results from chemotherapy.

- A study conducted at Carnegie Mellon University showed those with a network of friends and relatives were better able to deal with stress, took better care of themselves physically and emotionally, and had higher self-esteem than those without a variety of friends.

The medical profession has just recently begun to understand the importance of having a dependable social network, and the health problems that can develop without this network in place. Isolation, created by the need to be "the one and only" in your partner's life, is not only emotionally detrimental but, as the studies point out, can be dangerous to your health.

Besides taking time from work, as an obsessive lover, you may be reluctant to spend time with friends or family. You can't bring yourself to be away from your partner, even for a few hours. If forced to be apart, you call or text her. Keeping in touch helps to relieve your nervousness about what she is doing and who she is with. You probably can't focus on what is going on around you. Your friends have probably called, wanting to know where you have been, but your social life revolves around your partner.

You may have tried to isolate your partner. You may cause arguments when she wants to go out with friends or see her family. Or you might point out their faults, believing they are a bad influence. An obsessive lover may believe they have a right to keep their partner from her friends, to protect her from those who might take her away. But your partner has the right to be friends with whom she chooses, and to spend time with them.

Walt and Molly had been living together for several months. For a while, Molly met her friends one night a week after work. They usually had dinner together. Most of her friends were single, and Walt thought they tried to persuade Molly to leave him. He had met them a few times, and they didn't seem to like him.

Whenever Molly had plans to meet her friends after work, Walt was irritable in the morning. He wouldn't talk, he wouldn't give her a kiss good-bye. He couldn't focus on work and when he arrived home to an empty house and no dinner, he felt worse. By the time Molly would get home, he was miserable and they usually had an argument. He told her that her friends weren't any good for her. He believed that, once you were in a relationship, you should only hang out with other people in relationships.

True Love	When you are in a healthy love relationship, the emotional well-being of the other person is more important than your opinion of her friends.

Eventually, Molly stopped going. She was tired of fighting about it every week. Walt was happy, but she missed her friends and resented Walt's insistence that she find new friends whom he approved of. Although Walt succeeded in getting Molly to stay home with him, the loss of her freedom was a big price for Molly to pay. Walt didn't see it that way. He saw only that Molly was at home with him.

Walt's reaction to Molly going out without him is common in obsessive love relationships. Although he didn't specifically order Molly not to go out, he made life miserable for her when she did. Later, Walt was proud of the fact Molly chose to stay home with him and flaunted the fact that it was her choice, not his.

As an obsessive lover, you may completely isolate your partner eventually. You might opt to stay home instead of going to social events with your friends, letting her know that you are willing to give up your friends for her. "Why don't you love me the way I love you?" you might say, trying to make her feel guilty. You might find excuses to not attend family events. "After all," you say, "we only need each other."

Ignoring your responsibilities at work and isolating your partner from friends and family result from jealousy, usually without reason. Some of the suggestions in the previous chapter should help you cope with your feelings of jealousy.

When you hold someone so tightly, you are not only holding your partner back from enjoying life, you are holding yourself back as well. Your insecurities are causing you to miss out on having fun. Working on improving your own self-image, either through the exercises in this book or with a therapist, can help.

Communication in your relationship is also extremely important. When you are willing to express your own views, and listen to your partner's, you can overcome many problems and issues. Making sure your partner is happy should be your priority. Listen to how your behavior makes your partner feel. Work on accepting what she says and not what you think she should feel. If your behavior is causing pain or turmoil, you need to make changes. Your instinct may be that your partner should change to make you more comfortable, but relationships work both ways, and it may be you who needs to change to make her more comfortable.

Masking Emotional Pain

Fear of rejection, rejection, and constant worry or stress, are all part of obsessive love—and all cause emotional pain. You may have a hard time coping and turn to different ways to numb your feelings. In the end, most of the methods described here will end up causing additional problems.

As an obsessive lover, you may turn to alcohol or drugs. There are no statistics that link obsessive love to substance abuse. However, risk factors for substance abuse include poor relationships with your parents, loneliness, and low self-esteem. These are all thought to contribute to obsessive love as well.

When the pain of an obsessive relationship gets to be too much, you may turn to either alcohol or drugs to forget about it or numb it. This can happen when you are in a relationship and are having trouble dealing with the constant fear that your partner is unfaithful or may be thinking of leaving you. Or perhaps your relationship recently ended and you are having a hard time coping.

But this type of self-medicating doesn't work. What starts out as a way to ease the emotional pain you are feeling can become a problem in itself. Substance abuse is a physical dependency on either alcohol or drugs. If you have an addiction, you have developed a tolerance to the substance and will experience withdrawal symptoms if you don't use it. Not everyone who uses drugs or takes a drink becomes addicted, but many people do.

Did You Know?

MISC.

The National Institutes of Health indicate that men who have more than 15 drinks per week, women who have more than 12 drinks per week, or anyone who has 5 or more drinks in one sitting, are at risk for developing alcoholism.

Eating can also be used as a way to reduce stress or cope with pain. Compulsive overeating is also known as a food addiction, and can be used as a way to calm or soothe emotions. This type of behavior can lead to health problems, such as obesity, high cholesterol, diabetes, high blood pressure, arthritis, and heart disease.

In some ways it is harder to overcome an eating disorder than substance abuse. You can learn to completely abstain from drinking or taking drugs and still lead a normal, productive life. But you can't abstain from eating; you must learn to regulate something that you can't eliminate. These types of addictions might help for a little while. A bowl of chocolate ice cream can make you feel better, until the bowl is empty. In order to keep feeling better, you need to keep eating the ice cream.

With any addictive behavior, your feelings of jealousy are still there when the effect of the drugs, alcohol, or food is gone. On top of that, you have an additional problem to face. All of these can interfere with your job, cause problems with family, and cause financial hardship. Even so, if you are addicted, you will continue to use whatever substance you choose. These types of addictions usually require addiction counseling.

Case Study: Stan

Stan and Miranda were married and in many ways had a good life. But when Miranda received a promotion at work, it included six months of second shift work. She was excited about the new job and the new opportunity, and Stan was happy for her.

Once she started working second shift, Stan had a hard time. He found he was jealous every night. He knew he shouldn't be, but he couldn't help it. At first, he would drive by Miranda's job. He always saw her car exactly where it was supposed to be. When he called, she always answered the phone. But she did tell him not to call so she could get her work done.

Stan was a nervous wreck. He began eating from the time he got home from work until Miranda arrived home at 11:30 P.M. He ate cookies, ice cream, popcorn—whatever was in the house. Eating helped relieve the jealousy by making him feel good and giving him something to do.

At the end of the six months, Stan was thrilled that Miranda would be home again in the evenings—but he had gained more than 20 pounds.

Essential Takeaways

- When anger is used productively it can help make you closer to your partner.
- Writing down your negative thoughts can help you become aware of what you tell yourself and find positive alternatives.
- Learning to communicate with, and listen to, your partner helps you stay focused on their emotional well-being.
- Substance abuse and other ways to mask emotional pain only work for a short time, and end up causing additional problems.

Part 3

The Partner of an Obsessive Lover

Is your relationship smothering you? Do you wonder if it's normal for your partner to want to be with you all the time? Sometimes it is hard to see our relationships objectively; we aren't sure whether behaviors are normal or not. In this part we have some questions for you to think about to help you view your relationship in a new light and decide whether you might be in an obsessive relationship.

If your partner is obsessive, do your behaviors encourage or discourage his actions? No matter how much we don't want the obsessive behaviors, we sometimes have landed in such a relationship because it meets our emotional needs. As the partner of an obsessive lover, you'll read about which of your behaviors encourage your partner's obsessiveness and we'll offer tips on how you can make some changes in your actions to improve your relationship.

chapter 7

Is Someone Obsessed with You?

You are dating someone: he calls you a couple of times every day, he wants to see you every day. Is he attentive or is he obsessed? Or you are living with someone and he wants to know where you have been, who you have been with. He wants to be with you every day. He says he loves you so much.

When someone clearly steps over the line, following you or becoming overly possessive, it is easy to know he is being obsessive. But sometimes knowing where the line is drawn isn't so easy.

10 Questions to Ask Yourself

Each relationship is different. Just as each obsessive lover uses different ways to control their partner. New lovers may act differently than those who have been in relationships for months or years. Even so, most obsessive relationships share some characteristics.

Read the following questions and place a check mark next to each one that describes your relationship.

❏ Do you feel smothered by your partner's behaviors, or does your partner continually question you about where you have been and who you have been with?

❏ Does your partner accuse you of cheating without cause?

❏ Does your partner tell you he knows your feelings better than you, or try to convince you that you do love him?

❏ Have you broken up with someone and he refuses to believe it is over, continuing to pursue you even when you ask him to leave you alone?

❏ Do you receive phone calls, gifts, notes, or other unwanted communication?

❏ Does your partner follow you when you leave the house or does he check up on you by looking through your phone, e-mails, private diaries, Facebook page or other social networks, or calling your friends?

❏ Does your partner visit you unannounced, either at work or at home, to check on your activities?

❏ Do you feel anxious or worried about your partner's behavior to the point that it causes you physical or emotional discomfort, or stops you from going to work, going out with friends, or even completing daily activities?

❏ Does your partner argue with you or get upset when you make plans to go out without him?

❏ Do you avoid going out with friends or getting together with family because your partner doesn't want you to go?

Even one check mark is a warning that you may be in an obsessive relationship.

If you are in an obsessive relationship, you might find the behavior of your partner a bit annoying or you might be overwhelmed. You may feel *oppressed.* You may be fearful. Because each obsessive love relationship is different, you might not have the same reaction as someone else. No matter how you feel, if you don't want the attention, or you feel as if you want or need to get out, don't put up with it.

Definition

To be emotionally **oppressed** is to feel overwhelmed mentally or physically to the point of not being able to act.

The bottom line is, if your partner's behaviors make you uncomfortable, or if you are not satisfied with your relationship, it is time to make some changes. This may mean taking steps to improve your own self-confidence or finding ways to make your relationship better. It might mean leaving him. Throughout this chapter, we will talk about some of the ways obsessive lovers try to keep you with them and how you can work to create a healthy relationship with yourself and, if you choose to stay, with your partner.

Possessiveness vs. Affectionate Love

It feels good when the person you love pays attention to you. You want him to ask how your day was, listen when things go wrong, and be happy when things go right. You crave affection. You want a hug, a kiss, to hold hands, or to feel an arm wrapped protectively around you. You feel flattered. It makes you feel secure, safe, loved, wanted, and appreciated.

The obsessive lover fills our need for affection and attention. He wants to share every part of your life and be included in everything you do. People outside the relationship may be impressed with what looks like devotion when he accompanies you to the nail salon and waits patiently. They don't know that he doesn't want to let you out of his sight.

obsession Alert

Infatuation and obsession can look and feel similar. Infatuation is becoming engrossed in a relationship or carried away by feelings of love. Infatuation normally fades away in a healthy relationship. Obsession is fueled by a fear of rejection and is all-consuming. Obsessions don't normally fade away and often intensify over time.

Anna met Patrick shortly after she moved to Philadelphia. Everything was new and exciting, but it was also scary and lonely. Anna didn't know anyone other than people who worked in her office. She didn't have any friends yet. Patrick took away the loneliness. She no longer had to come home to an empty apartment with nothing but the television for company. Within weeks of meeting, Patrick was calling her several times a day and coming by every evening after work. They never made plans to see one another; Patrick was just always there, wanting to know everything about her day. He helped her decorate her apartment and came with her to out-of-the-way boutiques. No one had ever paid this much attention to Anna and she was thrilled. It made her feel good to know that someone wanted to be with her. She welcomed the attention and thought it might be love.

But as Anna made other friends and made plans to meet them after work, Patrick would sulk and make her feel guilty for going out, saying she didn't love him anymore. He would sit on her steps and wait for her to come home. Anna wanted to be with Patrick, but also wanted to meet other people in her new city. At first she thought Patrick's attention was great, but after a while, it became smothering. Patrick had crossed the line from being interested in Anna to being obsessed with Anna.

It is easy to confuse the desire to be with you all the time with love. We attribute certain behavior to love when it is really a desire to possess you as if you were an object. This is especially difficult if you are in a vulnerable situation, such as Anna. Other times you may be vulnerable when you are …

- On the rebound from a failed relationship.

- Unhappy in other parts of your life, such as work.

- Financially strapped.

- Self-conscious about your appearance.

- Feeling your biological clock ticking.

- Feeling insecure because all your friends are married or in a relationship and you are not.

- Approaching a "milestone birthday" i.e. 30, 40, 50.

If Anna had not been in such a vunerable situation, she might have seen Patrick's actions as smothering and stopped the relationship earlier. Looking back, she wasn't sure exactly when Patrick changed from being interested in her to being obsessed, but in the end, Anna needed to break free.

Before jumping into a relationship, think about what's important to you. If you need to, make a list of the things you are not willing to give up, such as seeing your family, spending time with friends, joining co-workers after work, or having an evening a week by yourself. A relationship should not stop you from caring for yourself. Set ground rules from the beginning and let your new partner know you want to be with him, but also need time to yourself.

If you are already in a relationship with someone who is possessive— someone who wants to monopolize your time or tell you who you should see and who you shouldn't—tell him how his behavior makes you feel. Set limits on how often you will see each other or how much time you will spend together. Don't let the relationship stop you from pursuing your own interests.

The Roller-Coaster Ride of Controlling Love

As the partner of an obsessive lover, you have probably experienced at least some controlling behaviors in your relationship. The need to control comes from the fear of losing you. In an effort to keep you in the relationship, your partner tries to control your actions. He believes this will prevent you from leaving. Living in a controlling relationship eats away at your feelings of self-worth. You end up feeling drained, exhausted, and worthless.

| True Love | Discuss your personal boundaries with your partner during a calm time. Explain which boundaries are flexible and can be negotiated, and which boundaries you will not bend on. For example, if he begins to scream at you during an argument and you are not willing to listen to that, tell him; explain what you will do when that happens. You might say, "It makes me feel nervous when you yell at me. Next time, I will not listen to you if you are screaming. I will walk away and we can begin again when you are calm." Make sure you stick to it. When he yells, say, "I am walking away now. We will talk again later," then go into another room. |

Controlling behaviors can come and go quickly, leaving you feeling like you are on an emotional roller coaster. One minute he is sweet, professing his love for you, the next he is putting you down. This type of control keeps you guessing and leaves you feeling confused. When he is controlling, you are ready to leave; then he apologizes or acts nice, and you are ready to stay. With the constant ups and downs, you end up wondering if you are crazy.

Amanda was in just such a relationship. Amanda's husband was obsessive, so she rarely left the house without him, except to work and grocery shop. When she lost her job due to layoffs, he rushed home from work to offer her support, taking her out to lunch to cheer her up. He let her know it would be okay, that he could take care of her. He talked about her abilities and how she would find another job. But when she started looking for another job, he became irritable and difficult, questioning her intently about every interview and finding reasons for her not to accept jobs. He told her she didn't need to work, she could stay home and take care of him and the house.

Controlling partners intersperse their behaviors based on your needs. They will provide support and encouragement, and then take it away. This type of behavior keeps you off balance, always wondering what is going to happen and believing your behavior is the catalyst for his angry outbursts. You don't understand how this person can be sweet, charming, and supporting one moment and angry the next. Instead of focusing on the obsessive, controlling behaviors, you believe the kind person is the "real" person—that circumstances are too stressful or that you didn't do something right.

This roller-coaster ride is typical in many obsessive relationships. It keeps you guessing and believing you have the power to control his moods. Obsessive lovers frequently offer support, help around the house, bring home gifts to make you feel special and loved. But these behaviors are part of an overall pattern, one that keeps you in line and keeps your obsessive partner in control.

Even early in a relationship, you can see controlling behaviors. Because obsessive love is an illusion, the obsessive partner uses control to make you into the person of their dreams, rather than the person you are. Or they may use control as a way to reduce their own anxiety about being rejected. Sometimes you miss clues, especially if you are a people-pleaser. You don't initially feel like you are giving in, since your partner's happiness is more important to you than your own—actually making others happy makes you happy. Eventually, though, you want to pursue your own interests and your partner doesn't want you to.

Did You Know?

Controlling behaviors develop as a defense mechanism against the fear of rejection, or as a learned behavior from experiencing this type of behavior as children, usually at home. Either way, through hard work people who are controlling can learn to have happy, healthy relationships. Counseling, therapy, and self-help exercises (see Chapter 13) can help you in learning healthy ways to relate to your partner.

Examples of Controlling Behaviors

Controlling behaviors can wax and wane in a relationship based on whether or not your partner is feeling insecure. The following are some examples of how your partner may act.

He questions you about what you do with your time. He wants a breakdown of every minute of your day. What did you do? Where were you? Early in the relationship, this level of interest may feel exhilarating to you, but in time you feel like you must report to him all of your activities. If you go out shopping, he asks when you will be back. If you are late, he wants to know why.

He argues with you when you have a different opinion. When you argue, you're never right. Your partner always wins the argument. He says your opinions are not valid, or don't make sense. He challenges what you think. If you are mad about something he did or didn't do, he will avoid the subject or turn it around to be your fault.

He makes decisions for you. He tells you whether to accept that new job offer, or what you should do on your day off. He makes plans for you and expects you to follow them. He tells you how to behave when you go out and corrects you if you've done something he doesn't like. He acts more like your father than your partner.

He chooses your clothes and picks out what you should wear. It's nice to hear that you look nice, and everyone has modeled an outfit hoping for a compliment. But your partner takes this further. Instead of a compliment, he'll say, "That's okay, but why don't you wear ...." Or he goes through your closet and picks out what you should wear. He goes shopping with you because "you don't have a sense of style." He is critical of anything he thinks may attract the opposite sex.

He monopolizes your time. If you have something you want to do he'll find other things for you to do with him, to prevent you from going out or pursuing your own interests. He may make you wait for him. For example, if you want to talk he will tell you he will be right there but then make you sit and wait. If you are going out and ready to leave, he might not be ready. He offers to take you somewhere expensive when you have other plans. He may just beg you to stay home with him and pout when you don't.

He tells you that he feels you don't love him when you don't take into account his needs (i.e., do what he wants). You reassure him all the time and try to please him—even if it's not what you want, you go along to get along.

He takes control of the money. Maybe he gives you an allowance or a weekly budget. He might question you every time you ask for money, even to go grocery shopping, and want to see the receipt when you return. He might have a savings account, in his name only, that he transfers money to so you do not have access to it. Sometimes he just keeps spending the money on other things and there is nothing left. If you don't live together, somehow you wind up spending only your money, even if you are doing what he wants to do.

He tells you what you think. Some controlling partners will continuously say, "I know you better than you know yourself."

He blames you for his behaviors. When you point out controlling behaviors, he will turn it around to be your fault. "I wouldn't be this way if you ...," or "You make me act this way ...," or even, "I just love you so much, that's what makes me act like this."

He puts you down. This can be direct put-downs, such as "You are stupid," and "You are fat," or can be more subtle, such as "You wouldn't understand," or "It's too complicated for you." He might make fun of you or mimic you when alone or in front of other people. He might not include you in decisions, which makes you feel less than competent. He may come behind you and "fix" whatever you have done, for example, fix your cooking, remake the bed. He may even claim that he is doing it to help you and leave you wondering why you feel so badly about yourself.

He's the Daddy/She's the Mommy. He takes care of you. You voluntarily give up control because no one ever made you feel cared about.

Coping with a Controlling Partner

As the partner of an obsessive lover, you want to make sure your behavior doesn't enable the controlling behaviors. Setting boundaries and sticking to them is hard. However, if you want to stay in the relationship and make it work, it is important to do so. When reading through the following tips, remember the goal is not to change your partner's behavior, but to change your reaction to the behavior. If his behavior still doesn't change, you may need to reevaluate your relationship.

- **Communicate with your partner.** Let him know what behaviors you don't like and why. Tell him what you expect and how you prefer to be talked to. Let him know which behaviors are unacceptable. Being quiet and not telling your partner how you feel allows the controlling to continue.

- **Don't lie.** Although it might be tempting to lie, especially if your partner wants to know your every move, lying will only make matters worse. Your partner's insecurities are driving his suspicions. Lying will give him further reason to be untrusting. Lying will also give him a good excuse to blame you for the problems in the relationship or his controlling behavior.

- **Look at how your own behavior might enable controlling behavior, then refuse to participate.** In controlling relationships there usually is one partner who controls and one person who is controlled. Sometimes both partners are controlling—just in different ways and at different times in the relationship. Many times people in a couple are more alike than different. There may be overt or covert controlling behaviors. If you refuse to be controlled, there is no one left to control. It will usually help to get a friend or counselor's input, as we often have a blind spot in seeing our own contribution to relationship difficulties.

In the end, you will need to decide whether the relationship is costing you too much. Make a list of what you have lost, given up, or spent. Make a list of how you have gained. Compare the quantity and quality of the items on these lists. Are there any deal breakers? If you have given up your dreams, lost your identity, or spend every day feeling smothered, it may be time to leave.

Misc.

Case Study: Erica

Erica and Greg have been married for over 15 years. Erica never thought Greg was obsessive or controlling, but lately she isn't sure. He had always liked buying her clothes—but that was because she didn't enjoy shopping and he did—so she let him. In the past couple years, since Greg lost his job, she noticed a number of changes. He wouldn't say she looked nice unless she was wearing an outfit he had bought. He found fault with little things, like how she cleaned the kitchen, and more and more would become jealous when Erica left the house. He checked up on her at work, questioning her about the men in the office. Who was she friends with? Who did she go to lunch with? Often he asked if she still loved him.

Erica thought Greg might be feeling insecure. He was trying to start his own business but it was going slowly. Erica was working two jobs and paying almost all the bills. She tried to be patient and not place more stress on Greg but his behavior lately had her on edge. It seems her life revolved around trying not to make Greg angry.

Erica was confused. How could she have not seen these behaviors sooner? Were they always there but she never noticed? She wanted to go to marriage counseling but Greg refused. Although she still loved Greg, Erica was tired of Greg's possessiveness and didn't want to spend every day worrying about what mood Greg was going to be in today. She decided a separation would be best.

Fear of Confrontation

For many people, it is easier to avoid an argument by being quiet than to confront your partner or get involved in a screaming match. You may be one of many people who find it hard to talk about their feelings, especially if they are angry ones. This fear can make you more vulnerable to being controlled.

Candace grew up in a home where arguing was not allowed. Her mother became extremely anxious any time voices were raised. When Candace fought with her brother, her mother would stop the argument and send them to their rooms for a little while. They could come out only when they were ready to apologize and speak nicely to each other. Conflict was avoided at all costs to keep her mother calm and happy.

Candace met Mark when she was 19 years old. By the time she turned 21, they were married. In the beginning, they got along well. But, as with all married couples, sometimes they didn't agree. When Mark got angry, he would scream and say mean things. Candace kept quiet. She didn't argue back or tell Mark what she thought, even when what he said hurt her. Because of her childhood, Candace lacked the skills to resolve conflict. She instead tried to keep Mark happy. She tried to guess what he wanted so he would never have a reason to get upset. She anticipated his moods and acted the way she thought would keep him calm. Mark's needs controlled Candace's life because she was afraid of any confrontation.

The fear of confrontation is not an excuse for someone to act controlling toward you. But if you have a hard time expressing your feelings because you are worried about their reaction, you are allowing the controlling behaviors to continue. Resentment and stress may build inside you until you feel like you are going to explode.

> **True Love**
>
> Healthy couples view conflict as a way to grow closer to one another. When conflicts arise, these couples look for a compromise, a way that both partners feel their values are intact. Conflicts should not be about power, control, or one person being right. During a confrontation, you should never insult the other person, and should accept and respect your differences. Both partners should feel comfortable expressing their opinions. Disagreements should remain about the issue, not about one another.

Dealing with confrontation takes practice. The following do's and don'ts can help give you the confidence to speak up when something is bothering you. In the beginning, you might need to work through it, step by step. As you become more confident, you will find some of the steps are no longer necessary.

Do remove yourself from the situation and prepare what you want to say. Write down how you feel and what you want to say. Continue by writing down all of the possible reactions your partner might have; think about how you would respond to each.

Don't jump into an argument without being clear about what you want to say.

Do start the conversation with "I." You are trying to get across how the situation made you feel, for example, "I get angry when you do this because …."

Don't start out with the word "you" or "I think you …." Beginning this way sounds like an accusation and will automatically put the other person on the defensive.

Do stick with the facts.

Don't over-embellish or exaggerate situations. Stick with exactly what happened.

Do be clear about why his behavior is a problem for you.

Don't expect your partner to be able to read your mind.

Do be clear about what changes you expect. How do you expect your partner to react to the situation in the future? What will you accept and what won't you accept?

Don't leave it up to your partner to interpret how he should act.

Do be willing to negotiate to find an agreement.

Don't accept lack of respect, humiliation, or intimidation as an end result.

Do clarify what you believe your partner said.

Don't tell your partner what he meant.

Above all, remain calm. This is about expressing how you feel and how you expect to be treated. You cannot change someone else's behavior, you can only change your reaction to it. Your focus needs to be about you.

Accepting Peace Offerings

The obsessive lover is looking for the impossible. He is looking for assurance that you will always be there, that you will always love him and you will love him with the intensity he needs. No matter how much reassurance you give, it isn't enough. As his obsessiveness escalates, you become agitated, uncomfortable, wary, and distant. Your partner seeks ways to get back control of the relationship by using sex and offering gifts.

Sex

Sex is a powerful tool and obsessive lovers use it to their advantage. He knows if he can get you to return to the bedroom, he has a chance to win back your love. Because it is so easy to feel close to someone after being intimate, he woos you, charms you, and even apologizes for his behavior. The romance of making love confuses you, drawing you back into the relationship. Sex is, in the obsessor's mind, a way to say, "See how much I love you." It is a resource used to lure you, as the partner of the obsessive lover, back to feeling secure. This may not be conscious but he knows from experience with you or others that you are drawn back into his orbit after sex.

obsession Alert

Some obsessive lovers use sex as a way to control their partner. They may demand sex, withhold sex as a punishment, or they may always wait for you to initiate sex as a way of feeling more powerful. This places the responsibility for intimacy, and the relationship, on you. In healthy relationships, both partners should have the right to say, "Not tonight, honey." In obsessive relationships, rejection may be used as a way to punish or demean the partner. If your partner is using sex as a way to exert control over you, it may be time to seek the help of a marriage counselor or therapist.

Gifts

Usually, obsessive lovers have spent enough time with you that they know what triggers romantic feelings and what makes you feel loved. They use this knowledge to find the perfect gifts that can give them leverage over their partner. It could be a handwritten love poem, or a seashell to remind you of the happy time you spent on vacation. It could be a bouquet of flowers. Whatever the gift, it is meant to serve as an apology or to manipulate the partner. The gift might be a way for you, as the partner, to back off from insistence upon respecting a particular boundary or just to reinforce the partner's belief that giving gifts equals love.

Unfortunately, gifts do not mean things will be different in the future and they do not represent an end to controlling behaviors. The gift isn't about you, it is about them. It is about fulfilling their need to have you remain in the relationship, to quell your fear or to return to the status quo.

Essential Takeaways

- The line between interested and obsessed is different in each relationship.
- Controlling behaviors come from a fear of losing you and as the fear intensifies, so do the behaviors.
- Being afraid to stand up for yourself frequently enables controlling behavior to continue.
- Obsessive lovers sometimes use sex or gifts as a way to bring you back into the relationship, to manipulate you into doing things their way or to ease your fear.

chapter 8

Identifying Contributing Behaviors

How your actions can enable obsessive behaviors

What emotional needs does your relationship satisfy?

Avoiding sending mixed signals

Why partners of obsessive lovers stay

It's easy to blame an obsessive relationship on the obsessive lover. He focuses too intently on his partner; she feels smothered and fights to regain her freedom. This is especially true when an obsessive lover has targeted someone he doesn't know or barely knows. In these cases, the partner or target doesn't ask for, or contribute, to the obsessive behaviors. She just wants to be left alone.

But in some obsessive relationships, although the partner probably doesn't like feeling smothered or trapped, she still may enable the obsessive behaviors without realizing it. In this chapter, we'll talk about how some partners do this and why. If this describes you, you can work to create a healthier outlook on love and, in turn, create a healthier relationship.

Are You Codependent?

If you are a *codependent* partner, you probably aren't overtly controlling. You might, however, have a fear of rejection, have a need for emotionally charged relationships, or need intense love to fill your own emptiness. Your relationship might fill a need for you to take care of someone. You might be ready to leave your obsessive lover one minute and ready to take him back the next.

Codependent partners act in ways that either encourage obsessive or negative behaviors—such as alcohol or drug use—or do nothing to stop or discourage the behaviors. They focus on their partner's problems and neglect their own needs. Codependents are attracted to partners struggling with a variety of problems, primarily addictions or other mental health problems—like those of obsessive lovers.

The following list describes some warning signs and behaviors of codependent partners. Put a check mark next to each one that describes you.

❏ Do you have an overwhelming need to fix, save, or rescue your partner?

❏ Do you consistently do more than your share in the relationship? Do you work harder to pay the bills? Do you do all the housework? Are you the only one who cares for the children?

❏ Would you feel guilty if you asked your partner to help more or if you stopped helping him?

❏ Do you want reassurance that you are doing a good job, are appreciated, and are loved? Do you seek recognition for all that you do?

❏ Are you afraid to leave your partner because you are afraid of being alone? Are you afraid your partner is going to leave you?

❏ Do you have a hard time saying no to your partner, even if it compromises your own values or places a hardship on you?

❏ Do you consistently sacrifice your own needs for the needs of your partner?

❏ Would your relationship feel empty if you were not taking care of your partner's needs?

❏ Do you feel offended, hurt, or angry if your partner says he doesn't want your help?

❏ Do you make excuses for your partner's behaviors?

If you checked one, you may have codependent tendencies; if you checked three to five answers, you probably want to learn more about codependency and take some steps to build your own self-esteem. If you checked more than five, you are probably codependent. Reading through this chapter and completing the exercises in Chapter 16 can help you break your cycle of poor or failed relationships.

True Love

Being codependent in a relationship often limits your ability to be yourself, enjoy yourself, and have fun. Even though it is difficult to leave an obsessive relationship, it helps to remember that many people find that they feel liberated and are able to relax and have fun once they separate from the relationship.

Meeting Emotional Needs

Codependency is a learned behavior and, like obsessive love, often has its roots in childhood experiences. Your parents may have neglected or abandoned you, leaving you with an emptiness inside. You crave love; you need to *feel* loved. And once you find someone to love you, you can't let go. You spend all your time trying to please your partner.

One type of person that codependents are attracted to is an obsessive lover. The intensity of obsessive love draws you in. It is exactly what you have been looking for—you think it's how love is supposed to be. Finally, someone wants to love you completely, make you the center of their universe. You can't believe how lucky you are. No one has ever loved you this way before. Your lover and your relationship seem perfect, at least in the beginning.

Kelly met Dan after a painful divorce. She had grown up with an alcoholic father and, even though she swore it would not happen to her, she married an alcoholic. Her ex-husband had expected her to take care of the house, pay the bills, and work full time. Her ex-husband rarely worked—and rarely paid attention to Kelly, unless he wanted something from her. Kelly stayed in the relationship for nearly 10 years, leaving several times before she finally left for good.

She was glad to be free of her ex-husband, but the loneliness and emptiness were back. When she met Dan, he immediately told her how beautiful she was. Kelly would say that was the moment she fell in love. Dan showered Kelly with attention. He called every day. He brought her flowers. He wanted to be with her all the time. Kelly thought she was in heaven. Finally, someone loved her.

At first, Kelly was flattered by Dan's jealousy. No one had cared whether she was around or not and Dan made her feel like she mattered. But Kelly was also used to being independent. As a child, she had fended for herself and she had been the sole breadwinner in her marriage. She came and went as she pleased; as long as she gave her ex-husband money for beer, he didn't care what she did.

True Love	Sometimes, both partners in a relationship are obsessive. Both are looking for the other person to fill their emotional needs. Perhaps there was a lack of affection or love during childhood and the partners are both searching to fill that void. When people are emotionally needy, their relationships tend to be intense and there is an insatiable need for affection and affirmation. To begin to heal and allow yourself to develop a healthy relationship, ask yourself what you wish your parents had done differently to show their love. This can help you discover what you are missing emotionally and help you explain to your partner what you need to feel loved and accepted.

In the beginning Kelly loved the attention, she told Dan everything she did, and answered all of his questions and dozens of daily calls. But as Dan became more and more possessive, Kelly fought back. She went out without telling him, and lied about where she had been. She would leave Dan for a few days and then return. She bounced back and forth, between needing Dan's love and wanting her freedom. Like many partners of obsessive lovers, Kelly's relationship filled the deep emptiness she felt inside. Past hurts were soothed by the intensity of Dan's feelings.

You may have been drawn into your current relationship because you wanted the deep emotional bond your partner promised. You may have fallen in love with being loved. But most people also need to be independent, to set their own hours, be their own person, and follow their own dreams. The price of being in an obsessive relationship is often the loss of all of that. For some, it is too high of a price and they want out.

The Need to Nurture, Save, and Help

Jealousy and possessiveness come from insecurities. Some partners see past these emotions and see the lost child inside. As the partner of an obsessive lover, if you are codependent you may want to help, nurture, or save your partner from the emotional scars of his past. You are sure your love is what he needs to heal, that your love is so strong he will stop being insecure and jealous. Your love will enable him to trust.

Like the young girl who constantly brings home stray kittens, you seek out needy partners to satisfy your *own* need to be nurtured. An obsessive lover needs you, and you need to be needed. This role is easy for women to fall into, as they are brought up to be the caretakers in a relationship. But men can have the need to be a savior or hero, as well.

All couples help each other from time to time. We all fall into situations we can't manage by ourselves and we need someone to help or support us. But if you're spending your time and energy trying to make your partner feel better, your need to nurture might stifle your own growth.

obsession
Alert

If you find most of your partners are needy, it may be because you are also needy. You are taking care of someone in order to receive love. When one person is needy and the other nurturing, the relationship is uneven. To find a partner who isn't needy, learn to take care of and love yourself. Once you can act loving toward yourself, you can be loving toward someone and accept their love in return.

Ella and Stephen were married. Stephen was extremely possessive. He didn't want Ella to leave the house unless he was with her. Ella understood that Stephen had been abandoned as a child and he was insecure. Ella made sure she didn't do anything to make Stephen jealous. When he said he didn't want her to drive, she said okay. When she went grocery shopping, he came with her. She didn't work outside the home. She watched the television shows he wanted to watch and wore the clothes he had helped pick out. She did this all because she loved him and she wanted to give him a home where he felt secure and loved. In turn, Stephen's constant attention made Ella feel cared about and cared for. It was easy to let him do things for her because Ella also needed to feel secure.

Ella thought she was helping Stephen, but both of them were stifled in their relationship. Stephen never had the chance to face and outgrow his own demons because Ella was there to face them for him. Ella was never allowed to grow, to find out what she liked in this world, and follow her interests.

Your relationship may not be as extreme as our example, but by allowing possessiveness to rule your relationship, no matter how much, does not help. True nurturing is helping the other person to develop, grow, and find his own talents. Rather than helping, codependency stops your partner from feeling any pain, from learning from mistakes, and from learning about healthy love.

When Both Partners Are Obsessive

Occasionally, both partners in a relationship are obsessive. Early in the courtship both you and your partner want and need constant reassurance and contact. Imagine Jean and Frank. Frank sends texts to Jean any time they are apart. Jean doesn't find them annoying—she eagerly waits for Frank to text or call her. Frank's work as a customer service rep gives him time to text as he is working. But sometimes, he is on the phone with a customer and the texts suddenly stop. Jean becomes nervous and starts texting Frank, over and over. She calls, leaving a frantic message asking what is wrong. Sometimes the situation is reversed and Jean can't take Frank's call. Frank gets anxious. He actually feels rejected. Frank calls and texts repeatedly.

As time passes, one partner usually begins to feel more secure in the relationship and begins to feel less of a need to be in constant contact and thus pulls away a little. The other partner usually becomes frantic at the perceived abandonment or rejection. The partner may find the extra intensity uncomfortable or unattractive. When the partner who is activated/triggered finally backs off and perhaps threatens to leave, that triggers the partner who had previously become secure to become more obsessive because they now fear abandonment. This may begin a cycle where one partner is always pulling in too close and the other is backing off, only to later reverse the roles. These lovers may break up and make up frequently. Make-up sex is usually very intense and bonding.

If they are able to stay in a long-term obsessive relationship, both partners generally have obsessive love tendencies. When only one person has obsessive love tendencies, the other person breaks the relationship pretty easily and rapidly when the partner begins being excessively jealous and possessive.

As an obsessive lover and an obsessive partner, you thrive on your partner's willingness to be involved in every part of your life, because it satisfies your need to be reassured of your partner's presence and love.

Sending Mixed Messages

You come home from work, tired after a long day. You have dinner and then settle down in front of the television with your boyfriend to relax. A friend from work texts you, asking if you can pick her up tomorrow because her car is in the shop. You text back, letting her know you'll be there.

Your boyfriend asks who texted you. "Someone from work needs a ride tomorrow."

He wants to know who. "Jenna," you answer. "I'm giving her a ride, her car is in the shop."

He grabs the phone to check the texts. You get angry and grab the phone back.

"It's not important, she just needs a ride to work. Can we watch the show?" You end the conversation, letting him know the subject is closed. He sulks, but accepts defeat.

The next night, the same thing happens, but he becomes more demanding, wanting to know who texted and what they wanted. You finally give in, telling him and then showing him the text to prove what you said.

Even though you tried and succeeded the first night to let your boyfriend know he needed to trust you, your actions the following night showed him the opposite. Your mixed messages let him know that persistence wins. As the partner of an obsessed lover, you want your partner to trust you, to take you at your word, and to accept that you are with him because you want to be. But your actions might be telling him something different. The following sections describe some of the ways you might be sending mixed messages to your obsessive partner.

The following is one of the most frequent and disastrous mistakes so many people make. Mixed messages can occur even after a relationship ends. Your ex calls, asking if he can see you. You agree to meet for a cup of coffee, but letting him know you don't want to get back together. Or you try to let your partner down gently and, instead of making a clear decision about leaving, you say you want to be friends and still stay in touch, but don't want a relationship. In obsessive relationships, these types of mixed messages are confusing. The obsessive lover hangs onto any sign of hope, even though you're just being polite and don't want to see him anymore. Frequent motivation is doing this to assuage feelings of guilt. It is better to be clear about your intentions and end the relationship entirely.

Making Excuses

You are out with friends and you get text after text from your boyfriend. Your friends keep telling you to turn off your phone and relax, but you can't do that. You know if you don't answer the texts it will only cause more problems—your boyfriend will come looking for you or start a big argument when you get home. So instead of turning off your phone, you make up a story. You tell your friends your boyfriend had some crisis at work and is worried about it. He is texting you to vent and cope with the stress he is under.

You know your partner's behavior is wrong, that it intrudes into other parts of your life, and that your friends think it's weird. You want to be with your friends, relax, and have a good time. But your thoughts are constantly going back to your partner and what mood he'll be in when you get home. You're ashamed that you can't stand up to him, and your embarrassment about your own actions causes you to make excuses. If you told the truth, you would have to own up to your part of the dysfunction in the relationship.

But this type of behavior can be confusing to your partner. When you are at home, you tell him you don't want him texting you when you are out with friends, but then you respond to his texts. You're sending mixed messages. In the long run, it is better to let your partner know in advance you will not be answering your phone or texts while you are out. Be ready to stand firm when you get home, and then turn off the phone and enjoy yourself.

To make it easier to follow through, leave the phone in the car or give it to a friend and tell her not to give it back until the evening is over. Initially this may make you quite anxious, but do not look to see if there are any messages.

Tolerating Excessive Behaviors

Your family is having a picnic and your boyfriend refuses to go. He says your family doesn't like him, and he doesn't want you to go, either. He tries to make you feel guilty. He can't believe you would choose to go over being with him. "If you love me, you'll stay home with me." You call your mom and tell her you aren't feeling well.

True Love	In a healthy relationship, both partners' needs and wants are important. When you begin a relationship, even if you are very easy going by nature don't let your partner choose every movie, every restaurant. Speak up, let him know what you like and what you expect. Take turns choosing the movie or the restaurant. Let him know that what you want is just as important as what he wants. If you don't, he will assume that he can make decisions for you.

You're at a party and you run into some old friends. You spend time sitting with them, catching up. You see your partner glaring at you from across the room and you know he wants you by his side. He doesn't know the person you're talking to and he's getting angry that you aren't paying attention to him. After a few minutes, you excuse yourself and join your partner for the remainder of the party.

A co-worker calls you about a work project. You talk for a few minutes and then get back to household chores. Your partner wants to know who called and why. You resent the questioning and tell him so. He continues to pester you and you finally give in and tell him what the phone call was about.

Every time you accept your partner's obsessive behaviors, you let him know that it is okay to treat you with so little respect. You may argue or fuss about his behaviors, but in the end, you give in and accept them. Your behavior lets your partner know that if he is persistent, you will eventually give in to his demands.

Taking the Blame

Often, your obsessive partner will blame you for his behavior. He might say, "If you didn't flirt so much, I wouldn't get jealous," or "If you would tell me who called, I wouldn't get so angry." After hearing this over and over, you begin to believe it. You begin to believe that you have control over your partner's actions. You have the power to make him trust you. And when he doesn't, it must be your fault. Codependents are focused upon trying to control their partner's problematic behaviors instead of identifying and solving their own problems. They are very susceptible to accepting the blame because they assume that if they try hard enough they can (control) make someone do something. That control is an illusion.

Case Study: Rhonda

Rhonda and Trent were in a relationship. Trent was jealous and told Rhonda over and over that she caused his behaviors. He said she dressed to attract other men and intentionally flirted in front of him. Rhonda didn't think she did that, but she started changing how she acted. She bought new clothes that were modest and wouldn't attract attention. Maybe she had dressed too sexy, she thought. She became reserved and quiet whenever there was another man around, so Trent wouldn't have a reason to be jealous. Rhonda believed that if she changed, Trent would, too. Unfortunately, even as Rhonda became less and less like herself, Trent was still jealous.

Trent's jealousy was never Rhonda's fault. No matter how much she tried or adjusted her own behavior, he would still be jealous, because jealousy comes from internal insecurities. External situations might trigger jealousy, but they are not the cause.

As you begin to take the blame, you change your behavior in an effort to keep your partner happy, to soothe his jealousy. Soon, everything you do revolves around keeping your partner calm. You stop talking to friends; you go out only when your partner allows it. You answer all of his questions. You feel like you are walking on eggshells in your own home.

Jealousy and possessiveness come from your partner's insecurities due to unresolved issues in his own life. You do not have the power to change these behaviors. It is not your fault and nothing you do makes him act in a certain way. You are responsible for your behaviors and your partner is responsible for his.

Reasons Partners Stay

Why would you stay in a relationship where your partner is controlling, possessive, and so obsessed with you that you no longer have a life of your own? The answer to these questions is not easy. No matter how bad the relationship is, there is an emotional bond between you and your partner. Your partner undoubtedly has good qualities that originally drew you to him. You have a history together. It is never easy to end a relationship and throw away the time you have spent together. When things are going well, you recall how good you felt in the early part of the relationship and hope everything will go back to those times. Generally there is a lot of vacillation and shifts in mood and feelings of hope.

Fear

It's a scary world out there, and even an uncomfortable situation is better than going out in the unknown world alone. Many partners of obsessive lovers, especially those who are codependent, are just as afraid of rejection, abandonment, and being alone. Leaving means facing the pain of being alone. It is easier to remain in an obsessive relationship than to leave and be alone.

Joan felt smothered by her husband, Larry. She worked as a cashier at a local department store and met her sister for lunch once a month; other than that, she only went out with Larry. She longed for the days when she was single, when she had a social life and looked forward to each day. She didn't know getting married meant she had to stop going anywhere unless Larry came along. Even when they went to family get-togethers Larry felt she needed to be by his side at all times. She wanted to sit in the kitchen with her cousins and gossip, but he would insist she sit by him—except, of course, when she got up to get him a drink or a plate of food.

Joan knew that it was not how everyone else lived. She would see her sisters and cousins sitting together, laughing and talking while their husbands were gathered in the other room. None of them seemed to even notice or care that their spouse wasn't at their side. Joan knew she should leave Larry, but the thought of being alone scared her to death. Larry made her feel secure and he always told her how much he loved her. She wasn't sure she could make it on her own. She had never lived by herself and the thought of it was overwhelming. Putting up with him needing her every moment was less frightening.

As the partner of an obsessive lover, you might feel the same as Joan did. No matter how smothering your partner's behaviors are, you know what to expect each day. You know you have a home and someone who comes home each night. You don't need to face being alone or feeling unloved. Staying is easier than facing your fears.

True Love

In healthy relationships, couples enjoy spending time with one another but also accept and encourage outside interests. If your partner doesn't feel secure with your being around other people, set limits. Reassure him that he is the most important person in your life, but he is not the *only* person in your life. Don't stop enjoying the company of your friends and family in order to satisfy a partner's possessiveness.

Low Self-Esteem

As the partner of an obsessive lover, you probably are insecure and have feelings of low self-worth. You don't think you can make it on your own—and your partner might remind you of this on a regular basis. Obsessive lovers often use put-downs as a way to keep you in the relationship. They make you feel you need them; that you aren't capable of managing a home by yourself. If you had low self-esteem when you entered the relationship, it might be even lower now. You feel you need your partner to survive. He takes care of you, pays the bills, feeds you. You need him because you aren't good enough to make it on your own.

And what about finding someone else? Would anyone else ever love you? Part of you knows you should be happy you have someone in your life. You have someone who loves you and wants you. You think that having someone who is jealous is better than having no one.

Finances and Children

Obsessive lovers use many different forms of control to make sure you don't leave them. As a partner of an obsessive lover, you might not work, or you might only work part time. Your partner might control the money that comes into the household, leaving you without resources to leave. Some partners of obsessive lovers need to ask for money even to go grocery shopping. This helps your obsessive partner feel secure that you won't abandon him.

Children can keep you tied to a relationship. If your partner is extremely controlling, he may use the children as a way to keep you with him. He might threaten to take the children away if you leave, holding it over your head. Or you may just be worried about not being able to care for them by yourself, not being able to afford to take care of them.

Cultural and Religious Reasons

We are brought up to believe that marriage is forever. When we separate or divorce, we feel we have failed. We think it is our fault that we could not maintain a relationship. Women especially tend to feel this way, because we are supposed to be nurturing and caretakers. When a marriage falls apart, we take the blame. This might be how you feel. You might see the end of your relationship as a reflection on you.

Our religious beliefs often define how we live. We want to be a good person and do what is right. Some religions disparage or forbid divorce. Your obsessive partner may use this as a way to keep you in the relationship. He will make you feel like you are a bad person or a sinner if you leave.

Or you may have been brought up believing that divorce is wrong. That no matter how bad the relationship is, it is an affront to God to walk out. You stay, feeling guilty that you even thought about walking away from your marriage.

Essential Takeaways

- An obsessive relationship can start out by filling your need for love.
- You may enable the obsessive behaviors and send confusing signals by getting angry one day and accepting obsessive behaviors the next day.
- When you accept obsessive behaviors you let your partner know it is okay to treat you this way.
- You may stay in a relationship because knowing what to expect, even if it is unhealthy, is easier than facing the unknown.

chapter 9

Breaking Up

Should you let your partner down easy or limit communication?

Preparing yourself for how your ex-partner might react

Caring for yourself emotionally after a breakup

Breaking up is hard. You must face the end of the dreams you had for your relationship. But sometimes, ending a relationship is for the best. The reasons are as unique as each relationship. You may feel your partner is too possessive; someone else may feel your partner's behaviors are appropriate and acceptable. You must decide if your relationship should end based on whether or not the relationship meets your own emotional needs.

In this chapter we'll talk about deciding how to end a relationship. Should you end it swiftly or let your partner down easy? And how can you take care of yourself after the breakup.

Is There a Best Way to Break Up?

Breaking up with someone is hard. It doesn't matter whether your relationship is new or you have been together for years. If you just recently started dating and realized you're not compatible, you still might feel guilt and sadness saying good-bye. If you've been together for years, a breakup ends many of your dreams and hopes for your future.

When you break up with an obsessive lover, the sadness you feel because of a failed relationship can be overshadowed by your partner's reaction. When faced with rejection, obsessive lovers might react by denying the relationship is over, becoming depressed and despondent, using drugs and alcohol, trying to win you back, stalking you, or, in extreme cases, becoming violent.

Even though you have left, your ex-partner's behavior can still influence and impact your daily life. It is impossible for you to turn off your feelings. If this has been a long-term relationship, you still care, you still love your partner, and your focus is divided between beginning your new life and worrying about how your partner is doing.

Did You Know?

Divorce or breakups put people through different stages similar to those you face with the death of a loved one. According to Phil Rich in an article in *Self Help* magazine, the four stages that occur after a divorce are:

1. Shock and disbelief

2. Initial adjustment

3. Active reorganization

4. Life reformation

People often move back and forth between stages as they redefine and explore their new life. The final stage doesn't really end but signals emotional growth.

Preparing for the Breakup

Leaving an obsessive relationship is never easy. At times it can seem like it will be impossible. But you must remember that you deserve to be in a healthy and loving relationship. You deserve to feel important, loved, and happy.

Don't threaten to breakup as a way to get your partner to act in a certain way. Threats will only make your relationship more difficult, as your partner will eventually realize that you're not serious.

For some partners of obsessive lovers, leaving the relationship is quick. They are decisive about moving on and ignore all attempts at contact by the obsessive lover. But for many partners, leaving an obsessive lover can be an emotional roller coaster. Following the steps outlined here might be helpful.

Think carefully about your relationship. Is your relationship worth saving or is it doomed? Remember, when deciding whether to end a relationship, one of the most important questions to ask yourself is, "Does this relationship enhance my life?" Relationships are not meant to cause pain and hurt (that's not to say that everyone in a relationship will never feel hurt or anger at their partner). A relationship is not meant to leave you feeling emotionally drained. Your relationship should make you feel good about yourself and make your life feel more complete.

Decide you want to leave. The first step in leaving an obsessive lover is to make up your mind to do it. Although this sounds easy, it is not. You may be conflicted, wanting to leave one moment, wanting to make the relationship work the next. Some partners of obsessive lovers can point to one moment in time when they resolved to leave. Maybe an incident made them understand that their partner was never going to change, or maybe it happened over a period of time, as the possessiveness and jealousy continued to wear them down. This is different for each person. One woman recalled hearing the song, "If You Don't Know Me By Now," playing on the radio. As she listened to the words, she knew it was talking about her life, if her husband could not trust her after 10 years of marriage, he never would. Another woman realized her relationship was over when she came home from visiting her mother and was accused of cheating. Some women may make the decision to leave, but spend months afraid to make it a reality.

Know you can leave. Your partner may make you feel guilty. He might focus on your weaknesses, making you doubt that you can survive without him. Or he may make you feel guilty, telling you how much pain you are causing him. Through all of this, you must remember that you can leave. You can live without him. You can have a new life.

Create a plan. If your relationship is extreme, giving you limited freedom, you might want to begin planning your escape months before you actually leave. Some women have hidden money over periods of time to make sure they have the financial resources to leave. Others have hidden extra car keys outside in the garden and made copies of documents, such as marriage certificates, mortgage information, and driver's licenses, keeping them at a friend's house for safekeeping. Make a list of what items or paperwork you will need and determine a safe place to keep the documentation. Your plan should also include where you will stay and how you will pay your bills.

Tell people you trust about your decision to leave. If your partner is obsessive, there is a chance he will become angry and upset or will come looking for you after you leave. Make sure you only tell people you are sure you can trust. You don't want this information getting back to your partner before you are ready. Let your friends know you may need their help when you leave. You may need a place to stay or help in staying away. If you aren't sure whether someone will keep your secret from your partner, keep him or her out of the process.

Talking to Your Partner

Before sitting down to talk with your partner, think about what you want to say. You might want to write it down. The conversation you are about to have will be emotional, for both you and your partner. You may have trouble remembering what you want to say when confronted with your partner's reaction. Having notes written down will help. Include examples of some of the behaviors you cannot live with.

If you are planning to talk with your partner, set up a time limit for the conversation. A conversation about breaking up, especially with an obsessive partner, can drag on and on. If you have a set time limit in place and stick to it, you can control how long the breakup takes. Have plans set up for after your breakup talk. For example, you might limit your conversation to one hour. Make plans to meet a friend somewhere one hour after you meet your partner. This will allow you to make an exit, saying, "I have plans to meet Pam at 8:00, so I need to leave now."

obsession Alert

Before you initiate your conversation, be sure you are safe. If you aren't sure how your partner will react or if you think you will be in danger, have someone with you or breakup from a distance such as through a note or e-mail. Although this sounds pretty callous, it may be the only way you can stay safe.

Initiate your breakup conversation when you are calm. If you blurt out, "I'm leaving you!" in the middle of an argument, your partner may believe that once you calm down you will be back. Instead, choose a time when you are calm and can remain determined about your decision. Let your partner know you have decided it would be best for you to end the relationship. Expect your partner to ask questions. He may want to know what he can do to make you stay. Decide beforehand whether you are going to answer these questions and how much you want to explain. If you are like many partners of obsessive lovers, you have probably explained many times already. Remember, this is your conversation, you can control how much you want to say and how long you want the conversation to last.

Be prepared for high emotions. If your partner reacts by crying, you can take a few moments to comfort him or let him recover but don't allow the crying to manipulate you or change your mind.

If your partner reacts by arguing with you, stop yourself from arguing back. Remember, it takes two people to argue. You are done arguing: you have made up your mind. Allow him a chance to have his say if you feel it is appropriate, but let him know that anything he says will not change your mind.

If your partner tries to make a deal, saying, for example, "If you stay and give me another chance, I will …," remember that no matter how many times you have tried to explain how you felt in the past, it hasn't done any good.

If your partner becomes angry or makes you feel concerned for your safety, end the conversation and calmly leave.

It is important to be honest and upfront when talking with your partner; however, it is also important not to make this conversation a time to air a laundry list of what you don't like about your partner. That time has passed. Stick to the important facts and issues.

Letting Go Slowly

An obsessive lover, as we have seen throughout this book, can't let go. He will take any sign of attentiveness as a sign of caring. If you call to see how he is managing, he will take this to mean you want to get back together. If you call to see if you have received any mail, he will assume you are using it as an excuse to talk to him. Any contact, no matter how small, will be seen as a possibility for reconciliation.

obsession Alert

An obsessive lover may not accept their partner has the right to break up with him. He believes he calls the shots and makes the decisions. If there is a divorce proceeding, he will do what he can to delay the process. Any contact or conversation will be used as a tool to once again be in control. By choosing to "let him down gently" you drag out the process and continue to let your ex feel he is in control.

Jenny and Terry had been dating for almost a year. Terry was ready to take the relationship to the next level. He wanted Jenny to move in with him, and assumed they would get married. He was focused entirely on the relationship. Jenny wasn't ready to move in and thought Terry was becoming too possessive. She told Terry she didn't want to see him anymore. Terry couldn't believe it and continued to call Jenny. Usually she turned him down, but sometimes she would give in and go out with Terry again. She felt conflicted; she liked Terry and enjoyed spending time with him, but couldn't take his possessiveness. She thought if they only saw each other once in a while, it would be better.

Terry, however, was confused. One day Jenny would tell him she didn't want to see him, the next week they would go out on a date. He held on tightly to the idea that Jenny would eventually move in with him.

Instead of breaking up, Jenny kept the relationship alive by trying, unsuccessfully, to let Terry down gently. Each time they would go out, Terry's hopes soared again. He didn't hear what Jenny said when she talked about seeing less of each other. He focused instead on every phone conversation, every date, and continued to plan their future together.

Jenny tried to make breaking up easier, but in the end she made it more difficult. Each time she got together with Terry, she became more stressed by his talk about marriage. Terry wasn't given the chance to move on, each time he called Jenny, he had a chance of her saying yes to going out for the evening. So he kept calling and kept hoping.

Breaking up with someone who is obsessed is difficult. As Jenny found out, there is no easy way to do so. Letting someone down easy can add to the pain and drag out the relationship. It sends mixed messages rather than a clear message that you are done with the relationship.

What to Expect

Each obsessive lover is different. Some may be extremely possessive and extremely attentive; others may be controlling, watching and questioning your every move. Just as obsessive lovers are different within relationships, they are different once the relationship has ended. Even so, there are some behaviors you can watch out for.

Depression

Some may become depressed and despondent. You don't have to worry about phone calls or gifts, instead you feel guilty and worry about his mental health. Each day you don't hear from him brings more anxiety. Instead of receiving daily calls, you are making the calls, checking in on him. You still love him, you still care, and you can't separate those feelings from your wanting to end the relationship.

Some obsessive lovers, in extreme cases, will threaten suicide. In most of these cases, this is an empty threat, a tactic to bring you back. However, all threats of suicide need to be taken seriously. How can you make sure your ex is okay while still maintaining distance in the relationship?

Jodi had ended her relationship with Travis. He had been extremely possessive and jealous when they were together. She had expected Travis to take the breakup hard and beg her to stay. But when she left, he simply looked sad. For a few weeks, Jodi thought everything was fine. She hadn't heard from Travis and, although there were times she missed him, she was happy with her decision.

Jodi was surprised when she received a phone call from Ben, Travis's best friend; he was worried about Travis. Ben said he had been calling and stopping by but Travis wasn't answering the phone or the door, and hadn't shown up at work for several days. Jodi drove over to check on Travis. He didn't answer the door but Jodi still had a key and let herself in. Travis was sitting on the couch. He looked like he hadn't showered in days, the curtains were closed, the apartment was dark. There were dishes on the kitchen counter and empty food containers scattered around. Travis just looked at her and then ignored her.

Case Study: Thomas

misc.

Thomas had been dating Chandra for several years. She was obsessive, following him to work meetings, sitting across the restaurant, hidden from view (or so she thought) to keep an eye on what he did and who he was meeting for lunch or dinner. Early in their relationship, Chandra had become friends with Thomas's mother and sister. Now whenever he went somewhere without her, she called his mother, complaining about how he treated her. Thomas would end up listening to a lecture the next day. He brought her flowers to be nice; she insisted he bought them because he felt guilty about something he had done. Thomas ended the relationship but Chandra couldn't accept it was over. She continued to follow Thomas and he thought he saw her peeking in his windows once, but by the time he went outside, no one was around.

One night, Thomas received a frantic phone call from Chandra. She was threatening suicide, "I just don't want to live if my life doesn't include you." Thomas rushed to her home, only to find her sitting in the dark waiting for him. She said she had realized it was a mistake and begged his forgiveness. This happened a few times before Thomas stopped coming over to check on her. The next time she called Thomas called the police and reported the call instead. When the police arrived, Chandra was sitting in the dark, waiting for Thomas. The police took Chandra to the hospital where she was admitted for a few days. Chandra never threatened suicide again.

Jodi began talking about anything just to get Travis to focus. She began to clean up: opening the curtains, picking up the trash, and washing the dishes. Travis sat on the couch. He kept saying, "See, I can't live without you." Jodi's guilt escalated, she felt responsible for Travis's depression and thought she hadn't done enough to help Travis through the breakup. She felt guilty that she wasn't this upset and had been enjoying the past couple weeks. Jodi started thinking there was something wrong with her, that she could be that uncaring. She started calling Travis and stopping by to check on him. Before she knew it, she was being drawn back into the relationship.

Jodi's mixed feelings are a common reaction. It is impossible to turn off your love for another person. You can't just one day stop caring, even when you know that the relationship is not healthy. When ending an obsessive relationship, it is easy to get pulled back in because of guilt or concern. Think about what situations may arise and make plans for how you are going to deal with it ahead of time. Instead of rushing over to check on Travis, Jodi could have met Ben somewhere and given him the key so he could check on Travis. She could have called the police and asked them to check on him. Jodi could have helped without becoming personally involved.

Self-Destructive Behaviors

Drinking, drugs, *high-risk behaviors*—an obsessive lover needs to find a way to mask the pain, to hide from the reality of the breakup. In the previous example, Travis felt the loss every moment. He may have, in some ways, enjoyed this feeling. His depression made him feel connected to his ex-partner. His actions were a way to connect with his emotions and feeling of loss. Others may use outward ways of avoiding their pain. They may drink too much, use illegal drugs, drive fast, or engage in other high-risk activities. They are using the high, whether from substances or adrenaline, to avoid feeling the pain.

High-risk behaviors are any behaviors, actions, or activities that are done without regard to safety or health. Some examples of high-risk behaviors include: having unsafe sex, excessive drinking, illicit drug use, driving fast, or driving under the influence.

Suppose, instead of a call from Ben saying he hadn't been able to get in touch with Travis, Jodi had received a different call. Ben and Travis were at a bar and Travis was drunk and wailing loudly about how he needed Jodi. Ben wanted Jodi to come to the bar and help quiet Travis. Jodi feels bad; she doesn't want Travis to be arrested for disorderly conduct because of her. She doesn't want him in pain. She goes to the bar, she quiets Travis down, and she takes him home. He wants her to stay the night. She sleeps on the couch, just for tonight, she tells herself.

The next day, Jodi leaves, she tells Travis she doesn't want to see him again. She goes back to her new life. But Travis has learned that Jodi will still come when he gets in trouble. He sees it as a good sign—she still loves him. For a few days, Travis stays away from drinking and focuses on calling Jodi to thank her. He sends her flowers. But as the days go by and he doesn't get the response he wants, he goes back to drinking, knowing that Jodi will come again if he needs her.

Jodi took responsibility for Travis's actions. She felt it was her fault that he was drunk and was willing to take the blame if he was arrested. She was still mixed-up, confusing love with guilt. She wanted her freedom but wanted Travis to be okay. Instead, Jodi could have told Ben she wasn't coming. She could have accepted that Travis was responsible for his own actions, not her. Even if Travis had been arrested, it was not Jodi's fault. By showing up and saving Travis, Jodi actually caused herself more problems. Travis is now sure that he can get Jodi to come back.

Promises to Change

When faced with the prospect of losing you, losing the relationship, many obsessive lovers will promise to change. They may beg you to stay, tell you they have learned, the future will be better, they will stop being possessive, they will stop being controlling, they will stop being jealous. Partners of obsessive lovers often make several attempts to leave, believing the promises and giving in because you still believe in the relationship or because you are also afraid of being alone. Eventually, though, partners will tire of the promises and the temporary attempts to change.

Greta had been in an on-again, off-again relationship with Jeff for a couple years. Greta always felt her needs were ignored but every time she tried to leave, Jeff would beg her to stay, promising he would change. He said he would pay more attention to Greta's needs, he would not get angry when she went out with her friends, and he would try to be less jealous. Each time, Greta believed Jeff and returned to the relationship. But the changes Jeff promised usually only lasted a few weeks, a month at the most, and then he would return to his old behaviors. The possessiveness, the jealousy, the neediness would all return.

Greta was stuck in the cycle of broken promises. Finally, she realized that all of Jeff's words were just that: words. She accepted he was not going to change. Finally, Greta made a plan to leave. She contacted old friends and found a new place to stay, someplace where Jeff wouldn't find her, and began her new life.

Often the obsessive lover will panic at the thought of losing the relationship. He will tell his partner whatever she wants to hear. He might even mean everything he says. He may want to change. But without working on the underlying reasons for his behaviors, change is unlikely.

After breaking up with an obsessive lover, you might be tempted to give in and see your ex. The constant barrage of phone calls, gifts, or flowers may wear you down. But sending gifts and flowers, or calling every day, are selfish acts. Your ex-partner did not care about your happiness when you were together, and he doesn't care now. What he wants is to have you back under his control. During the relationship, you were willing to forego your happiness and put his needs first, and he wants that back.

Stalking and Violence

In extreme cases, the obsessive lover may stalk you, follow you, become excessive in their attempts to contact you, or become violent because of anger or the need for revenge. In the last part of this book, we discuss what you can do to protect yourself against a stalker or violence. If you are experiencing this type of reaction after you have broken up with someone, you should involve the police and discuss legal options to put an end to it. If your ex-partner is violent you do not want to handle the situation yourself and put yourself in a dangerous situation.

How to Cope

Being in an obsessive relationship takes an emotional toll and your self-esteem takes a beating. Leaving an obsessive relationship can be even more difficult. Your obsessive partner may know your weaknesses and might know exactly how to make you feel guilty or get your sympathy. During this time, your emotions are in turmoil. You don't want to be in an oppressive relationship, but you feel tied to it.

Missing Your Obsessive Partner

If you have been in a long-term obsessive relationship, leaving is even more difficult. You don't want to stay but you are used to the relationship; in some ways, you depend on it just as much as the obsessive partner does. If your relationship has been intense, it may have taken over your life. You think about the relationship the moment you wake up, and your days are filled with making sure your partner is happy. Even though it may be your choice to leave, it is still difficult. You aren't used to thinking about yourself first. You probably resent the time and effort it takes each day to keep up with your partner's needs. Even so, you miss him. How could you want out of something and yet miss it when it is gone? You are confused, alone, and lonely.

Tanya was in an obsessive, controlling relationship for 10 years. She worked part time as a receptionist in a doctor's office, but often her husband, Joe, was jealous and would stop by the office when she was there. On the days she worked, he asked questions about who came to see the doctor, who she talked to, and who talked to her. Even though she enjoyed the work, the barrage of questions about the time she was at work made her dread the days she went to work. Most of her days were spent at home. She made sure the house was clean, the laundry was done, and that dinner was on the table when Joe came home from work.

After years of living like this, Tanya decided she'd had enough and left. She thought it was going to be easy. She looked forward to evenings at her new apartment without someone questioning her every move. She looked forward to going to work without wondering if Joe was going to stop in to bother her. So Tanya was surprised when her life felt empty. Instead of enjoying her evenings, she felt lonely. Instead of feeling great at work, she looked up anxiously when the door opened and found herself hoping Joe would come in. She didn't understand. She didn't like the oppressed feeling she had when she was with Joe, but she didn't like the feeling of being without Joe either. She didn't know what was wrong with her.

Tanya, like many partners of obsessive lovers, had learned to adapt to and depend on the needs of their partners. When you spend so much time focusing on the needs of another, you come to need the attention of your partner—leaving the relationship behind feels lonely. As the partner of an obsessive lover, it is important to take care of your emotional health, both during the relationship and after you end the relationship.

As you begin your new life as a single person, act like you are single. Put away or replace any mementos from your previous relationship. Put away pictures of the two of you together. If you are living in the same house you had lived in with your partner, contact utility companies and request the bills be put into your name alone. If you have moved into a new home, decorate it with things that reflect your taste. Begin to develop your own personality and life.

Remember, though, that emotions are not good or bad. Emotions just are. It is normal in all separations to go through ups and downs. If you find yourself fighting the urge to call your partner, make a list of some of the controlling and obsessive behaviors that you resented. This will help you to remember why you left and help you stay away. If you find yourself focusing only on the negative and holding on to resentment, so much that you find it difficult to move on and explore the world on your own, you might want to make a list of the good moments so you can keep a balance. This may be a good time to join a support group or participate in a group activity at the gym, your child's school, or your church or synagogue. Try to keep busy and socialize with people to distract you from negative thinking.

Accepting Change

It is scary to think about rebuilding your life, alone. But with separation, whether it is a breakup or a divorce, there is one thing certain: your life will change. Embracing change starts by knowing what you want. Take some time to think about what you need and want. Although you may not be ready to focus on some of your goals, it is good to list your individual goals and think about what you want out of life.

As the partner of an obsessive lover, especially if your partner was controlling, you may wonder if you can make it on your own. You might think you need your partner to take care of the finances. Years of listening to put-downs can leave you feeling as if no one will find you attractive. Your fear of starting over can make you second-guess your decision to leave. Take your life one day at a time. Learn to be your own best friend, be accepting of your weaknesses, and vow to make one positive change or take one step forward each day.

Choose one goal and list the steps needed to make this goal a reality. By narrowing down your goals to one, you lessen the chance of becoming overwhelmed with all of the changes in your life. As you begin to work through the steps, you will feel a sense of accomplishment. With each step you complete, change will seem a little less scary.

Paula left a six-year obsessive relationship. She had worked part time but didn't make nearly enough money to support herself. At first, she was living with a friend, but her first goal was to find a full-time job so she could live on her own and not be dependent on her friend. After a hard day searching for a job but coming home without any good prospects, Paula would feel discouraged. At those times, she started second-guessing her choice to leave, wondering if her ex-partner was right: she couldn't make it on her own.

Instead of focusing on the negative, Paula would create a story of what she wanted her life to look like. She envisioned her new apartment, what types of furnishings she would pick out, what types of foods she would stock in her kitchen. These were all choices Paula had never made on her own; she had allowed her ex-partner to pick out the living room couch, the kitchen table, and the accessories. Now, she started poring over catalogs, thinking about her tastes. This exercise always helped her renew her goal of finding a full-time job.

Explore Your Own Interests

Just as Paula allowed her ex-partner to choose the furnishings for her house, you may have gone along with the activities your partner wanted to do. His needs probably came first. If he liked attending sporting events, you might have spent your weekends at baseball or basketball games. You may not have had an opportunity to explore your own interests.

Focusing on yourself might be a new experience. Take your time and enjoy it. Learn what interests you. What makes you smile? What makes you feel content? At first, you might feel uncomfortable or selfish focusing only on your own needs. But what you learn will help you in future relationships. For example, when your partner asks what you want to do, do you immediately answer, "Whatever you want"? This could be an automatic response, or an indication that you never took the time to find out what you like to do. Now is your chance. Look at each day as an opportunity to explore your own interests. When you do date again, make sure you have an answer to, "What do you want to do?"

Did You Know?

There is no set time for getting over a breakup. For some people it is weeks or months, while others do not feel whole again for years. It is an individual process. If you are in the process of a divorce or breakup, give yourself time and be patient with yourself. Don't set a time limit, allow yourself to grieve. The death of a relationship affects us in much the same way as a death.

Take Care of Yourself

As with your interests, you probably kept your needs on the back burner. Your partner's needs came first. If you were sick, you still made dinner. If you were stressed, you still made sure the house was clean. How you felt was secondary to what your partner needed and what your relationship required.

But a stressful life can lead to health problems. Separating from your partner is stressful. It is time to focus on your needs. During the time right after you separate, make sure you eat right, get plenty of rest, and find time each day to relax. Postpone nonessential tasks until later, when you are feeling stronger and more confident.

Essential Takeaways

- Although it may seem kinder to let your partner down easy and stay in touch, an obsessive lover will take any contact as a sign you want to get back together. It is better to stop all contact.

- Create boundaries for yourself, such as not answering the phone or not accepting gifts or flowers.

- Obsessive partners can react by becoming depressed, using drugs or alcohol, or acting out against you. Some will act in those ways in an effort to bring you back into the relationship.

- When you leave an obsessive relationship, it is normal to go through periods when you miss your previous partner.

- As you start your own life, it is important to take care of yourself, explore your own interests, and develop your own personality.

chapter 10

Managing Finances on Your Own

What is financial or economic abuse?

Breaking financial ties with your obsessive lover

Becoming financially independent

Starting out on your own is scary. If you've been in an obsessive relationship, you may not have had any control over the finances or the house. You may be insecure about managing money or think that you can't make it on your own. In this chapter we'll talk about what you can do to manage your finances and get back on your feet.

When Obsessive Partners are Financially Abusive

As the partner of the obsessive lover, you may be kept in the dark about financial matters. Money, and the access to it, gives you the ability to leave the relationship. An obsessive lover often needs to control the finances to ensure you can't pack your bags and move. Here are some of the ways obsessive lovers use finances as a way to control you:

- Wanting you to quit your job and stay home, or wanting you to work only part time.

- Controlling the checkbook and bank accounts and giving you an allowance for food, household items, and other necessities each week. You may have to itemize your spending for your partner each week.

- Putting all assets in his name, including the bank accounts, house, and cars. He may try to change ownership of any assets you had prior to the relationship so they are in his name.

- Having you use direct deposit at work so your pay goes into the household checking account—which is in his name.

- Destroying or hiding your credit cards or pressuring you to close your accounts.

Financial control or *economic abuse* usually includes put-downs as well. Your partner may continually remind you that you are not smart enough to handle the money, that you spend too much money, or are not responsible. In reality, your partner is scared that you will leave. He believes if he takes away your ability to earn a living or manage the household finances, he takes away your ability to leave.

Definition

Economic abuse is sometimes listed as a subcategory of emotional abuse. The purpose of economic or financial abuse is to create complete dependency on the abuser. Besides financial, this type of abuse can also include: refusing to share in housework or child care; restricting the use of the family car; or not allowing the partner to attend work or school, or to better themselves in any way.

Diane had been in a relationship with Jerry for three years. His constant jealousy finally drove her away. She had always assumed that, as the relationship developed and grew, Jerry would become more confident in her love and the accusations would end. She had moved in with him, spent every evening at home, and yet he was still intensely jealous, showing up at her job, calling her 10 times every day. Her boss had spoken to her several times about the many disruptions Jerry was causing. Nothing she said worked. She professed her love every day, but still his jealousy kept getting worse. In the end, Diane still loved Jerry, but she just couldn't take his insecurities.

Diane moved in with a friend temporarily. She didn't have a lot of room to store her belongings so she packed her things and left them in the basement of the house she had shared with Jerry—telling him she would be back to pick up the rest of her things in a few weeks. Jerry was sure she would return to him and everything would be fine again.

Diane was shocked when she went to the bank to withdraw money and found she had no money in her checking account. A year or so ago, Jerry had suggested they put each other's names on the bank accounts, "just in case." She had agreed. Now she remembered they had gone to her bank and added his name, but never got around to adding her name to his account. At the time she hadn't thought much about it because she trusted Jerry, but now she realized he had emptied her account and she had no access to her money. She closed the account to stop him from doing it again, but the money she had to move to her own apartment was gone.

When Diane called and confronted Jerry, he told her it would all be fine. He was "saving" the money in his account. He would transfer it back to her account when she came back home. Diane was devastated and wondered if she was doing the right thing.

For a few months, she felt conflicted. She had started a new life and didn't have to come home each night to face Jerry's jealous rages—but at the same time, she didn't feel free, not while she knew she needed to see him to get her things. She would replay conversations with Jerry where he had told her she couldn't do it; she couldn't manage money or take care of herself. She was filled with self-doubt, but she was determined.

Every conversation was strained and stressful. Jerry kept assuming she would be back; she kept telling him she wouldn't. Her life, even though she was through with the relationship, was still on hold. She needed to start from scratch, to work her way from nothing and begin building a life where she was in control.

Did You Know?

MISC.

In the article, "Economic Abuse: The Hidden Side of Domestic Violence," Jennifer Kuhn, manager of the Economics Against Abuse program at the Allstate Foundation, writes that economic abuse, such as ruining someone's credit score or denying access to money, can cause lasting emotional scars that may be more difficult to overcome than physical abuse.

Joint Assets

When leaving an obsessive partner, you want to separate yourself emotionally and physically. The less contact you have, the more your ex-partner will understand you want the separation. Part of this process is dividing any property you may own with your partner, as well as creating two individual financial situations—instead of mingling your finances with those of your ex-partner.

If you were married, some of this will be done in the divorce decree. Even so, you want to be as knowledgeable about the process and your financial situation as possible.

Gathering Information

Usually one partner knows more about the household finances than the other. In obsessive relationships, this is often the obsessive lover. If you are considering leaving, take some time to prepare. Gather information and learn about the financial responsibilities and obligations in your home. For example, here's some of the information you will need:

- Previous tax returns.

- A copy of any wills that have been executed.

- Insurance policies including auto, health, and life.

- Any written agreements for business transactions.

- Pay stubs for both partners for the previous three to six months.

- Bank account records including checking, savings, certificates of deposits, retirement accounts, stocks, annuities, etc.

- A list of all debts including home loans, car loans, personal loans, and credit cards. Include account numbers, balances, and contact information for each.

- Any other documentation on income or expenses.

True Love

Economic abuse can include one partner running up a large debt or becoming overextended on credit cards without the other's knowledge. If you are separating or in the process of divorce, contact the credit card company and put a hold on your account to make sure no additional debt is incurred. You may want to establish credit in your own name before you leave if you don't have a card solely in your name.

Learning about your family finances not only helps during divorce proceedings but helps you in setting up your own household. It is important to know what debts you will be required to pay, at least in part. It is important to know your household income and, if you are filing for spousal or child support, how much you may be entitled to. Gathering information is the first step toward eliminating the financial ties you have with your partner.

Dividing Property

If you were married, you are probably legally entitled to some assets. These assets may include your home, your car, cash assets, furnishings, stocks, the cash value of insurance policies, and pension funds. Generally, divorce settlements call for "equitable distribution" of assets. This is not necessarily the same as equal distribution. Some of the factors that are taken into consideration when dividing property are ...

- Each person's contribution to the marriage, including nonfinancial contributions.

- If the property is a gift or inheritance. They are usually considered to be the property of the individual who received it and are not included in the property distribution.

- What each partner brought into the relationship.

This means that if a car or home is in your partner's name, you may still be entitled to some of the equity in the property. In some cases, assets are divided according to the needs and desires of the partners. Other assets may be sold in order to be divided between the partners.

Dividing Debt

Just as you are entitled to some of the assets from your marriage, you are also responsible for the debts incurred during the marriage. There are several different ways debt can be divided. One person can take responsibility for the debt in return for either reduced or increased spousal support; the debts can be divided, with each partner being responsible for their portion of the debts; or assets can be sold in order to pay the debt off.

Misc.

Case Study: Evan and Stephanie

Evan and Stephanie had been married for nine years. Stephanie had worked as a sales representative for a pharmaceutical company when she first met Evan. At first he told her he was proud of her achievements, but once they were married he always found ways to criticize her job. She worked long hours and he would complain when she wasn't home for dinner. She sometimes had to travel and he managed to start an argument each time she went out of town. He called her constantly at work and started fights with her in the morning, causing her to be late. Stephanie's performance at work suffered and eventually she lost her job. Evan wanted her to stay home for a while and take a break from the demands of work.

At first, Stephanie enjoyed her time at home. She liked not having to be somewhere early in the morning and meeting her friends for lunch. But when she was ready to start looking for work, Evan caused a huge fight. He liked her being at home. Stephanie finally relented because she was ready to start a family and wanted to stay home if she did have a baby. However, that never happened.

Years later, Stephanie was completely dependent on Evan financially. Through the years she had slowly handed over the financial decisions to Evan. She wasn't sure why, it just seemed easier and wasn't worth the arguments that occurred when she tried to voice her opinion on their financial decisions. Now, she had no idea how much money they had in retirement accounts, checking accounts, or savings accounts. Evan kept most of the information at his office.

Stephanie felt trapped. She needed to ask Evan for money to go grocery shopping and even then he questioned how much she spent. He came with her if she wanted new shoes or new clothes because he didn't want to give her the bank card. Stephanie knew she should leave Evan but didn't have the money to go anywhere. She had lost touch with friends and was too embarrassed to go to her parents. She felt stuck, alone, and miserable.

Slowly, Stephanie started putting together the pieces of their financial life: finding small clues in Evan's wallet, phone numbers on his cell phone. She realized Evan was hiding mounting debts and using her Social Security number to take out loans. Stephanie finally contacted an attorney to talk about divorce. When she left, she had no money whatsoever, but she was free and happy.

Even though your partner may not have shared information or allowed you to be part of financial decisions during your marriage, you can take control of your situation by gathering information and learning about your individual situation and rights.

Taking Responsibility for Your Own Finances

Like Diane earlier in this chapter, many partners of obsessive lovers find themselves in situations that were meant to prevent them from leaving. For partners who have been out of the work force or working part time, full-time employment is either hard to find or they no longer have the skills to get a decent paying job. Others may have no knowledge of what it takes to run a household financially. They may never have paid a bill or even seen the bills.

Dealing with money problems—on top of the emotional turmoil that comes about from leaving an obsessive relationship—can cause partners to crumble and end up back with their obsessive partners. Throughout this section, we'll focus on ways to create a budget and offer tips for living on one income.

Budgeting

If you are living with your partner and you leave the relationship, your income changes—no matter what. You might have relied on your partner's income or even if you worked, you are now living on one income instead of two. Your expenses need to match (or hopefully exceed) your monthly bills.

Creating a financial plan, or budget, should consist of the following:

1. Income

2. Expenses

3. Income and expense comparison

4. Create new income opportunities

Make a list of your monthly income. This should include your take-home pay from your job (or jobs), child support, spousal support, and any other income you receive on a regular basis. Make a second category for any income you receive sporadically.

Make a list of all your fixed or recurring monthly expenses. This should include car payment, rent or mortgage, insurance, cell phone, utilities, and other bills you will need to pay on a monthly basis. Go over the list carefully to see if you can reduce or eliminate any expenses. For example, can you lower your cell phone or cable bill by choosing a less expensive service plan? Can you eliminate your landline if you have a cell phone? Can you eliminate any extra insurance payments such as vision insurance? Your final list should be all bills which are absolute necessities.

obsession Alert

Some women who have been economically abused have no control over the monthly bills and may not even have access to what bills are paid, which ones are due, and how much money is required to run the household. If your name is on the bank account, request a copy of your past three to six bank statements. Make a list of every bill that has been paid so you can form a picture of what you will need if you leave.

Your next list should be expenses you incur on a regular basis but are not necessities. This list might include manicures, morning coffee, and eating lunch out. If you're not sure what expenses you incur, look over your bank statements for the past two months and list everything you have spent money on. Does your monthly income exceed your expenses? Or, like many recently single people, do your expenses exceed your income? If so, the first expenses to be cut should be those that you incur but are not necessary.

If your expenses are still too high, go through your expenses to see what else you can eliminate or reduce. Think about your wants versus your needs. What expenses are absolute necessities and which are luxuries? Remember, these cuts are temporary. You can begin adding expenses back in as your income increases.

What can you do to increase your income? Can you take on a second part-time job, or if you are working part time can you look for full-time employment? Do you have strong skills in some area that you can use to do consulting work? If you have been out of the work force or are working part time, you might want to look into going back to school or attending some night classes to brush up on your skills and learn new ones. This does not increase your income immediately but will help you build self-confidence and find a more suitable job in the future.

Asking for Assistance

Some partners who have suffered financial abuse may find it necessary to apply for emergency financial assistance from government agencies or local community-assistance programs. If you need help, a domestic violence or homeless shelter may be able to provide information on any financial assistance you may qualify for and help you through the application process. In addition, you can ask if there are any grants or financial assistance for job training, vocational counseling, or for purchasing clothes for work or job interviews. Check with your local public-assistance office for additional resources in your area.

Creating a budget is the first step. Now you need to stay within your budget. Each month you are able to make it on your own and make your own financial decisions will build your confidence. If you have credit cards, put them away or destroy them. You don't want to have the ability to give in to temptation and buy unnecessary items.

Tips for Staying on a Budget

Living within your budget can be hard, there are always surprise expenses not included in the budget. Even going to the doctor can cause you to go off the budget or come up short at the end of the month. Rather than get discouraged and doubt your ability to manage your finances, use the following tips to help you live within your means:

- Look at your budget and decide how much money each month you can save. If you are living paycheck to paycheck or do not have enough to cover basic necessities, it is going to be hard to come up with an amount of money to save. But saving is important. Start with a small amount. Open a savings account and transfer the amount you decide on each month. This way, should you have a month where sticking to the budget is impossible because of unforeseen expenses (you need to go to the doctor, your car broke down), you will have an easier time making ends meet.

- Take out, in cash, your spending money each week. If you have allowed yourself $50 for the week, it will last longer if you see the cash each time you buy something. You can see how much you have left for the week and plan accordingly.

- If you have balances on your credit cards, choose one card at a time and send money over the minimum payment due. Once that balance is paid off, start on the next credit card until you have paid them all off.

- Continue to monitor your spending. It is easy to set up a budget and then not worry as long as you have money to pay your bills. Instead, continue to monitor your spending habits and your monthly bills to watch for ways you can save money.

- Make a list before heading out to the grocery store or any other shopping excursion. Buy only what is on your list to avoid impulse shopping and coming home with a lot of items you don't need.

- Allow yourself a little money to do something fun once a month. It's hard to stay on a budget if you are always feeling down about not having money. Allow for a little extra to go and do something you want, such as go to a movie, go out to dinner, or get a manicure. Think of it as a reward for staying on budget the rest of the month.

- Give up bad habits that cost money. If you smoke or drink, this is a great time to quit. You are starting a new life, make it a healthy life. You'll also see the savings.

- Balance your checkbook monthly. If you have never balanced a checkbook, the customer service reps at the bank will be glad to help you. Balancing your checkbook can catch mistakes that might cost you money in overdraft fees.

- Lighten up. We all go off our budget sometimes. If you stumble on following the budget, don't be hard on yourself. Accept the mistake or indulgence and get right back on track.

Small Expenditures Add Up

Keep track of every cent you spend. Sometimes we don't realize how much money we are spending. Paying $0.65 for just one donut each day before work adds up to $130.00 per year. Paying attention to your small purchases helps you limit spending.

If your ex-partner believes you can't make it on your own because you are too "stupid" to understand finances, use this as motivation to stay on budget. Your independence depends on it.

Planning for the Future

As a newly single adult, you probably don't have much room in your budget for your future. But there is also a possibility that your obsessive partner took it upon himself to manage your financial security. That security is now up to you. If you work, you might have a retirement plan at work that is in your name. Your ex-partner would not have been able to move that money without your permission. Check to see whether you have a retirement plan and find out how much money is in it and how much you can afford to contribute to it on a regular basis.

Become Informed

The obsessive lover who uses economic abuse as a way to keep you in the relationship depends on you not knowing about the family financial affairs. The best way to prevent or overcome economic abuse is to learn as much as you can about your financial situation.

If you don't have a retirement plan, start thinking about how much you will need to save for your future. There are many different ways to save, from government-approved plans to whole-life insurance policies. Begin researching your options by reading about retirement planning in books or on Internet sites. Check with friends and relatives to find out if someone can give you advice and explain the different ways to save money for retirement. The more you learn, the easier it will be. Even if you don't have the money in your budget right now, start learning about your options. When you can afford to save, you will know exactly what you want to do.

Essential Takeaways

- Obsessive lovers frequently control the household finances in an effort to keep you in the relationship.
- When leaving an obsessive partner, it is important to separate yourself emotionally, physically, and financially.
- If you are married you are entitled to some of the assets of your marriage, despite your obsessive lover trying to keep you in the dark.
- Some partners of obsessive lovers are unprepared to take on the responsibility of managing their own finances.

chapter 11

When You Have Children

Explaining about healthy relationships,
even if you aren't in one

Helping your children manage their emotions

Does staying in an unhealthy relationship
help your children

Nonconfrontational ways to talk to your former partner

When you have children, you might wonder how you can teach them to have healthy relationships if you are struggling in an obsessive relationship. Or, if you have left, you might find it difficult to talk with your previous partner, even when you are talking about your children. In this chapter, we'll talk about teaching your children about relationships, helping them cope with separation or divorce, tips for talking with your previous partner, and how to manage if your partner uses your children as pawns.

Talking to Your Childen

You and your partner formed your ideas of love early in your lives. A home where parents were neglectful can cause someone to be insecure in their adult relationships. The relationship you had with your parents helped shape your ability, or inability, to form healthy love relationships as an adult—and the same is true for your partner. You might also recreate your parents' relationship with one another. If one parent was overbearing, jealous, and possessive, and the other parent accepted this behavior, you might believe this is what love is. Or perhaps you don't consciously think this is love, but you unconsciously respond to the same dynamics you saw growing up. That type of relationship automatically feels more familiar.

Teaching Children About Healthy Relationships

In just the same way, your children are learning about love and relationships from you and your partner. How you and your partner interact on a daily basis will form the model your children use as adults. If you are in an obsessive relationship, if your partner is jealous and possessive, if your partner doesn't trust you or doesn't respect you, your children will believe that this is how you treat someone you love. If you are afraid, if you spend your time trying to appease your partner, your children will see that love makes you scared or that love is one-sided. They will absorb this dysfunctional example no matter what you tell them to the contrary.

Did You Know?

Misc.

According to the National Campaign to Prevent Teen and Unplanned Pregnancy, teens say parents have the greatest influence on their decisions about relationships. Teens agree that they listen to parents more than their friends, the media, other family members, or even their girlfriend or boyfriend.

Communication is essential to teaching your children about developing healthy relationships. Although the ideal is to be in a healthy relationship and teach by example, if you are not you can still help your children learn and understand what constitutes a good relationship. Talk openly about respect, valuing and appreciating your partner's good attributes, and how marriages and all relationships require compromise.

If you are in an unhealthy relationship or you are separated or divorced, explain that people continue to change and grow throughout their lives. Point out that as a child grows up, they change. Their needs change. Their view of the world changes, too. Use examples such as outgrowing television shows and toys. Older children might be able to relate to changing friends. Your teenage daughter may have been best friends with Mary last year, but this year her best friend is Joan. There's nothing wrong with Mary, but your daughter realized she had more in common with Joan. Explain that sometimes grown-ups do this as well. Sometimes they marry someone and, as time goes on and they have new experiences, their views change. They no longer have as much in common with their partner.

Let your children know that, no matter what changes between two people, it is never acceptable to hit or be disrespectful to another person. If your spouse is disrespectful, puts you down, or is demeaning to you in any way in front of your children, stand up to him. Let him know this behavior is unacceptable. Remember, your children will model their relationships after yours. Instead of focusing on your partner, focus on what behaviors you want your children to see and learn. Act respectfully, but also demand respect. If this is difficult, you may want to read Chapter 15, where we talk about setting boundaries within your relationship.

Explain to your children that you do not have the power to change someone else. You only have the ability to change your reaction and responses to their behaviors. If your spouse is jealous and possessive, you cannot stop him from being that way but you can change how you react to him. Your children have watched your interactions with your partner over and over. Help them understand the best way to react to the situation. If necessary, explain why you reacted in a certain way. Let them know that just as their friends have a right to voice their opinions and talk about their needs, both partners in a relationship have that right as well.

Relationships are built around two people and, as such, will be filled with differing opinions. Teach your children it is important to respect different opinions, even when you don't agree. Let them know both partners in a relationship need to take the time to listen to the other. Help your children see that conflict is not necessarily a bad thing. Conflict can help you resolve problems when you calmly and respectfully talk about your differences.

Tips for Helping Your Children Cope

Whether you are still with your obsessive partner, planning to leave, or have already left, your children feel the tension and stress in your household. There are a number of ways you can help your children cope with the disruption in their lives:

- Give your children unconditional, unending love. Let them know every day that you love them. Let them know that, no matter what problems you and your partner have with each other, it is no reflection on how much each of you loves them.

- Let your children know the problems in your relationship are not their fault. Let them know grown-ups sometimes fight and sometimes find it best to live apart. You don't need to give a lot of details on what the problems are, you just need to reassure your children they did not cause the problems.

- If you will be separating, try to tell your children together. This will let your children know that you both care about them.

- Be prepared for a range of reactions. Initially, a child may want to know where he will sleep or how he will get home from school each day. Later he may be angry, anxious, or withdrawn. Accept each stage with understanding and compassion.

- Continue your child's routine as much as possible. If your son is in sports or your daughter takes dance lessons, try your best to keep up these activities to give your child a sense of stability.

- Expect your child to follow the rules of the household. It is tempting to be lenient or lighten up on the rules because your children are going through a tough time; but they need the consistency and to know you still love them enough to care about their behavior.

If your child is having an especially difficult time dealing with the stress in the household or with the changes of separation, consider talking with a counselor. Your child might benefit from having a neutral person to talk to.

True Love

As a parent, you know what is best for you and your children. You make decisions for them every day. Some children will react with anger or resentment, or may not agree with your decision to separate or divorce. If you feel it is the best decision, don't waver because your children are upset by it. As long as you continue to reassure them of your love, as they get older, they will understand you made your decision based on what was best. They will accept that your actions were not made selfishly or rashly, but with everyone's best interest in mind.

Should You Stay for the Children?

Separation or divorce is a big decision, one of the hardest you will make in your life. Going through a divorce is difficult for everyone involved: you, your spouse, and certainly your children. For this reason, many partners of obsessive lovers will choose to stay in an unhealthy relationship. They muddle through their days, refusing to dwell on their unhappiness or believing they are doing the noble thing, sacrificing their happiness for their children.

Divorce should be a last resort. You should make every attempt to make your marriage work. But when it doesn't—when you have exhausted all your resources, when you are sure the marriage is never going to work—you aren't helping anyone, your children included, by staying and being miserable.

**obsession
Alert**

As you move closer to making a decision about leaving, your obsessive partner may sense something is wrong and increase his efforts to control you. He may become more jealous and feel that you are being influenced by your "secret lover." He may try harder to control your actions, not wanting you to leave the house without him or not trusting you to even go to the store. This is because he is becoming even more insecure in the relationship as he feels you slipping away.

Divorce itself is not what hurts children. It is the way people get divorced that hurts children. If you get divorced and remain angry or resentful, you will pass these emotions on to your children. They will also be angry about the divorce. If you divorce with a commitment to remain civil—even friendly—with each other, to communicate openly about your children's needs, and to work together for the good of the children, you help your children deal with the separation in a healthy way.

It has been said that you cannot give freely what you don't possess. If you are not happy, you can't share happiness with your children. Children have a more difficult time living in a home without love or one filled with anger than learning to live in a divorced household.

As a parent, your life after your divorce will influence your child's overall emotional well-being. If you leave and find a healthy relationship, your child has the opportunity to see how a healthy relationship develops. You, as the role model, have shown that you do not have to accept a situation that makes you unhappy; you have the ability to make positive changes in your life.

Case Study: Phyllis

Phyllis had divorced her husband several years ago. At first, her son, Chris, then 10 years old, was upset. He would spend weekends with his father and return angry and withdrawn. He blamed his mother for taking his father away from him. For a few days, he didn't even want to talk to his mother. Then his father remarried, and Chris had a chance to see his father's obsessive love behavior.

One weekend when Chris was with his father, his new wife went out with friends. His father told Chris they were going out to dinner, but before going to the restaurant, his dad parked the car outside his wife's friend's home and they sat there for a couple hours, just watching the house. When Chris complained he was hungry, his dad became angry. He started talking about how "she" was probably in there with someone else. Finally, Chris's stepmother came out of the house with her friend and they drove away. Chris's dad followed them to a restaurant and snuck inside to see who they talked to. Chris never got dinner, but he wasn't hungry anymore. He was disgusted with how his dad acted and how he stalked his step-mom. He finally understood why his mother had left.

Imagine the guilt you place on your child if you tell him you stayed because of him. As he grows up he realizes that you sacrificed your own happiness to stay in an unsatisfying relationship. He may feel your unhappiness is his fault; that, if he hadn't been around, your life would have been better. If you ask grown children whether they would have preferred their parents stay together and be unhappy, or divorce and seek a more meaningful life, many would tell you they would prefer their parents were happy in their lives.

Whether or not to leave is a hard decision. There is no easy answer. But if you decide the obsessiveness of your partner is too difficult to deal with and is leaving you drained, unhappy, and compromised as a parent, you might be able to offer your children a better life away from your partner.

Separation or Divorce and Children

If you have chosen to separate from or divorce your obsessive partner, the previous lessons are still important. But on top of those, you need to continue to assure your children that the separation doesn't change how you feel about them. Address how life is going to be different. You might be going from a two-income household to one income. You might have a contentious relationship with your partner. Try to keep your feelings for your partner out of your conversations with your children by focusing on respecting people you disagree with.

When Children Are Used as Pawns

If you have left an obsessive lover, chances are he is not ready to accept it. He may still feel possessive or believe you belong to him. Sometimes obsessive partners use their children either to keep an eye on their estranged partner or as a way to seek revenge on their partner for leaving. Either way, your children will feel used. This type of behavior can severely damage their self-esteem.

True Love	When you use your child to get revenge or punish your former partner, you actually give them control of the situation. You are letting them determine what you do. Gain control over your life by focusing on your needs rather than focusing on your ex.

Dawn and Robert had been married for over 10 years. They had two children, Matt, 8 years old, and Tommy, 6 years old. Robert had always been jealous, but Dawn, like many women, thought that with time the jealousy would lessen. It didn't, actually, it had continued to get worse. Now that both her sons were in school, Dawn thought about going back to work. She had worked as a bookkeeper for several years but had quit to stay home when Matt was born. Now, she longed to be back among other women and wanted to get a part-time job while the boys were at school. Robert wanted her to stay at home, taking care of the house. "What if one of the boys is sick? What are you going to do then?" Robert asked. Dawn said her mother had offered to help when that happened. Robert continued finding reasons she should not go back to work, insisting it was better for the family if she was at home.

Dawn found a job and Robert was furious. Dawn finally tired of his daily tirades and moved out, taking her sons with her. Robert did not think she would make it and was sure she would come running back, telling him he was right, that she belonged at home. But she didn't. With her mother's help, Dawn started working full time, got her own apartment, and was happy with her life.

Every other weekend, the boys stayed with their dad. Robert was sure another man was to blame. Dawn would not have left on her own—someone must be influencing her. He started questioning his sons about what Dawn was doing. When they were reluctant to "tattle" on Mom, Robert started paying them for information. If they told him who she talked to, what she did, or any other information, he gave them a dollar or two, but they weren't supposed to tell their mother. The boys felt so guilty and conflicted about trying to hide from their mother what was going on that their schoolwork suffered, they had trouble sleeping, and they acted up at home.

obsession Alert

Your former spouse knows your hot buttons. He understands how to get you angry, what makes you happy, and what hurts you. He uses this information to get a reaction from you. A negative reaction is better than no reaction at all. If your former partner tries to use your child to get a reaction from you, no matter how upset you are, don't let him know. Your reaction will only fuel his need to do it again.

Unfortunately, many obsessive lovers use their children to get back at their partner for leaving. For most, open communication has never been a strong suit. They are used to having their way. Walking out was the ultimate insult. It showed you were no longer willing to be controlled or intimidated. This can cause your former partner to lash out even more, and using the children is just another way to punish you. As the partner of an obsessive lover, you might be angry and resentful of the way he treated you in the marriage. You might be scared or worried. You might have financial concerns and blame your former partner for the pain you are feeling.

Some of the ways parents use children after a divorce or separation include …

- Using the children as messengers by asking them to relay messages or angry remarks.

- Talking disparagingly about the other person to or in front of your children.

- Making up lies or stretching the truth to place the blame of the separation on the other partner.

- Fighting in front of your children.

- Questioning them about the other person's actions or behaviors.

- Withholding visitation rights to punish the other partner, or not allowing the child to call and speak to the other parent.

- Punishing the other parent by cancelling visitation at the last minute, showing up late, or not showing up at all.

- Going against the other parent's decisions or discipline in order to make it more difficult for them.

- Asking children to take sides or asking them whom they love more.

When relationships are strained, as they are at the end of an obsessive relationship, it can be easy to fall into the habit of talking to your child as if she were your friend, sharing your disappointments or anger at your partner with her. But this can be devastating to your child.

Communicating with Your Partner

It is difficult to maintain communication in obsessive relationships. The more contact you have with your former partner, the more he continues to believe the relationship isn't over, that there is a chance you will be back. Try the following tips to keep up communication without having to speak with your ex-partner every day.

Use e-mail or texting whenever possible. E-mail is less personal. You can say what you need to say, let him know your child's schedule, update him on grades, or inform him about upcoming events. And you can verify exactly what was said. By not speaking directly to him, you save yourself the stress of listening to him ask when you are coming back. You are happier and he is kept up-to-date on the children's activities. Pause before you hit the send button and look over what you wrote to make sure that what you wrote isn't open to misinterpretation. Some people find themselves "arguing" via text or e-mail. Don't do it.

Use an online calendar to keep track of sporting events, parent-teacher conferences, dance recitals, family parties, and any other important events in your child's life. You can update the calendar with the score from your son's baseball game or highlights of the game. Give your former partner access to the calendar and ask him to fill in events that are going on in his house. You will both know exactly what is going on and can keep up with what is going on at the other person's house.

True Love

If you must have a face-to-face meeting with your former partner, treat it as a business appointment. Set up a specific time to meet, be on time, and dress as if you were going to a business meeting. This will set the tone for the meeting and keep it cordial and focused. Once you have finished discussing the reason for the meeting, say your good-byes and leave. Don't linger and give your partner an excuse to ask personal questions about your life. If there is still a lot of tension between you, try to meet in a public place. Don't involve alcohol.

When you must speak with your ex-partner, keep the conversation focused on your children. Let him know if he changes the subject or wants to discuss your relationship or question you about what you are doing, you will hang up. He can call back when he is ready to talk about the children. Stick to it. After a few times, he will realize you are serious and stay focused during the call.

Set up the pick-up and drop-off of your children at a neutral location. Don't invite him in your home if you don't want him there. Don't go to his house if you don't feel comfortable doing so. Instead, meet at a friend's house, a relative's house, a restaurant, or some other public place to avoid being alone with your former partner.

If it is impossible for you to communicate civilly with your former partner, you might want to consider *mediation*. A mediator is a neutral third party who works with both you and your partner to help facilitate conflict resolution.

Definition

Mediation uses a neutral third party to help reconcile differences. In a mediation session, the mediator cannot give advice and cannot act as an attorney for either party. He can point out things each partner should be aware of and remind the partners what they are trying to accomplish. Some child-custody courts will recommend mediation as a way to resolve differences and come to a mutual agreement. Mediation sessions are confidential.

Essential Takeaways

- Even if you are in an unhealthy relationship, you can help your children understand healthy relationships by teaching them about valuing another's opinions, appreciating another's strengths, and the ways people sometimes grow apart.

- Many people believe it is better to stay in a relationship "for the good of the children," but children also benefit from having parents who are happy, healthy, and satisfied with their lives.

- Some obsessive lovers use their children as a way to show their anger or take revenge on the partner who left.

- Using methods such as e-mail or texting can help you communicate with your former partner without talking to him.

Part 4

Freedom from Obsessive Love

How you view yourself plays a large part in how you relate to your partner. If you have a poor self-image, it can have a negative effect on your relationship. In this part we'll talk about how our self-image develops and what you can do to change it.

Many people work through these issues on their own; others need some extra help and assistance through therapy and counseling. We'll talk about what happens in psychotherapy and what changes you will be working toward. We'll also discuss the differences between individual and marriage counseling to help you decide which is best for you.

Giving up on an obsessive relationship doesn't mean giving up on love. For obsessive lovers, we provide information on learning how to form a healthy love relationship by accepting your role in the relationship and learning how to balance your need to be with your partner with their need to follow their own interests. For the partners of obsessive lovers, we offer information on how to improve your present relationship, move on if you feel it can't be saved, and make changes to prevent you from becoming involved in another obsessive relationship.

chapter 12

How Self-Image Influences Relationships

How self-image develops

Measuring your self-esteem

Focusing on positive thoughts

Changing your attitude to change your relationship

We need love. It is a biological need. Babies who don't bond with their caregivers can develop failure to thrive, with weight gains below normal for their sex and age. As adults, healthy love relationships are associated with better health and longer lives.

Love makes the world go around, or so the saying goes. Love does provide us with meaning in our life. We will, in the name of romance, go to great lengths to woo our potential partners. Love and romance are found around the world, in every culture. We all want to be loved unconditionally, to be accepted completely, and to know that our love is everlasting.

Although obsessive love isn't really love, it is driven by the same needs: to be accepted, to be wanted, and to be loved. How well our relationship meets our needs is influenced by how we think about ourselves, and vice versa.

In this chapter we'll talk about how obsessive lovers and their partners view themselves, and what steps they can take to improve their self-esteem and, in turn, improve their relationships.

For Obsessive Lovers

One of the differences between a healthy relationship and an obsessive relationship is the need to be reassured that love will last forever, that commitment can be proven and guaranteed, and that security can be ironclad. As an obsessive lover, you have a deep need to know your partner will always be there. Your emotional needs drive who you choose for a partner.

Creating a New Self-Image

In our childhood we learn how to love and what to expect from love. We learn from how our parents loved and treated us and by watching the adults in our life. If your childhood was filled with rejection, abuse, neglect, or abandonment, you may have entered adulthood feeling unloved and unlovable. These feelings seep into your relationships. Your insecurities influence your behaviors. We talked about how childhood experiences can contribute to obsessive love behaviors in Chapter 4. Learning to create healthy love relationships is dependent upon separating your *self-image* from these experiences.

Our **self-image** is how we view ourselves. A self-image contains words we believe describe our individual traits. You might describe yourself as dependable, reliable, trustworthy, and outgoing. This is your self-image. Your self-image is created through personal interactions, achievements, and perceived failures. A self-image can be positive or negative. Some aspects of our self-image can be unconscious.

Your self-image is influenced by many factors, such as what others think about you, what your parents told you as a child, what friends and previous lovers have said, and what you tell yourself. When a child is neglected, abused, or abandoned, his self-image might contain words such as unlovable, not good enough, thoughtless, or selfish. As you enter adult relationships, this self-image comes along. When you believe you are unlovable or not good enough, you believe it is only a matter of time until your partner figures this out and leaves. Many of your decisions and many of your thoughts, revolve around this deep-seated insecurity.

On top of self-image, you are afraid. You have found someone to love you and every day you worry that she will leave and you will be alone. If that happens it means that everyone, yourself included, was right: you are unlovable. Remaining in the relationship is a matter of survival. It is the only thing that can help you maintain any positive sense of self.

Through positive experiences outside your home, you may have developed a healthy self-image as a student, a business woman, or a parent, but still have a damaged self-image as it pertains to relationships. This dichotomy can be very confusing to the person.

Self-Image Inventory

The good news is that you can change and improve your self-image. The first step is to understand how you think about yourself. The following is a list of questions. Fill in each blank honestly. The answers give you a list of traits and characteristics you feel best describe you. Remember, there are no right or wrong answers and nobody else needs to see what you have written.

1. When I compete with someone, I feel like I will _____ win. (always, often, occasionally, rarely, never)

2. I am _____. (very interesting, somewhat interesting, boring, very boring)

3. When someone compliments me, I _____ feel embarrassed. (never, occasionally, frequently, always)

4. When I first meet someone, I make _____. (a good impression, an average impression, no impression, a bad impression)

5. My confidence level is _____. (high, average, low, nonexistent)

6. I _____ I will reach the goals I have set for my life. (believe, don't believe)

7. I think I am _____. (very mature, mature, somewhat mature, immature)

8. When I'm around people I don't know, I am _____. (very comfortable, comfortable, somewhat nervous, nervous, very nervous and uncomfortable)

9. I _____ feel inferior to other people. (never, occasionally, sometimes, usually, always)

10. I _____ feel good about myself. (always, usually, sometimes, occasionally, never)

11. I _____ need recognition and approval from others. (never, hardly ever, sometimes, frequently, always)

12. I _____ have good problem-solving abilities. (always, usually, occasionally, rarely, never)

13. I _____ enjoy my life. (always, usually, occasionally, rarely, never)

14. I am _____ afraid of making mistakes. (never, rarely, sometimes, usually, always)

15. I _____ think other people have a high opinion of me. (always, usually, sometimes, rarely, never)

Look over your answers. Do you have a positive or negative view of yourself? You might have some areas where your self-image is high and some where you aren't so sure. You may have good self-image in areas outside of relationships, so the number of items you have answered negatively does not indicate the extent of the problem.

Using your answers as a starting point, you can begin to work to improve how you see yourself.

obsession Alert

People with low self-esteem may be suspicious of partners. Because they don't like themselves, they can't believe someone else could like them. They believe the person is with them for some ulterior motive, or become jealous and possessive because they don't believe the partner is going to stay with someone unlovable.

Steps to Improving Self-Image

Before you begin taking steps to remake your self-image, you must accept who you are at this moment. If you're an obsessive lover and looking to make positive changes in your life, then your self-image is already lacking. You might see yourself as a loser, someone not worthy of having a relationship. You might not blame your partner for not wanting to be with you—after all, you don't even like yourself.

You are who you are as a result of all your past experiences. Each relationship, each job, each achievement, and each failure has added, positively or negatively, to how you view yourself. This is who you are, at this moment. But it doesn't have to be who you are tomorrow, next week, next month, or next year. You have the ability to change who you are and what you think. The first step is to change from thinking, "I am not a nice person," to "I have done things that I am not proud of, but I am willing to change. I am a good person."

By accepting your previous controlling or obsessive behaviors, without attaching guilt or shame, you can accept who you are. Only then can you move forward.

The next step is to look at your answers in the previous section. What areas of your life are most troublesome? What situations cause you the most negative thoughts? If you answered that you feel very uncomfortable when around people you don't know, think about what you say to yourself in those situations. Do you think, "I'm not good enough to be here—they won't like me ... I don't fit in"? What else happens in that situation? Does your heart feel like it is pounding in your chest? Do you feel nauseous? Do you sweat? Do you become so nervous you can't focus, can't follow a conversation, can't talk without stumbling over your words?

Chances are, these negative thoughts are controlling your relationship. Think about times when you are feeling jealous. Why do you worry your partner might find someone else? Your thoughts might include:

- I am not good enough for her.

- She will find someone better than me.

- She probably wants someone with more money than me.

- She deserves someone nicer than me.

According to Mark Tyrell, co-author of *Self Confidence Trainer*, as people become healthier in their outlook and improve their self-esteem, they use "I" less often. As you meet your own emotional needs in a healthy way, you focus your attention on people and situations outside of your own realm. In other words, you find positive ways to channel your energy.

Jealousy isn't about the other person, it is about your feelings that you aren't good enough. If you can learn to change these thoughts, you can improve your relationship.

The next step in changing your self-image is to understand how you view the world. Here are some negative ways someone with a poor self-image may interpret situations:

- **You view the world in black and white, all or nothing.** "If she doesn't love me, nobody will."

- **You confuse feelings and facts.** When you feel strongly about something, you assume it must be true. "I feel like she wants to leave me."

- **You see only the negative.** You forget your partner gave you a kiss, said she loved you. You only remember she went out without you.

- **You jump to negative conclusions.** "I texted her an hour ago and she hasn't texted back—she must be with someone else."

- **You minimize the positive.** "She said she loved me, but that isn't as important as her actions, she still went out."

Understanding how you view the world and interpret events can help with the next step, which is replacing negative thoughts with positive thoughts. Using a piece of paper or a journal, draw a line vertically down the middle. On one side, write down every time you catch yourself thinking something negative. On the other side, write down a positive thought to replace it.

This takes lots and lots of patience and hard work. You've spent years perfecting your negative-thought processes. It's going to take practice to change them, and you will have stumbles along the way. Forgive yourself and keep working to change. Keep reminding yourself, "I can do this." Congratulate yourself each time you catch yourself saying something negative and changing it to something positive.

As you work to change your negative-thought patterns, it will become easier. The mind is very powerful: the more you tell yourself you are lovable, the more you will believe it! People in your life, including your partner, will begin to notice a difference in you. You will feel a renewed sense of self-confidence. Not only will you like yourself more, but you will gain a better appreciation and respect for those around you.

For Partners of Obsessive Lovers

The obsessive lover isn't the only person in the relationship with self-esteem issues. As the partner of an obsessive lover, you may also have a negative view of yourself. Some partners have fallen into the relationship accidentally. They met and were charmed by an obsessive lover and were drawn into the relationship unwittingly. Others are attracted to obsessive lovers because they are drawn to the intensity of the relationship.

Misc.

Case Study: Monica

Monica grew up with an alcoholic mother. Her father worked two jobs and was rarely home. When he was home, he was distant. Monica spent most days caring for the family. Most mornings began by waking her two younger brothers up, getting them breakfast, and sending them off to school. Then she would check on her mother and bring her some water or coffee—even though her mother was never up before noon—before she went to school herself. After school she took care of her brothers, made dinner and helped them with their homework. Her mother didn't do much except sit, drink, and yell at her. Monica tried to keep the house clean, her brothers quiet, and everyone happy so her mother didn't have a reason to yell—but that didn't usually work; she found a reason anyway.

When Monica got married, her daily routine didn't change much. The only thing that changed was who she took care of. She still cleaned, cooked dinner, and tried to make sure her husband didn't get upset. She always put his needs first and did whatever he said. He yelled when things weren't the way he wanted. He got angry if she talked to another man. One day, she was talking with her neighbor and he forbade her to speak to him again. Monica thought this was the way life was. She didn't know differently.

For some partners of obsessive lovers, their childhoods were just as troublesome as Monica's. Your parents may have left you alone, or to fend for younger brothers and sisters. Or, in some cases, your parents may have expected you to take care of *them*. You learned that nurturing someone was the way to find love. You learned your own needs weren't as important as your loved one's needs.

If you were criticized excessively you may have grown up believing you couldn't do anything right. You may seek out the approval of your partner, afraid to make him angry, afraid of speaking up, afraid of making mistakes. Your self-image depends on other people's approval. Your decisions are based on making others happy, with no thought for your own happiness. (Everyone is criticized.)

Accessing Your Strengths and Weaknesses

Just as the self-image inventory in the previous section for obsessive lovers helped to focus on how to improve self-esteem, truthfully considering the following statements can help you look at your behaviors to see where you can work to improve how you view yourself. Put a check next to any sentence that sounds like you.

- ❏ I find it difficult to accept when other people are disappointed in me.
- ❏ I have apologized for mistakes even when I didn't think it was my fault.
- ❏ I feel good when I am taking care of someone else but feel guilty if I do things for myself.
- ❏ I feel insecure and unsure of myself in new situations.
- ❏ I am embarrassed when someone gives me a compliment.
- ❏ I avoid doing new things because I am afraid of failing or looking silly.
- ❏ I let my partner make decisions because I would probably make the wrong decision.
- ❏ I find it difficult to express my opinions.

❑ I don't like meeting new people; I find it intimidating.

❑ I often feel ashamed of my behaviors.

❑ I feel uneasy if my partner is not with me.

❑ I worry about what my partner thinks or if I am doing a good enough job.

❑ I don't talk about my opinions; no one cares, and I'm probably wrong.

❑ I am easily swayed by my partner's or other people's opinions and beliefs.

❑ I am often tense, anxious, upset, or depressed.

Each statement you marked represents a way in which you limit yourself. If you checked that you worry about what your partner thinks, you are probably making decisions based on whether your partner will approve, not on what is best for you. Each check is an area of your life you can work to improve.

True Love	We have healthy relationships when we have a positive self-image and view of the world. Set aside 10 minutes each day to focus on yourself and clear your mind of all the negative people and situations around you. Sit quietly, imagining yourself in a peaceful setting, maybe sitting near a brook listening to the sounds of nature or on a beach on a sunny day. Focus on your imaginary scene, bringing in the sounds and sights. For 10 minutes, allow yourself to be happy and peaceful. No matter what is going on around you, you can take 10 minutes to yourself. Even this short of a time can help you gain perspective and improve your view of your life.

Changing Your Attitude

As with the steps outlined for obsessive lovers, partners of obsessive lovers can improve their outlook about themselves, their lives, and their relationships, too. By changing your attitude and improving your outlook on life, you can make positive changes. Your relationship will be more satisfying—or the new and improved you might decide the relationship is no longer good enough, that you want and deserve more respect. The following steps can help you change your view of yourself.

Practice speaking positively. Every time you tell yourself something positive, you take one step toward improving your self-esteem. Start out by telling yourself one positive thing each morning. It doesn't matter what it is. It could be, "I look nice today." Something simple can make the difference in your level of confidence all day. Each day, add one more positive thing. If your partner puts you down, immediately counter it with something positive. Within two weeks, you should set a goal to tell yourself at least 10 positive things each day. As you continue, you will begin to feel more self-assured.

Visualize how you want to be. Visualization is a powerful tool used by many successful people. What do you want to be like? Do you want to be a confident person? Do you want to be able to stand up for yourself? Think about how you picture yourself during a confrontation. Do you see yourself keeping your mouth shut, being afraid of speaking your thoughts? When your partner puts you down or forbids you from going out, what is your response? Instead, imagine yourself standing up for what you believe and what you want. Give your imagery as much detail as possible. The more you visualize how you want to be, the more you will believe that image and work toward it.

Remind yourself you can do anything once. It may be frightening to think about standing up to your obsessive partner. You may worry about his reaction. It is easier to think about doing something once. It gives you strength knowing it is a single event. It does not take as much courage to do something once as it does to commit to changing forever. But once you do it once, remind yourself that if you did it once, you can do it again.

Set your standards based on your abilities, not others'. When you compare yourself to someone else, you usually lose. For example, "I can't cook as well as John's mother." Immediately you have rated your cooking as inferior. Change that thought to something positive, "I like the way I cook meatloaf." Instead of using the word "better" use the word "different."

Make a list of your positive traits and read it each day. What do you do well? What are your strengths? No matter what it is, write it down. Keep your list in a place you can see it each day and read it as often as possible. The more times you read it, the more you will begin to believe it. Ask friends, co-workers, and family to help you compile a list if you feel stuck on this task.

Is your partner controlling your life? Can you give examples? If you think your obsessive partner is controlling, take a few weeks to write down examples as you observe your interactions. Does he always choose where you go when you go out? Write it down. Does he make all decisions? Write down times he negates or ignores your opinion. Think about how you feel when he makes decisions for you or ignores how you feel. Once you have a written log, you can discuss with him specific examples of his behaviors and how his actions make you feel.

Raising your self-esteem and improving your attitude toward yourself is hard work. It takes time. Allow yourself to make mistakes. If you catch yourself thinking negative thoughts, don't belittle yourself, correct the negative thought and replace it with a positive thought.

As you continue with these exercises, you may find your relationship beginning to change as well. Your partner may not understand why you are speaking up or why you are less willing to be his doormat. Accept these changes. Either he will change with you or he will revolt by increasing his controlling behaviors. You have the ability to decide what happens next in your relationship or whether you want to end the relationship. It is your choice, not just your partner's choice.

Essential Takeaways

- You create your self-image based on what your parents told you, what friends and past lovers have said, and what you tell yourself. With commitment, patience, and practice, you can change your self-image.

- Your self-image influences your relationships. If you have a negative self-image, your relationship with your partner can be filled with suspicion and jealousy.

- Looking at your behaviors can help you see what areas you should work on to improve your self-esteem and, in turn, improve your relationship.

- Using strategies such as positive self-talk and visualization can help you to feel better about yourself.

chapter 13

Counseling and Therapy

It's hard to admit that you need therapy or counseling. You might feel that you are admitting weakness or that something is wrong with you. But sometimes the reasons for your fears of rejection and abandonment can be too much for you to fix on your own. A therapist or counselor can offer support and encouragement as you take your journey of looking into the past and facing what you find there. Therapy helps you learn how to not repeat the past. In this chapter we look at some of the different methods and processes therapists use to help obsessive lovers and their partners overcome their fears and learn to develop healthy relationships.

Psychotherapy

Many people manage to overcome behaviors associated with obsessive love on their own. But many others, even if their relationship is over, end up in similar relationships over and over. They may control their obsessive behaviors for a while, but they haven't confronted and dealt with experiences from their past that caused the fear of rejection or abandonment, so they risk repeating obsessive behaviors in every relationship. *Psychotherapy* or counseling can help.

Psychotherapy uses psychology to treat behavior disorders or mental illnesses. It is sometimes referred to as talk therapy, but uses insight, suggestions, encouragement, and instruction to help you make positive changes in your life.

As the partner of an obsessive lover, you might also end up in obsessive relationships again and again. You might get tired of the controlling and obsessive behavior of your partner and leave, but you still gravitate to those tendencies, so when you find another partner the same type of relationship develops. If you are finding this in your life, you probably could benefit from working with a psychologist, therapist, or counselor.

Besides using therapy to change obsessive behaviors, some other reasons to consider counseling are:

- You are unhappy in your relationship and are confused as to whether you should try to make it work, learn to accept it, or end the relationship.

- You know the relationship is not good for you, but you are unable to end it.

- You are paralyzed at the thought of leaving the relationship, either because you are afraid to be alone or because you are afraid of what your partner might do.

- You are hopelessly obsessed and feel your life is out of control; you don't think you have any power over your feelings or acting in inappropriate ways.

- You see a pattern of failed relationships but can't figure out why you are always attracted to the "wrong" person; or your partners are always leaving you because you smother them.

Psychotherapy or counseling can help you recognize the thought processes that lead to obsessive behaviors, support you as you look back at your childhood or early experiences to find what caused your fears, and show you how to confront those situations and change the direction of your life. This type of treatment usually consists of a session once a week, normally one-on-one. Sometimes group sessions with others facing similar situations can also help.

Finding the Causes of Obsession

Facing your past—the fear, the hurt, the rejection, the neglect, the abandonment—is hard. It takes courage. Most people find the process easier with a therapist's support and encouragement.

One goal of psychotherapy is to help you change your current behaviors. But sometimes you can't do that until you understand and resolve what has happened in the past. As an obsessive lover, you probably think or act in certain ways because of what happened to you in your childhood. It is hard to imagine that events that occurred 10, 20, or 30 years ago have any impact in your current relationship, but they do.

obsession Alert

Some obsessive lovers enter therapy with the goal of fixing their relationship. But psychotherapy is meant to focus on you. Your therapist will help you identify and focus on unhealthy behavior patterns and thought processes then find healthy ways to replace them. If you are obsessive, you will need to stop blaming your partner for your behaviors and focus on yourself.

If your needs to be loved and accepted weren't met as a child, if you were abandoned or neglected, you might search your whole life for answers, trying to find out why your parents did not love you. You might look to your partner to provide the love you never received. When you ask your partner for reassurance that their love will be everlasting, you are really asking her not to hurt you like your parents hurt you. You are asking your partner to erase the pain you felt many years ago, and build the sense of self-esteem and well-being that was never developed inside you. Unfortunately, you are asking your partner for the impossible.

Martin became obsessive in every romantic relationship he had. When Martin was a teenager, his girlfriends would say he was intense. In the morning before school, he would wait for them by their bus. After school, he rushed to be with them for the few minutes before the bus arrived.

He would call them as soon as he got home and again after dinner. He professed his love immediately. When someone broke up with him, he moped around school looking like a lost puppy for weeks. Then he would "fall in love" again and start the whole process over.

As an adult, Martin was just as intense in his relationships. He wanted and needed to be with his current partner, Jane, every moment. He couldn't bear to be away from her. Whatever Jane did, Martin wanted to be right there with her. "Not because I don't trust you," he would say, "I just love being with you and don't want to miss a minute of your life." He gave in to whatever Jane wanted. He let her choose the movie or the restaurant. It didn't matter, as long as he could be at her side. Jane started out enjoying how much Martin loved her. As time went on, she longed to be able to do something, anything, by herself.

Jane finally asked Martin to attend counseling with her, so they could find a way to be together without her feeling crowded. During their sessions, Martin talked about his childhood. His parents both lived at home with him, but they were emotionally distant. He remembers sitting for hours, watching television or reading in his room, with neither parent speaking to him. It wasn't that they purposely ignored him or were mean, they just seemed to forget he was there. The only time he received any attention was when he followed his mother around. As a small child he would follow her everywhere, talking away. When he stopped talking, the conversation ended. He again seemed to disappear to his mother.

True Love	Sometimes true love is shown through your commitment to change yourself, not the relationship. Showing your partner you are willing to attend therapy, and be honest and open with the therapist in order to make positive changes in your life, can help to build trust. If necessary, couples or marriage counseling can follow individual counseling.

The therapist helped Martin to see that he was still following his mother around, but using Jane instead. He was afraid that if he left Jane's side, she would forget about him. He couldn't chance having Jane go somewhere without him. The threat of being ignored was more than he could stand. Jane and Martin worked closely with the therapist to help Martin understand and overcome his fears. While the therapist continued to work with

Martin to resolve his childhood issues, they also made a schedule to slowly give Jane time to herself.

In this example, as in many cases, Martin needed to understand where his fears came from before he could find a solution. This relationship could have ended with Jane fighting against Martin's overbearing need to be near her at all times, not wanting to deal with the obsessiveness of Martin's love. Instead, Jane wanted to find a solution, so she worked with Martin. Once she understood how his childhood played a role, she could understand Martin's actions and work with him to create a life together.

Thoughts vs. Feelings

It is sometimes difficult to separate our thoughts and our feelings. We mix these up so much in our minds that we think they are one in the same. But thoughts are much different from feelings, and it's important to know the difference and know whether your thoughts or your feelings are driving your actions.

To begin to understand the difference, pay attention to what words you use to describe your thoughts. For example, you might say, "I felt she was at the store for too long." But being at the store for too long is not a feeling. You might have said, "I felt worried and concerned because she was at the store for so long." Your feelings were "worried" and "concerned."

Feelings are emotions, thoughts are ideas or perceptions. Your feelings drive your obsessive behaviors. By separating your thoughts from your feelings, you can better understand why you react in certain ways.

obsession Alert

According to a 1995 *Consumer Reports* survey, psychologists, clinical social workers, and psychiatrists were all rated approximately the same in their effectiveness in helping their clients. Psychologists receive training in therapeutic techniques, social workers help you find access to local social supports, and psychiatrists can offer therapy as well as prescribe medication. Your relationship with your therapist will play a major role in how effective your treatment is.

A therapist can help you to identify the feelings behind your thoughts. If you are controlling your partner's behaviors because you think she is cheating on you, for example, your therapist can help you focus on the feelings—such as jealousy, fear, or insecurity—behind these thoughts. The therapist will help you look at the evidence for or against your belief that your partner is cheating. Once you realize there is no reason to believe she is cheating, the therapist can help you understand that changing your thoughts will change your feelings and will, in turn, change your reactions to your feelings.

Changing Behaviors

Sometimes identifying and understanding the reasons for your obsession, such as Martin did in our last example, is motivation enough to change your behaviors. Sometimes understanding your past makes it easier, but changing behaviors is still difficult. After years of acting in a certain way it is hard to change, even when your behaviors are destructive to yourself and your relationships.

Changing obsessive behaviors and thoughts is a gradual process. No matter what the underlying cause, you have adopted certain behaviors through the years to help you reach your goal: undying love and security. These are now learned behaviors and, in order to change them, you have to unlearn them.

A therapist or counselor can help you learn new ways of reacting to situations. For example, if your current way of thinking is, "She's late; she must be cheating on me," your goal would be to ask yourself some questions before jumping to conclusions. You may ask yourself, "Is there a reason she's late tonight? Is she caught in traffic? Has she stopped at the store?" You can learn to replace your irrational thoughts with new thoughts. As your thoughts change, your feelings change, which in turn changes your behavior.

Vaughn was always jealous. He worried incessantly about Bonnie finding someone else. When Bonnie went out, he constantly looked at the clock, getting more agitated with each passing minute. Sometimes, when his jealousy became unmanageable, Vaughn would get in his car and go looking for Bonnie to bring her home. Usually, she met her friends at a local club and he would show up and insist she come home. Bonnie would get angry when Vaughn showed up. If he controlled his jealousy and didn't go after Bonnie, they would end up fighting anyway because of his pent-up emotions. Bonnie was ready to end the relationship, but Vaughn agreed to work with a therapist.

Vaughn felt that his jealous feelings took over, that he no longer had control of his actions: the thought of Bonnie cheating drove him to be controlling or angry. The therapist began by challenging Vaughn's belief that he could not help himself. The therapist pointed out that a thought is neither good nor bad, and it cannot make you do anything. By separating his thoughts from his feelings, Vaughn admitted that it was his feelings of jealousy that pushed him to go looking for Bonnie. In doing so, Vaughn had to accept responsibility for his actions. Previously, by attaching feelings to Bonnie's actions, he could place the blame on her. He could say, "If she didn't stay out so late, I wouldn't get jealous." He began to view his actions as a result of his feelings rather than Bonnie's behavior.

obsession Alert

Many obsessive lovers believe their behaviors are impulsive, that their feelings of jealousy take over and they can't control their actions, but this is not true. Following your partner takes thought. You decide to pick up your keys, get in your car, and drive to where you believe your partner is. At each point, you could decide to stop, but you don't. Jealous and controlling actions are not usually impulsive but learned responses. Therapy and counseling provide you with strategies to unlearn these behaviors.

Conflict Resolution

As an obsessive lover, as you work on resolving issues from your past and changing thought patterns, you may also need to work on finding healthy ways to resolve conflicts. You and your partner probably have unproductive ways of solving problems. You now need to find new ways to deal with anger and conflict.

Anger Management

Anger and aggression are frequently confused. Anger is a normal human emotion; aggression is a behavior that is meant to threaten or harm a person or property. Anger in itself is not bad, but when it gets overwhelming, too intense, or too frequent, it can lead to acts of aggression, including violence, verbal abuse, and intimidation.

How you handle anger is a learned response. When you act out inappropriately each time you become angry, those responses become a habit. As an obsessive partner, you may have been dealing with anger inappropriately for a long time. There is a good chance you have shown, verbally or physically, aggressive actions when you become agitated or upset. You can unlearn those reactions and replace them with more positive and constructive ways of coping with your anger.

Most people believe the goal of anger management is to eliminate anger, but that isn't true. It is to teach appropriate ways of coping with this emotion. The first step is to learn to be aware of your anger. You probably feel a number of physical and behavioral cues that let you know your anger is building: increased heart rate, feeling flushed or hot, tightness in your chest or arms, clenched fists, raised voice. These help you measure your anger level. Paying attention to these cues lets you know when you need to take action so that your anger doesn't escalate to the point that you are out of control.

Therapists use a variety of methods to help you cope with overwhelming feelings of anger. Some are …

- Relaxation techniques.
- *Cognitive behavioral therapy,* to change thought processes.
- Communication skills.

Definition

Cognitive behavioral therapy (CBT) is based on the concept that how we think is related to how we act. CBT focuses on present behaviors rather than past events. The goal is to change the thinking process behind the actions.

There are both immediate and long-term relaxation techniques. The immediate strategies include deep-breathing exercises, catching and changing your thought process, and temporarily leaving the situation. Long-term solutions include maintaining a daily exercise program and working to change your belief system.

Cognitive behavioral therapy works to change thought processes. When your partner has gone out with friends and is not home when you expected her, you get angry. But it is not the event which makes you angry, it's how you interpret what's happening. As you wait for your partner, you talk to yourself. You might start with, "She is late, she wants to see someone else, I've seen the way she looks at other men, she doesn't love me …." This self-talk is causing the anger. Your partner being late shouldn't make you angry by itself, especially when you don't know the reason why. You have created a reason for her lateness and it is your fabrication that has made you angry. Cognitive therapy teaches you to change your self-talk. You may say to yourself, "She's late, I hope everything's okay. I'm sure it is—she's capable and able to take care of herself. She loves me and will be home soon." These thoughts instill confidence rather than anger.

Communication, as we've addressed in past chapters, involves using "I" statements rather than "you" statements. When expressing your anger, focus on how you feel not what the other person has or has not done. Be especially careful not to blame or make others responsible for what you feel or do.

Once your therapist has helped you become aware of your anger and taught you techniques to manage it, he may help you to create an anger control plan. This involves determining which methods work for you. It may be a combination of techniques, or it could be one method when your anger is mild and a different one when your anger increases. As an obsessive partner, your anger probably escalates as you cope with feelings of jealousy. Your anger control plan provides you with concrete steps to take to make sure your anger does not escalate.

Problem-Solving Techniques

How do you resolve problems in your relationship? Have you developed unhealthy habits? Do you always need to be right? Do problems make you feel threatened? Do you panic when there is a conflict, thinking your partner will leave?

Your therapist or counselor can work with you to develop steps for you to take when faced with a problem or conflict. A basic problem-resolution model looks something like this:

First, identify the problem. This requires using some of the methods described in the last section, such as separating your emotions from your thoughts so that you can focus on the real problem. Imagine your partner is planning a weekend trip to visit relatives. You don't want her to go. You see the problem as her leaving for the weekend. She sees the problem as you being too controlling. You cannot work together to solve the problem because you each have a different issue. What is the real problem? Do you have valid reasons for not wanting her to go? Is she ignoring certain responsibilities at home? Or is she right—you are being controlling?

> **True Love**
>
> When partners in healthy relationships work together to identify and solve a problem, each partner has the opportunity to present possible solutions. Together the couple can decide on the best solution. In controlling relationships, the controlling partner frequently wants his idea to be used and often ignores suggestions from his partner.

When you have focused on the real problem, try to look objectively at the emotions behind the problem. What are you feeling? You might be insecure, fearful, or concerned for her safety. In order to find a resolution, you have to separate thoughts from emotions. Talking about your feelings will help you separate them from the objective facts of the situation.

Next, decide whether this problem needs to be solved. Some problems in life don't need to be! They may just go away or resolve themselves and have no further impact. But others, when ignored, fester and grow, causing resentment and anger. If you ignore this problem, what will happen? When your partner leaves for the weekend, will you get over it, go about your business, and see her on Sunday? Or will you spend your time being angry and upset? Will you follow her? Call or text her constantly? Try to ruin her plans? If so, your actions will probably cause even more problems later on. Therefore, you have a problem—your insecurity, not the fact that she is going away—that needs to be addressed.

So you need to make a plan of action. In the last section, we talked about creating an anger control plan with your therapist. You and your therapist can create a control plan for dealing with jealousy as well. Your action plan might include focusing on the underlying reasons for the jealousy: your insecurities. It may include repeating phrases, such as, "I know she loves me and she will be back on Sunday. It is important for her spend time with her family." It can include finding activities to keep busy, such as getting together with friends or doing chores around the house.

In the beginning, you will lean on your therapist for support and encouragement. Your therapist will provide practical solutions for resolving conflicts and past issues. But the goal of therapy is for you to learn the techniques and strategies so you can employ them in everyday life. Many people see working with a therapist as a sign of weakness, but it takes real strength and courage to admit you need help. Your determination to live a better life and find peace and happiness in your relationships will help make therapy a successful journey.

Couples Counseling vs. Individual Counseling

Your partner may have suggested couples or marriage counseling as a way to get your relationship back on track. You may be feeling as if your relationship is falling apart. If you haven't yet spoken with a therapist or counselor, you might see these problems as relationship problems. You might believe you need to work on these problems together. But obsessive behaviors are often not a relationship problem, they are an individual problem, one with its roots in your past. It is quite possible you will need to work on your individual problems before you can work on your relationship problems.

misc.

Is It Time to See a Therapist?

How do you know if it is time to see a therapist? If you answer yes to any of the following questions, you might benefit from seeing a therapist or counselor.

- Have you tried to stop your obsessive behaviors but have been unable to do so?
- Does your jealousy interfere with your relationship?
- Do you feel you cannot control obsessive actions and behaviors?

Randy and Sandra attended their first marriage counseling session together. They began to explain some of the problems they were having. Sandra was feeling smothered in the relationship. She felt Randy wanted to control everything she did and was overbearing and jealous. Randy talked about wanting to take care of Sandra. He wanted to protect her but felt she was always fighting him. For example, Randy explained, last week Sandra had a job interview in a different section of town. He didn't feel it was safe and he wanted to drive her. He just wanted to protect and take care of her. Sandra insisted she was able to go by herself. She didn't need Randy to drive. She wanted a partner, not a protector.

After listening for a while, the counselor suggested individual counseling for Randy and that they later return to marriage counseling. He wanted to work on Randy's insecurities. He thought the problems within the marriage could not be resolved without Randy first addressing his personal issues.

If you have begun therapy as a way to save your relationship, you may be going into it for the wrong reasons. As an obsessive lover, you might go into therapy with the goal of becoming the person your partner wants you to be. You want to become loveable. You still can't imagine life without your partner, so therapy is seen as a way to keep your relationship.

The goal of therapy should be to make you whole. By doing so, your relationship should also improve, but you or your partner might also see the relationship as unhealthy and decide to end it. The focus of your therapy needs to be on you. It needs to be on making yourself the best you can be, delving into deeply buried experiences and coming to terms with your childhood so you can emotionally grow.

As an obsessive lover, you have made your partner responsible for your happiness and satisfaction. When you use phrases like "You made me do it" or "If you didn't stay out late, I wouldn't get jealous," you are giving your partner the power to keep you calm or make you angry. Individual therapy works to change those perceptions and give you the power to control your emotions. Once you have worked on yourself and found self-confidence within, you may no longer want to be in the relationship. You may find the relationship does not satisfy your needs.

For others, individual therapy is a beginning. As you work on improving your outlook about yourself, you find your partner to be even more attractive. You begin to focus on her achievements, her abilities, and the positives she brings to the relationship. You learn to appreciate and respect her. You find the relationship new and improved. And issues like her going away for the weekend stop being problems you have to get over—they stop being problems at all.

Measuring Progress

You have agreed to therapy. You know there are some problems in your relationship. You are even willing to admit you might be too controlling. How do you know if your hard work is helping? What should you be looking for?

Case Study: Philip

Philip began counseling because his partner, Joan, wanted him to. It was the only way she was willing to stay in the relationship. Philip didn't really think he needed counseling, but didn't want to lose Joan, so he agreed.

At the start of the sessions, the therapist asked Philip what he wanted to gain from the therapy. He said he wanted to stop being controlling and obsessive. He wanted to trust Joan. Together the therapist and Philip set some goals:

- Understand the emotions behind the need to control Joan's actions.

- Develop strategies to stop the feelings of jealousy.

Philip wanted to start with the second goal. He wanted to stop the feelings and be done with therapy, but his therapist believed uncovering the emotions behind the jealousy was important and should be addressed first.

Philip talked about his childhood. It was pretty uneventful as far as he was concerned. He grew up in a middle class neighborhood. His parents were together. He had a younger brother who was disabled. His parents had spent a lot of time taking him to doctors, working with the schools to make sure his brother received services, and giving him the extra attention he needed at night. Philip understood this, logically; he loved his little brother and wanted him to get the care he needed.

But he also remembered times when he needed his parents and they didn't have the time. They would miss his parent/teacher meetings because his little brother's meetings lasted longer. They missed his baseball games because his brother needed to go to the doctor. Philip accepted this as part of life and never resented his little brother. But emotionally, Philip felt he wasn't as important as his brother, that he didn't deserve the same amount of love. At the deepest level, he was worried that Joan would decide that he wasn't worth loving and leave.

Philip had never associated his childhood with his jealousy. Even now, he didn't resent his brother or his parents. But being a child who received only "leftover" attention played a big role in how he approached his adult relationships. With the help of therapy, Philip began to focus on the reasons he was lovable. He was surprised that the second goal, to stop feeling jealous, began to take care of itself as he worked on the first goal.

At the start of therapy, you and your therapist should outline some goals. These goals need to revolve around you, not your partner or your relationship. Each person's goals will be individual to their situation. Together you can check these goals on a regular basis. As your therapy continues and you make changes in your life, your goals can change as well.

As counseling progresses you may have an increased awareness of how your beliefs and behaviors interfere with your ability to have healthy relationships. You will start to recognize controlling or obsessive behaviors and learn to focus on how your feelings are affecting your thoughts, rather than on your partner's actions. You may be able to replace negative thoughts with more positive thoughts. Even when obsessive thoughts continue, they may not be as disturbing or as frequently disruptive as they were in the past. As you become more self-aware you will get more satisfaction out of life.

Essential Takeaways

- A therapist or counselor offers support and encouragement when you are looking into your past for reasons for your present behaviors.
- A therapist or counselor helps in developing specific strategies for dealing with anger and resolving conflicts to help your relationship grow stronger.
- Counseling for obsessive love is a way to improve your outlook on life but is not a relationship "fixer."
- As you make progress in counseling you will be able to recognize obsessive behaviors and immediately correct them.

chapter 14

For Obsessive Lovers: Breaking the Cycle

Obsessive behaviors are a choice

Finding the right mix: loving without being possessive

Relationships are 50/50

You want to learn how to have a healthy relationship. So far, we've gone over how your self-image impacts your relationship and how you can take steps to start improving your confidence. And we've talked about what you can expect from therapy.

You may have started all this with the hopes of saving the relationship you were or still are in. Along the way, you may have realized you're not in a healthy relationship—or your partner may have left. Now that you're looking to the future, with your current partner or not, there are steps you can take to make sure that, this time, your obsessiveness doesn't interfere with the love you want and deserve.

Coming to Terms with Your Role

One of the hardest parts of changing your life is coming to terms with your role in a failed or failing relationship. How did your behaviors contribute to the downfall? Did your behaviors hurt your partner? As difficult as it is to answer these questions honestly, without doing so you risk repeating your behaviors in your future relationships.

Accepting Accountability

If you've worked with a therapist, you've probably looked at your childhood to find where your obsessive behaviors originated. You have discovered hurts, rejection, neglect, or abandonment. You know that how you act in your adult relationships reflects how you were treated as a child. You know your behaviors were a result of your insecurities and you are working on improving your self-image. You are working to separate how people whom you trusted treated you in the past from how you see yourself now. You can understand why you have acted in controlling or obsessive ways.

But knowing and understanding doesn't make your behaviors right or acceptable. You are still responsible for the pain your actions caused your partner or ex-partner, intentionally or unintentionally. It is easy to blame your parents, the unfortunate situation you may have endured during childhood, or just life. But in order to move forward, you must look at your actions and take *personal accountability* for your behaviors.

Personal accountability is taking responsibility for your role in how your life has turned out. When you accept personal accountability, you no longer believe things just "happen" to you, or place the blame for events or feelings on someone else.

Some obsessive lovers place the blame on themselves but excuse the behaviors because the obsessions are uncontrollable. "I can't help myself," many will say. You feel as if there was nothing you could do once the obsession took hold of you. This type of thinking allows you to absolve yourself of responsibility. But obsessions can be controlled. Your obsessive and controlling behaviors are a choice.

Brian and Silvia had broken up. Brian was having a hard time dealing with the breakup and would drive by her house every evening after work, even though her house was in a different part of town. He couldn't help himself, he thought. He got in the car planning to drive straight home, but once he started thinking about Silvia he headed toward her house instead.

Brian made the decision to drive past Silvia's home. He had plenty of time to think about the decision and plenty of time to turn around and go home. At every red light and stop sign, Brian decided to continue to Silvia's house instead of changing direction. Brian felt so strongly, he thought he could not fight his emotions.

Brian actually thought about Silvia all day. He thought about driving by her house, but then would dismiss it. He went back and forth all day, knowing he shouldn't drive-by but feeling he needed to see her, and if not her, her car or her house. Maybe he would even see Silvia out in the yard. Brian spent the day trying to fight the desire to drive-by. By the end of the day, he didn't think he could fight it any more. He felt he needed to drive-by. But this belief stopped Brian from taking full responsibility for his actions or moving on from his relationship with Silvia.

Brian has to accept that his actions are his choice. And if they are his choice, he can choose not to drive-by. Additionally he has to accept that his past obsessive behaviors were also his choice. Instead of driving by Silvia's house, Brian could go to the gym, stay late at work and complete a project, call a friend and meet for dinner, or go to a movie. By having a list of alternative activities, Brian has a better chance of changing his behaviors.

obsession Alert

If you are working to control your obsessive behaviors and your relationship has ended, it is a good idea to rid your life of triggers—photos, memorabilia, or anything that reminds you of your relationship. If you're still in a relationship, you might want to take a break from the relationship while you work on yourself. This can take a few days, a few weeks, even a few months. If this scares you, just remember that you're working on your behaviors in order to improve yourself which, in turn, will improve your relationship. Taking some time to work on your emotional health should, in the end, make the relationship stronger.

When you realize and accept that your behaviors are a choice, you'll see that you have a choice to not behave in an obsessive way. You have control over your actions. You can choose not to drive by your partner's house or you can choose not to call. It is not always going to be easy. You may still want to do those things; you may still think you need to see her or hear her voice, but remember, these are wants not needs and you have the choice whether to act on them or not.

Making a Commitment to Change

As we discussed in the previous chapter, therapy for obsessive behaviors is not meant to keep you in the relationship or keep your partner in your life. It is to help you change your outlook, your self-image, and to help you focus on having your emotional needs satisfied in a healthy relationship. This healthy relationship may be with your current partner, or it could be a future relationship with someone else.

As with therapy, your commitment to change has to be about you. You have to have a desire and a willingness to create a more fulfilling life for yourself. By doing so, your current and future relationships will be different. They will be based on mutual respect and love rather than control. You will not need to worry when your partner goes out for the evening with friends, because you trust her. You are confident in her love.

When you are jealous and mistrusting, you're miserable. You can't eat, you can't sleep. You feel unloved. The very emotion you are trying to protect— love—is the one that's out of reach. You are unhappy and unsatisfied with your life. Again and again, past relationships have turned out the same. You always end up feeling abandoned or rejected. Your approach of being obsessive, jealous, and controlling isn't working.

You deserve more. You deserve to be content, to feel appreciated and loved. You need to try something new. Make a commitment to change and find healthy ways to show your feelings for someone and, in return, you will receive the love you seek.

So how do you decide to change? The first step is to tell yourself you will change. Not that you want to change, but that you will change. Repeat it over and over. "I will change, I will change …." Write a list of reasons why you want to change. Read your list often to continue to give you motivation. The second step is to tell yourself that you will do what you need to do to change, "I will put in the time and energy needed to make change happen."

Obsessive and controlling behaviors are learned behaviors. Therefore, they can be unlearned. Imagine you work for a furniture store. Your sales manager has taught you to be aggressive. As soon as a customer walks through the door, you are to go over and ask what they are looking for. You are to stay with them, pushing for the sale. You are supposed to lead them to this week's sales. You are paid on commission, so, if you don't make the sale, you don't get paid.

Did You Know?

A 2006 study at the University of Alberta in Edmonton, Canada, showed that, despite knowing a behavior is wrong, we can't usually change unless we understand the underlying reason for the behavior. So knowing your obsessive or controlling behavior is wrong probably isn't enough motivation to change it. You may need to work with a therapist to unlock the childhood experiences that have led to your behaviors and insecurities.

When the store goes out of business, you get a job at another furniture store. You are being paid a salary plus commission. When a customer comes in, you rush over. But your manager pulls you aside, saying, "We don't want to be too pushy. We want our customers to feel comfortable and be able to look around. Instead, offer them a cup of coffee. Keep it upbeat and positive. If they're just looking, we want them to feel like they want to come back again. Keep your eye on them and ask if they have questions once in a while. When they engage you in conversation, you will know they want more information."

This is a whole new way of selling for you. You have to unlearn your past habits and learn new ones. Sometimes you forget and fall back into your previous sales techniques. As time goes on, that happens less and less. The more you work on the new way of selling, the better you get. As you get better, you get more sales, which motivates you to keep working on the new way.

This example illustrates how you have to approach your commitment to change. You won't be able to change every behavior overnight. It will take time. But as you practice, as you remind yourself of the new behaviors, you will make progress and will see and feel a change in yourself and in how you relate to people in your life.

The next step in committing to change is to understand what you need to change. Make a list of all the ways you act obsessively. Take a week or two to keep track of your actions and your thoughts. Your list might look like this:

Sunday: Couldn't stop thinking of Tracey, wanted to call her. Finally called and she told me to stop calling. I kept thinking of her but now I thought there must be someone else. I wanted to drive by her house, but I didn't.

Monday: Still couldn't stop thinking of Tracey. Went out at lunch and drove by where she works. I saw her car in the parking lot. I still couldn't stop thinking about her.

Tuesday: Gave in and called Tracey again. I hung up without saying anything. I just needed to hear her voice. I thought about her all day at work.

obsession Alert

At the end of a relationship, some obsessive lovers use passive behaviors rather than following their partner, driving by, or making numerous phone calls. These behaviors, such as overeating or not leaving the house, can be just as destructive as the outward behaviors. If you are making a list of obsessive behaviors, include these types of self-destructive behaviors on this list.

From your list, you can see what behaviors and thoughts you need to stop or change. Your commitment for the next week might be:

- No phone calls, not even hang-ups
- No driving by her house or work

You have now made a commitment to change. Tell yourself you can do this for one week. You can't accept anything less. If you aren't sure you can make it, call a friend or relative and ask for their help. Over the next week, whenever you are feeling like you are about to give in, call your friend instead. Lean on him for emotional support. Talking about it will often reduce the need to do it. You can make a list of diversions besides calling your friend. Go to a support group, go to the gym and join in a basketball game, find something—anything—that will get your mind off of contacting your former partner.

When you make it through one week, make a commitment for one more week. Take little steps. As you continue to add a week at a time to your behavior changes, you will find it gets easier. You will also begin to see that these actions really are choices. Each time you make the choice not to act on your thoughts, you become stronger.

Learning Balance

In every relationship you've had, you've become obsessive. You don't know how to be in a relationship without being obsessive. If you don't show these feelings, it seems like you aren't showing your love. How do you balance these feelings? How do you show someone you love her and want to be with her while still giving her freedom?

MISC.	**Case Study: Robert**

Case Study: Robert

Robert's relationship with Casey had recently ended. It was a volatile relationship right from the beginning. Robert's unfounded jealousy would make Casey mad and they'd end up screaming at each other. Then they would make up, and life would be good again, for a while. Robert would end up blowing up about something—Casey didn't call him back or she looked at some other guy. Sometimes Robert didn't even need a reason, his imagination would get the best of him and he would become enraged. Sometimes Casey would leave, only to come back a few days later to try to make it work.

When Casey left for good, Robert tried everything to get her back. But this time she wasn't willing to try again. Eventually Robert started dating again. He met some nice women but, after Casey, they all seemed boring. No one excited him like Casey did. No one made him feel intensely possessive. He wanted to feel the strong emotions he had felt before. To Robert, that was love.

Usually in obsessive relationships you have isolated your partner. You may have tried to keep her all to yourself. You discouraged or tried to stop her from seeing family and friends. In the process you isolated yourself as well. You probably stopped calling friends; you made excuses to not go to family events. You passed up opportunities to attend work functions or meet co-workers after work.

Without your partner in your life, you feel like you have nothing. In order to create a balance in your life, it is time to reach out to those you have neglected and develop new interests. Call friends, reconnect with family, show co-workers you want to be friends. Find classes on topics you are interested in. Go to the gym or enroll in a sports league. Rekindle the things you used to find enjoyment in.

Just as you saw therapy as a way to get your partner back, you might see joining classes or going out with friends as a way to pass the time or alleviate your pain until your partner comes back. But these activities should become a part of your life. This is what brings balance to your life. If you are looking to create healthy relationships, remember that you and your partner can and should maintain interests outside the relationship. Obsessive relationships have little or no room for anything other than the relationship; healthy relationships have plenty of room for outside interests and sharing time with one another.

Once you become aware of how your actions and thoughts are obsessive and controlling, you might worry that you will repeat the pattern in your next relationship. Alternatively, you might remain emotionally distant, afraid that, by opening yourself up to love, you are opening yourself up to rejection and once you worry about rejection, your obsessive feelings will return. Even though breakups are hard, they are sometimes for the best. A relationship might be unhealthy, or you might not have much in common; you may date someone but deep feelings never develop. Some relationships are not meant to be.

In your past, you've seen breakups as someone abandoning you. But it is not always about you. Your partner may not want to continue a relationship for a number of reasons:

- She may not be emotionally ready for a commitment.
- You may have met and "clicked" but she is involved with someone else.
- She has personal problems that have nothing to do with you and she needs time to sort through her life.
- She is focusing on her career rather than a relationship right now.

- She has her own relationship issues she needs to work on.

- You argued all the time and were unhappy most of the time—you just didn't get along.

- You had different philosophies of life, different religious beliefs, different financial goals or spending habits.

- You had little or nothing in common except sexual chemistry.

True Love

As a former obsessive lover you may go from not accepting any responsibility in a failed relationship to feeling totally responsible. As you learn how your behaviors affected your previous partner, you take on the role of making sure nothing goes wrong in the next relationship. True love, however, accepts that there are two people in any relationship and both are responsible for the outcome.

As you can see, sometimes relationships end through no fault of your own. You did not do anything wrong, it just wasn't meant to be. Every breakup or rejection is not a personal attack. If the relationship does not meet your needs, you have the ability to walk away. A healthy relationship meets the emotional needs of both partners. The only way to develop a deep, healthy, loving relationship is to take the chance and trust yourself to treat her with respect and love.

In relationships, you are used to the deep, intense feelings of obsession. Will you be able to enjoy a relationship without feeling so passionately for the other person? You have thrived (or thought you did) on the excitement and the passion of an obsessive relationship. Anything else seems boring to you. But in obsessive relationships, the passion you craved was also filled with hurt, pain, and turmoil. These emotions did not bring the satisfaction and contentment you were looking for.

As you move from being an obsessive lover to a healthy lover, your idea of love changes. A deep emotional commitment does not have to come with pain. Healthy relationships offer passion and excitement based on intimacy and true love.

Understanding Compromise

As an obsessive lover, your past relationships were often one-sided. Things were done according to your needs. You used controlling or *manipulative behaviors* to make your partner follow your lead. There was no room for compromise. This was the only way you could feel secure in the relationship. Through working on your self-image, working with a therapist, and learning about healthy relationships, you have learned that such a one-sided relationship is not emotionally beneficial to either you or your partner. You need to learn a new way.

Manipulative behaviors are those that you use to get someone to do something you want. Although behaviors are different depending on the person, some common manipulative behaviors include:

- Making the other person feel guilty if she doesn't do what you want
- Pestering the person until she gives in
- Being extra nice just to get something in return
- Being intimidating

Relationships are built around two separate individuals. Both people have their own wants, needs, and desires. Both people have their own ideas about how things should be done and what they want from the other person. In the past, you wanted everything. But now, you are open to discussion.

Carl and Megan had been dating for about six months. Carl, a former obsessive lover, was trying hard to not be obsessive or controlling. He sometimes found it difficult because he had spent so many years in other relationships where he called all the shots. He would jump back and forth. Sometimes he would get upset if Megan wasn't available and he wanted to go out. He was afraid to show it, afraid that being upset made him obsessive and would make Megan feel smothered.

One week, he was invited to a party by a co-worker and he wanted to take Megan with him. When he called and asked, she told him she had already made plans. He was disappointed. This party was important to him. His boss was going to be there and he wanted to make a good impression because he was up for a promotion. He was nervous and wanted Megan there for support. But if he told her he was disappointed, would that be seen as controlling? Was he trying to manipulate her into changing her mind and coming with him? Or was he allowed to say he was disappointed because that is how he felt?

Carl was confused about how to handle the situation. In the end, he said, "I'm sorry you can't come. I would have really liked you there with me because it's an important night for me. But I understand. Can we get together on Saturday so I can tell you about it?"

True Love In true love, there is a balance. You need to be assertive enough to make sure your emotional needs are met without being manipulative or controlling.

Carl chose to tell Megan how he felt without demanding she come with him or trying to make her feel guilty and change her mind about coming. In the end, Carl decided that ignoring his feelings would only make things worse, but he found a way to express those feelings and still respect Megan's choice. He attended the party without Megan and was surprised that he had a good time. The next day he met Megan for dinner and told her all about it.

This was all new to Carl. He was not used to making compromises. He was used to being the more important partner in a relationship, not because he felt superior but because anything less was too scary. In his past relationships, he would have said, "How can you not come? This is an important night to me. Don't you love me? If you loved me, you would come." He would not have accepted anything less. Even if Megan had refused, he would have called and asked her again and again every day until the day of the party. Carl was proud of himself for having made the right choice. He had learned that his feelings were important, and Megan's were, too. He learned to compromise and was rewarded by Megan's reaction. Not only did she want to see him again, she complimented him on understanding that she was not able to accompany him and said she hoped next time she would be available.

Essential Takeaways

- Before you can make changes in your life, you must accept responsibility for your actions and the pain you have caused your partner.
- Keeping track of your obsessive thoughts and actions can help you decide what behaviors you need to change.
- Healthy relationships are built by fulfilling the needs of both partners.
- Every breakup or rejection is not a personal attack.

chapter 15

For Partners of Obsessive Lovers: Finding Love on Your Own Terms

Creating emotional distance

Rekindling lost relationships

Looking to the past to make a better future

Making your needs important

Ending a relationship is hard. Even when the relationship was difficult or obsessive, it hurts when it is over. As the partner of an obsessive lover, you share a powerful emotional connection. You were deeply involved in the relationship. You tried to make it work. And now you have left. The smothering questions, the overbearing behaviors were all too much to take. You were sure you would feel better once you left, but you feel guilty, ashamed, sad, and lonely.

In the beginning, you may feel a sense of loss, but you might revel in your newly gained freedom. It's simple human nature to forget about bad times in any context, and you will probably miss your former partner when you are remembering the good times. But this is a time to regain your sense of independence. Future relationships will be more satisfying if you know what you want and are willing to pursue your own interests.

Breaking Emotional Ties

You know you've made the right decision. You can't feel oppressed one more day. Then your partner calls, sounding so sad, so sorry—and all of a sudden, you aren't so sure. You wonder if maybe this time he means it, maybe he really understands why you left, how serious you are, and he's willing to change.

But then you remember: You've done this before. You've told him how you felt. How you feel trapped when he wants to go everywhere with you. How you feel humiliated, angry, and resentful when he doesn't trust you. How you feel like a child when he questions you endlessly. You have told him and told him and told him. Usually he changes for a little while. Or maybe he just tells you he has. Then, when you get comfortable again, the obsessive behaviors start again.

You remember all of this and it reinforces your desire to be out of the relationship. You're again sure that you're doing the right thing. You are determined to stay away and stay strong. You hope next time he calls you won't cave in.

Your obsessive partner will take any attention as a sign that you are willing to reconcile. Suppose you say, "I don't want to see you. I want to be alone for a while." You are trying to be nice about the breakup, keep things civil, avoid any angry outbursts. Your partner, however, hears the words "for a while" and believes that, if he waits long enough, you will come back. After all, you're still being friendly to him. Even if you don't talk to him, he might believe you really will come back eventually, especially if you have broken up in the past and ended up together again.

MISC.

Case Study: Sasha

Sasha ended her relationship with Bryan after five years. She still loved him, but he was just too obsessive. His jealousy and possessiveness were too much, and Sasha needed to get away. She had left before, but this time she was determined to stay away. Living with his neediness was not good for her health; she was having stomach problems from the stress.

Living on her own was harder than she expected, though. Sasha wasn't used to having to pay the bills and run the household. Bryan had made most of the decisions for her. Now she didn't have anyone to lean on.

Bryan was still calling Sasha and that made it even harder. He would call every morning and several times each evening. Most of the time Sasha didn't answer the phone, but she knew it was him. There were evenings when she felt alone. Those nights, when the phone rang, she would answer and talk to Bryan. He wanted her back, he'd say. He was sorry, he would change, he said. She wanted to believe him but at the same time, she had heard it all before. Afterward, she always felt worse.

Finally, Sasha couldn't take it anymore and told Bryan to stop calling. She told him she wasn't going to answer his calls because it was too stressful. She cut off all contact. If the phone rang in the evening, she unplugged it. If he came over, she didn't answer the door. She couldn't talk to him because talking made it worse. If she was going to make it on her own, she needed to disconnect from him.

It is easier to put physical distance between you and your former partner than emotional distance. You can move to your own apartment, even move to a different town, but it takes more time and more effort to create emotional distance. But it is important to separate emotionally as well as physically when ending an obsessive relationship. Here are some suggestions:

- Stop all contact.

- Set clear limits and boundaries.

- Find someone else to emotionally vent to.

- Allow yourself time to mourn the relationship.

- Let go of guilt and feelings of responsibility.

- Take time to get to know yourself.

Give yourself two weeks with absolutely no contact. It is hard to have emotional distance if you are still accepting calls, leaning on your former partner for emotional support, or giving in and calling him when you are feeling alone and lonely. Don't pick up the phone if you think it is him. Don't respond to text messages. Be wary of answering social networking messages or IM's from screen names that you don't recognize. This period will allow you to adjust to your life without your partner. Many partners of obsessive lovers find this time exhilarating. They find they enjoy the feelings of freedom. Once the two weeks are over, you might find you want no further contact.

You may not be ready to stop all contact. You can still set limits on when and how often you will be in contact. Keep to these limits and set goals for more and more time in between contact. While it is always better to stop contact if you are going to stick with it, you can make things worse if you are inconsistent. Setting limits you can stick with is better than saying "no contact" and then giving in and talking to your former partner. Inconsistency often backfires and leads your former partner to persist even longer in trying to get you back.

Setting personal boundaries is as much for your former partner's benefit as your own. Knowing whether you will talk, how often, and what you will talk about, sets boundaries for both of you. Sometimes, especially if there are children involved, communication with your former partner is necessary. But you can set rules such as "I will talk to you on Saturday mornings and let you know how the week went. I don't want to discuss my life or yours. Our discussion will center around our child's life." If there are no children, you may not have any reason to speak with your former partner. Let him know you will not answer the phone if you don't want any contact.

Trying to End the Relationship

As you try to disconnect emotionally from your former obsessive partner, he will probably work hard to hold on to your relationship. Be clear and firm with your boundaries. If you don't want any contact, tell him so. If you don't want to speak with him on the phone, tell him not to call. There is a good chance he will not accept the boundaries you have set at first. Use caller ID, voice mail, or e-mail filters to reduce the contact. Don't answer your door unless you know who it is. A therapist can help you cope with the stress of ending a relationship with an obsessive lover and help you to understand why it is so hard for you to stick to your new boundaries. Therapists can help you to set goals and develop techniques to stop yourself from giving in.

If you find yourself wanting to call your former partner to vent about your day, call a friend instead. Even in the worst relationships, there are times when you received needed emotional support. When you needed to vent about your job, your car breaking down, having a bad day, someone was there to listen to you. Suddenly, you have to face these moments alone and it is scary and depressing. Let friends know in advance you might need to call just to have someone listen. Your friends will understand and might be glad to fill in as a shoulder to lean on. If you don't feel that you have enough friends with whom you can be open, consider joining a support group.

Of course, you need to give yourself time to mourn the loss of your dreams and hopes. Even if you had a poor relationship, when you end it you feel sad. In the beginning you had dreams for your future together. Those dreams are now gone. Mourning gives you closure; you are saying good-bye to your relationship.

Throughout your obsessive relationship, you probably took care of your partner. This might have been physically: making sure dinner was cooked, the house was clean, and clothes were washed. It might have been emotionally, taking steps to make sure he wasn't upset. When you leave you worry about how he will manage. Will he become depressed? Will he drink too much? Will he eat right? During the relationship you were so in tune to his needs, you ignored your own. It feels strange to not spend your days taking care of him and instead focusing on your own needs. You feel guilty thinking about yourself. Let go of the guilt. You need to focus on you. Your former partner is an adult and can take care of himself. Your responsibility now is to yourself.

Obsessive lovers are often controlling. During your relationship, you may have given in to what your partner wanted. You went to restaurants he liked, you went to movies he chose, you spent your weekends doing things he wanted to do. But what do you like? What activities do you enjoy? In the months after your breakup, take the time to explore different activities and find out what you enjoy.

Reconnecting with Friends and Relatives

How many friendships have you ignored during your relationship? As the partner of an obsessive lover, you probably focused so intently on making your partner happy you turned down invitations so often friends stopped asking you to go out. Relatives probably no longer expect you at family functions.

Now that you have ended the relationship, it is time to rekindle lost friendships and reconnect with your family. Start by making some phone calls. It may feel awkward at first, but friends will be glad to hear from you. Be honest about where you were and where you are now. They may be surprised and some will undoubtedly be happy you are finally free from the control imposed by your partner. Some may say how much they didn't like your former partner. If you are feeling guilty about leaving or wavering in your determination to stay away, lean on your friends and ask for their support. Most will be more than happy to help.

Some friends may tell you how much they didn't like your former partner. You may or may not be ready to hear what they have to say. If you are feeling guilty, wondering if you should go back, hearing your friends' opinion can help you stay strong and remember why you left and why you want to stay away. On the other hand, you might not want to continue to rehash all of the bad feelings and moments of your relationship. Be honest with your friends. Let them know what you need and what will help you heal and recover from the stress of the relationship.

Some friends may be hesitant to share their feelings, fearing that you will get back together with your previous partner and their comments will drive a wedge in your friendship. If you want to hear honest opinions, reassure your friends that your friendship is important. Let them know you want to know what they saw. You want to better understand what happened in your relationship so you can see warning signs earlier in any future relationships.

Did You Know?

According to a survey by eNation, 43 percent of people called friends or family for help during a breakup. According to the survey, other ways to cope include watching a lot of movies, going shopping, and going on vacation.

Margaret had recently left her obsessive partner, Wayne. Margaret and Wayne had been living together for three years. In the beginning of the relationship, Margaret had kept in touch with friends, meeting them once a month for a girls' night out. But not only did Wayne not want her to go, her friends didn't understand what she saw in Wayne and why she stayed with him. Margaret was caught up in the relationship, sure Wayne was the man of her dreams, and so she ignored what her friends thought. When she was with her friends, they tried to talk some sense into her by pointing out all of Wayne's faults. This made Margaret uncomfortable and she began to avoid going out, at first she made excuses, and eventually they stopped calling.

Now, Margaret was on her own again. She finally understood what her friends had been telling her. Wayne was controlling. He was obsessive. Wayne was all about Wayne. He didn't care if she was happy; he only cared about her making him happy. It had been a hard lesson to learn, but since she left she was able to see that they were right.

She was embarrassed, though. She was afraid to call, afraid her friends had lost respect for her, or would say "I told you so." It was several weeks before Margaret picked up the phone to call her best friend, Karen, and even then she chickened out a few times before dialing the number. But Karen was so excited to hear from Margaret, and thrilled she had left Wayne. They talked for an hour, as if they had never stopped talking. They laughed, they cried, and they made plans to meet for dinner the following night. Margaret felt great and couldn't wait to see her friend. Later that night, several other friends called Margaret. Word had gotten around about her breakup, and they were calling to offer support and let her know they had missed her.

Like many partners of obsessive lovers, Margaret had forgotten to take care of herself and nurture her own emotional needs. Her friends were more than happy to welcome her back and give her the support she needed. Reach out to those you have ignored or neglected. If you're worried about the reaction of your friends, start slow. Call one friend and make arrangements to get together. During the first weeks and months after your breakup you might need the emotional support of friends, don't be afraid to ask for their help.

You might have also neglected your family. Relatives, like your friends, are often seen as a threat to your relationship. Your former partner could have discouraged you from attending family functions or keeping in contact with your parents, siblings, and cousins. It's time to reach out and reconnect. The good thing about family is their willingness to forget about the past and make you feel welcome. If you're happy, your family is happy for you.

As you begin to rejoin your friends and family, remember how much you enjoy and need their company and support. When you're feeling lonely or vulnerable, reach out to these people. Their insight into your behaviors in the beginning of your relationship can help you avoid the same mistakes next time. Vow that in your next relationship you will not allow your partner to come between you and these valuable people or dictate who you can be in touch with.

It is always difficult and painful to end a romantic relationship. It is possible, though, to use the ending of a relationship as an opportunity for growth. Use this time to learn about yourself. What do you want in future relationships? What did you enjoy about the relationship? What did you not enjoy? Use your analysis (and when a relationship ends you will analyze it) to help you decide what you want and need from future relationships.

Future Relationships

You fell into an obsessive relationship before and are afraid that you will do the same thing in your next relationship. Even if you are not yet ready to start dating, you need to begin the process of learning what you want from a relationship and how you plan to make sure your partner gives you respect and love.

What Went Wrong Last Time?

It may seem strange to look back at a failed relationship to find out what you need to do in the future, but figuring out why you ended up in an obsessive relationship can help you avoid it the next time. In Chapter 8, we looked at what situations in your past played a part in your obsessive relationship. You may have been neglected in your childhood and the intensity of an obsessive relationship made you feel loved and wanted. You might have lived with controlling or judgmental parents, so your former partner's behavior might have seemed normal to you; you associated control with love. You might have been the caretaker of your family from a young age, and the neediness of your former partner drew you in to the relationship.

Understanding the emotional needs or patterns your previous relationship filled can help you to not make the same mistake. If you grew up in a home with controlling parents, it is time to take control of your own life so you don't rely on a partner to control your actions. If you feel the need to take care of everyone around you, it is time to take care of yourself first. As with obsessive lovers, working with a therapist or counselor can help you come to terms with situations in your childhood and help you develop the confidence you need to create healthy relationships.

Setting Boundaries

We all set boundaries all the time. At work you develop relationships with co-workers and bosses. Each relationship has boundaries. You might choose to keep relationships professional, not getting together socially with people you work with. This is setting boundaries. You might have neighbors you are friendly with but you don't share too many personal details. This is setting boundaries. You automatically set these boundaries to protect yourself emotionally.

Romantic relationships need boundaries as well. Setting boundaries means creating rules that protect us emotionally within a relationship. Boundaries let each partner know what to expect. They form the basis of how you expect to be treated and what you will accept and what you won't. By outlining your emotional boundaries with your partner, you show that you are taking care of yourself and you expect your partner to respect those boundaries.

 When explaining your personal boundaries to your partner, the point is to defend your emotional well-being, not to make your partner feel bad. When your partner has pushed or crossed a boundary, broach the subject later, when you are both calm, and keep the conversation focused on your needs rather than his behaviors.

Some guidelines to setting personal boundaries in relationships are ...

- Be self-aware.
- Be confident when talking to your partner about your boundaries.
- Set boundaries to protect yourself physically, emotionally, and spiritually.
- Be firm and direct.
- Enforce the boundaries you set.

What do you want? What will you accept? What makes you uncomfortable? Do you know? If you aren't sure what your boundaries should be, start paying attention to how you react to different situations. When do you become nervous? What causes knots in your stomach? What makes you want to run away? Use the following checklist to help you. As you read through the examples, place a check mark next to each statement you agree with.

- ❏ I do not like people to go through my personal belongings without my permission.
- ❏ I feel uncomfortable when someone criticizes me.
- ❏ I shut down when someone yells or screams at me.
- ❏ I am uncomfortable if someone tells off-color stories or jokes that degrade other people.
- ❏ I do not like someone to be in my personal space.
- ❏ I have a right to privacy.
- ❏ I have a right to request help around the house.
- ❏ I have a right to be by myself if I want.
- ❏ I have a right to get together with friends, by myself.
- ❏ I have a right to change my mind.
- ❏ I expect someone to understand if I cancel a commitment or a date if I am not feeling well.
- ❏ I have the right to feel safe in my home.
- ❏ I don't have to give in to my partner just because they keep begging me to do what they want.
- ❏ I don't have to talk or text immediately just because my partner calls or texts.
- ❏ I don't have to have sex just because my partner wants to have sex.

The above are examples. You might think of many more, or you can use those you checked as your boundaries. If you checked that you feel uncomfortable when someone criticizes you or you shut down when someone yells, you could set a boundary like this: "It makes me feel uncomfortable when you criticize or yell at me. If that happens, I am going to leave the room and we can talk again when you are willing to be more respectful to me."

Next, *be confident.* Body language is just as important as words. Explain your boundaries in a calm, neutral tone and use "I" statements instead of "you" statements. For example, "I like talking to you during the day, but please do not call me when I am at work," or "I feel uncomfortable when you raise your voice. I am asking you to talk to me without yelling."

Just as important as setting boundaries to protect your emotional well-being is making sure you are physically safe. You should never allow anyone to use physical force or intimidation to control you. "I will not accept being physically harmed in any way. I will leave you if you even threaten to harm me." Your spirituality and beliefs should also be protected and respected at all times. Do not allow someone to make fun of or criticize your beliefs.

When explaining your boundaries to your partner, you do not need to explain or defend your reasons. Do not use language that can be misinterpreted; for example, don't say, "I prefer that you not yell at me." That can sound too flexible. Instead state, "I will leave the room if you yell at me."

obsession Alert

When approaching your partner about emotional boundaries, be clear about the consequences of not respecting your boundaries but don't make any threats you are not ready to carry out. For example, don't say, "If you yell at me I will leave you," if you are not ready to leave. Instead, say "If you yell at me, I will leave the room until we can talk calmly." If you use threats and are not willing to carry them out your partner will not feel it is necessary to respect your boundaries. All boundaries should include: "If you …, I will …," and "If you continue, I will …."

If you set a boundary, make sure you follow through. If you do not, your partner will assume your boundaries are flexible and you can be taken advantage of. If you say "I will leave the room if you yell at me. We can talk again later when you are willing to talk without yelling," make sure you actually leave the room if your partner begins to yell.

If you're not used to having or enforcing boundaries in your life, you might feel uncomfortable or even guilty at first. You're used to placing your needs behind the needs of everyone in your life, especially your partner. But in order to create a healthy relationship, both you and your partner need personal boundaries. Face your guilt, but acknowledge that you must do this in order to take care of you.

Making Changes in Your Present Relationship

You may choose not to end your relationship. You may choose to stay and try to make your relationship work. You can still make some changes. Remember, however, that you can't change your partner's thoughts, feelings, or behaviors. You can only change your reaction to them.

The previous section on setting boundaries is a good place to start. Complete the checklist. How many of these boundaries are being overstepped in your current relationship? Which boundaries are most important to you? Start with those.

If you have been accepting obsessive and controlling behavior, you will probably encounter some resistance. Your partner might say you're being unfair. If you already feel guilty about setting boundaries and caring for yourself, this resistance will be difficult. Be strong. Remember why you are now choosing to protect yourself emotionally, physically, and spiritually. In the end, setting boundaries and taking care of yourself will result in better relationships. If your partner won't respect your boundaries, you need to decide if you can stay in the relationship. If you're working with a therapist, she can help you. If you aren't seeing a counselor, you can seek out support groups to help you stay strong and keep your focus on keeping yourself healthy.

MISC.

Controlling Behaviors vs. Boundaries

When you first begin to set boundaries, your partner might accuse you of trying to control him. Controlling behavior is telling the other person how to act or behave. Setting boundaries is giving a clear explanation of what you expect and how you will act if your boundaries are not respected. You are not telling your partner how to act, just how *you* are going to act.

Mona and Tim had been together for two years. Tim was obsessive from the beginning. Mona had accepted his behavior as a sign that he loved her, but she also thought the jealousy would subside as the relationship got stronger. What was at first flattering was now smothering. Mona decided she had enough. Her choices were to leave or to make some changes.

Mona didn't want to leave; she loved Tim and had already invested two years of her life in the relationship. She didn't want to start over. A friend at work had told Mona about a women's group she belonged to, and Mona had attended a few meetings. Tim wasn't happy about it, but Mona had insisted. The support group gave Mona the courage to try to make positive changes in her life.

At one of the meetings, the group worked on personal boundaries and Mona filled out a worksheet similar to the checklist in the previous section. It made her realize how much she allowed Tim to walk all over her. Mona decided to start standing up in her relationship. Rather than making major changes, she decided to start small. Her first change had been insisting on attending the weekly meetings. She didn't intend to give that up, no matter how much Tim fussed. She needed these meetings to keep up her determination and strength.

Then, Mona chose one personal boundary at a time. She was easily intimidated by Tim's yelling during arguments; no matter what they argued about, she gave up. She decided she wasn't going to do that anymore. She told Tim that she didn't like it when he yelled, it made her uncomfortable. She said if he chose to yell, she would leave the room until he was ready to talk. At first Tim said, "Yeah, sure." He assumed she wasn't serious. But the next time Tim yelled, Mona walked away. Tim was furious. She didn't give in. She would not continue the argument. The first couple times, Tim would follow her, yelling. She ended up getting in the car and taking a drive to let him know she was serious. Eventually, Tim got the message. He hasn't stopped yelling, but he yells less than before. Mona thinks they are making progress. Two months after her first women's meeting, Mona is still going. She is standing up to Tim during arguments. She feels stronger and is ready to tackle another personal boundary: asking for help around the house.

Changing a relationship where the rules have already been set is difficult but, in some cases, it can be done. Change takes time, so be prepared to see small changes very gradually. Sometimes change occurs only when you are preparing to leave the relationship. Only you can decide if it's too little, too late. Having a support network helps. You should not take responsibility for trying to change your partner's behaviors. By changing your reaction to those behaviors, however, you focus on what you need. It's up to your partner to choose to change or not. It's up to you to decide whether to accept his behaviors.

Essential Takeaways

- Stopping all contact with your former partner can help you see the relationship more objectively.
- Rekindling friendships you neglected during your relationship provides needed emotional support.
- Becoming aware of your personal needs is the first step to setting boundaries.
- It is difficult to change a relationship after boundaries have been violated, but it is possible in some cases.

chapter 16

Self-Help Exercises

Keeping a log or journal of your relationship

Changing how you talk to yourself

Deciding who you are and who you want to be

Using friends for support

Throughout this book we have provided you with strategies, suggestions, and guidelines to help you overcome obsessive love. Whether you are an obsessive lover or the partner of one, you can benefit from the suggestions previously mentioned and those outlined in this chapter. Some of the exercises have been described in previous sections but are described in more detail here.

The exercises in this chapter are meant to help you change your patterns of thought. Some will assist you in freeing yourself from feelings that are holding you back. Each can move you closer to your goal of overcoming obsessive love in your life. Choose the exercises that work best for you.

Writing

Writing down your thoughts can help. "I'm not any good at writing," you might say. It doesn't matter. What you write doesn't have to be art, and it doesn't have to be for anyone's eyes but your own. Writing can take on many different forms. Writing can help you look at situations in your life more objectively and help you express feelings you may be uncomfortable saying aloud.

Keeping a log can be as simple as documenting events—the date, what happened, and your reaction to it—or more like a journal or diary, with long, detailed entries. As an obsessive lover, logs help you to see patterns in your behaviors and thought processes, and help you identify triggers. If you are the partner of an obsessive lover, a log helps you keep track of the behaviors you are uncomfortable with and how you reacted to those behaviors.

obsession Alert

You can use a relationship log to look for patterns in your past relationships. Make a list of past partners and relationships, including physical characteristics, personality traits, and notes on your relationship. Look over your list to see if you identify patterns of what is attracting you to a certain type of person. Are you attracted to a particular physical appearance or characteristic, regardless of their personality? Are you attracted to outgoing personalities but have trouble with deep emotional connections? Were past lovers charming but controlling? Did you have instantaneous sexual attraction and relationships that moved quickly? By listing all your relationships and partners, you can begin to see your patterns of attraction to help you choose future partners.

Noticing Your Behavior

By keeping a log of your relationship, you will automatically begin noticing how you have acted. This is particularly important for obsessive lovers. If you are trying to change, having a log of what you do and paying attention to how often you use controlling or manipulative behaviors is the first step to learning more constructive and healthy behaviors. You can't possibly change behaviors until you know which behaviors to change.

Marcus, while working with his therapist, began a log of his obsessive behaviors.

April 17: Patty had the day off work today and had planned to meet her sister for lunch and shopping. I thought about taking the day off, too, so I could go with her, but there was an important project due and

I needed to be there. I went to work but had a hard time concentrating. I kept thinking about Patty going to lunch with her sister. I imagined the conversation, "You need to leave him, Patty; he isn't any good for you." I know her sister doesn't like me. At lunch time I thought about checking on her but didn't know what restaurant they went to. I did call Patty several times, but she didn't answer and didn't call me back. By the time I got home, I was frantic. I was half expecting her not to be there, to have left me—but there she was. I know I shouldn't feel like this, I should trust Patty, but something seems to overtake me and I become desperate. I don't think I would be able to go on if she left.

Marcus's therapist worked with him on finding healthier ways to think. First, she said, he could and would go on if Patty left. He could replace that thought with, *It would be difficult if Patty left and I would be really hurt, but I would be okay.* By reframing his thought that he could not live without Patty, he could alleviate his feelings of desperation. The therapist also pointed out that Marcus did not call in sick or leave work early to check on Patty—both actions Marcus would have taken just a few months ago, as documented in previous entries. The log was helping Marcus to see his progress.

Your log doesn't need to be as detailed as Marcus's. Your log can just be every phone call and text each day. Include the time, who made contact (you or your partner), the reason, what you hoped would happen, and the result. At the end of the day, add up the total number of calls and texts, both made and received. During the first week, observe the patterns, for example, in the reasons contact was made.

The following week, make goals for the number of calls and texts. For example, if the previous week had 100 total calls and texts, you can set a goal for 90 calls and texts this week. Each week, look over your log and set a goal for the following week. Besides the number of calls, your goals may include not calling when you're angry, or not initiating calls. Your goals should be achievable, to give you success to build on. Reducing the number of calls from 100 to 0 might be unrealistic and set you up to fail.

No matter how much you believe you can't live without your partner, broken hearts do heal. There is no set time, for some it is days, for others months. Loneliness is not caused by the absence of someone else but by an emptiness inside that only you can fill. The old adage, "No one can make you happy except you," is true. Only you have the power to change your life.

Finding Patterns

As the partner of an obsessive lover, a log of your relationship serves different purposes but can be just as helpful. You can see how your behaviors may influence events. Do your behaviors enable your obsessive partner in any way? You might be used to your partner calling or texting you excessively. When you don't receive one, you panic and think something is wrong. You text a message, "Is anything wrong?" You may not even realize that you miss your obsessive lover's frequent texts until they don't come, and your behavior has encouraged and enabled his behavior. A log can help you see these patterns.

After you have left the relationship and you are feeling lonely, wondering if you should go back, a log may help you to look over behaviors and see patterns or remind you of his obsessive behaviors. Janet had left Don but was having second thoughts. She remembered the good times and felt guilty. She wondered if she had overreacted. She read over some of the entries she had written down. One entry was:

June 29: I went to the pool to relax. Don didn't want me to go, he wanted me to go with him to some sporting event. He got mad and started telling me I didn't love him. I got mad and went to the pool anyway. He called me about 10 times but after the third call I stopped answering. He showed up at the pool and said he decided not to go with his friends. He stayed at the pool, complaining. He doesn't like the pool, why did he come? He couldn't stand me in a bathing suit in public; some other guy might look at me! Instead of relaxing, I was miserable. Finally, I gave up and left. Don acted like nothing was wrong and wanted to go out to dinner. I was too furious and wouldn't go. He couldn't understand why I was so mad. The whole weekend was ruined.

After Janet looked back over some of the entries, she remembered why she had left and why she wanted to stay away. She couldn't go anywhere by herself. She had felt trapped. There were some positive entries in her log, when she and Don had a good time, but the obsessive, destructive entries outnumbered the good. The log she kept helped her stay focused on creating a new life.

Remembering What Really Happened

When you remember events from your relationship, do you filter out the moments you want and forget the rest? Do you only remember the happy moments in your relationship but forget the fights and unhappiness? Often, we filter our memories, choosing to twist or distort what really happened. This frequently happens after a relationship has ended. You feel lonely and begin to think back, focusing on the reasons you should return to the relationship, idealizing the relationship. A log or journal can help you recall more details.

Dawn was separated from Danny. He had been calling her, sending her flowers and apologizing; she was feeling herself being drawn back into the relationship. She thought about the time they had gone to the carnival, Danny had won her a stuffed bear, he had been sweet and attentive, going on the rides she liked. She remembered the night as one of the good times in their relationship. It made her miss Danny.

But the next day, Dawn came across a diary she had kept. She read through the entries and came across the one she had written about going to the carnival.

Danny was so sweet at the carnival last night. I wish he could always be like that, but I know he was just being nice because of the fight we had earlier. My new job is driving Danny crazy. The other night I had to

> *work late to get a report finished and he called over*
> *and over. I couldn't get anything accomplished and*
> *was late getting my report to my boss. I was so mad!*
> *We had a big blow-out. I told him I was going to leave*
> *if he didn't stop being so ridiculous. I need my job and*
> *want to do well. I can't help it if he doesn't trust me. I*
> *haven't done anything and wouldn't. If only he could*
> *always be like he was at the carnival.*

Dawn hadn't remembered the fight. She had only remembered Danny being nice. Once she read the entry, the whole fight came back to her. She remembered how he wanted her to quit her job because he didn't like her having to work late sometimes. She had been so furious, that was why he had been so attentive, she had threatened to leave.

Even if you did not keep a log or journal while you were in the relationship, you can still write down your memories. They may be somewhat distorted, as Dawn's was in the beginning, but as you continue to write you will remember more—the good times and the bad. It may not be a completely accurate history of your relationship, but it will be worth it if you are honest with yourself. You might want to ask friends to help you remember your feelings during certain events.

Withdrawal

Some people feel actual withdrawal symptoms when a relationship ends, such as depression, loss of appetite, and nervousness.

Letters to Yourself

What would you tell a friend in your situation? Whether as an obsessive lover or as the partner of one, what advice would you have for someone else? Writing letters to yourself can take on many shapes unique to what works best for you. Below are some examples of different letters:

> *Dear Jenny,*
>
> *You are doing great. I know it is hard to come home to*
> *an empty house. You really miss Pete the most when*

*you first get home from work and have to think about
the long, lonely night ahead of you. It would help to
have a list of things to do by yourself in the evening.
You could start painting again, you always liked that.
You could rent some of those chick flicks Pete never
wanted to watch. You could call a friend and make
plans to meet for dinner. You could read a book. These
are all things Pete always complained when you did
because they took time away from him.*

Love,
Jenny

**True
Love**

Mark a calendar with things you plan to do every night this week. That
way, you have something to look forward to when you come home from
work. Monday could be a day to go buy supplies. Buy a great big, fun
calendar to hang in the kitchen. Buy paints and canvases. Decide on some
movies. Contact friends to meet later in the week. Make Monday your
planning day. You can do this. You are worth it.

Hey Hank,

*This is hard—really hard—but you can do it. You can
go on with your life. Remember how selfish Sharon
was? Remember how she wanted you to do everything
for her but never wanted to do anything for you?
Remember how she didn't want you to even go see
your mom? She was needy. She was controlling. You
deserve better. One day, Hank, just one day at a time,
and pretty soon you won't even think about her.*

Sincerely,
Hank

Notice how each person used a different approach. Jenny wrote a letter
reminding her of activities to keep busy and the reason she couldn't do
these things when she was with Pete. Hank's letter was a reminder of what
was wrong with Sharon. Your letter needs to address your needs. You could

use notes taped to your mirror or refrigerator or send yourself the letter in the mail. Whatever works to help you cope with your situation.

Affirmations

As we have discussed throughout this book, both obsessive lovers and their partners frequently have low self-esteem. *Affirmations* can help you cope with negative thoughts and fears. You can say them silently or aloud. The more you repeat affirmations, the more you believe them. You might want to make a list of affirmations and tape it in several places throughout your house so you read and repeat them often. Repetition is the most important part of using affirmations to improve your life.

Definition

An **affirmation** is a declaration that something is true. They are often used to overcome negative thought patterns.

Our subconscious has certain beliefs and patterns, and it continues to follow these to reinforce how we think. For example, if you believe you are stupid, every time you make a mistake you tell yourself, "See? You are so stupid." This thought reinforces your negative view of yourself. Affirmations work to change these beliefs. Your affirmation would be "I am an intelligent person." As you repeat this to yourself, several times every day, you will begin to change your negative view of yourself into a positive view.

Some examples of positive, self-confidence-building affirmations are as follows:

- I can make my own decisions.
- I deserve to be happy.
- I have the power to change myself.
- I deserve to be loved.
- I am lovable.
- I am caring, supportive, and loyal.
- I am good at_____.

Affirmations should be clear and concise. They should be believable or should contain a goal. If you are overweight and you use an affirmation of, "I am thin," your mind will automatically reject this with, "You are not thin." You have now negated any good from using that affirmation. Instead, use an affirmation such as, "Every day I make progress toward my weight goal."

Changing Your Thoughts

As an obsessive lover, you might have a continuous flow of negative, self-depreciating thoughts. You might think, "She doesn't love me, I am not good enough for her, she wants someone with more money; she deserves someone better than me." As the partner of an obsessive lover, you might think, "I am stupid. I can't do anything right; if only I could be better, he wouldn't be so jealous." The more you tell yourself these things, the more you believe them. In order to change your self-perception, you need to change your thoughts. You have the power to control your life by controlling your thoughts. You can take charge of how you think.

Rewording Self-Talk

The first step to changing negative thoughts is to keep track of how you talk to yourself. Keep a log of what you tell yourself. In the beginning, you may be amazed by how often you put yourself down. Use a notebook and draw a vertical line down the middle of the page. On one side, write down any negative thought you say to yourself. On the other side, reword what you have said.

We usually repeat, over and over, what we heard in our childhood. If our parents told us we were lazy or useless, it is what we continue to tell ourselves as adults. It is possible, with hard work, to change how you talk to yourself.

Reword the negative thought to make it a positive affirmation. For example if you thought, "I am such a loser," reword it to "I am a capable person," or some other affirmation that works for you. Write it in your notebook. Each time you hear yourself repeating, "I am such a loser," change it to the alternative you wrote down. Alternatively, you can reword your thought to be in the past tense. "I always do something stupid" could be changed to "I used to do things without thinking, now I think first."

This will take some practice. You need to be aware of your thoughts and remind yourself to change your thoughts and why you are doing this. This takes patience and hard work. As you work at it, you should notice less negative self-talk.

Stopping Obsessive Thoughts

You can't stop thinking about her; no matter what you do, thoughts of your partner intrude on your life. Whether you are with your partner or have separated, you have to train yourself not to think about her. The permanent solution is to work on the reasons for your obsession: your insecurities about love.

We've talked about facing your past in depth, and that is certainly important, but it isn't going to happen overnight. You need to be able to get through the next hour, the next day, the next month. How are you going to be able to get on with your life when you can't get through an hour without obsessive thoughts about your partner? Use these thought-stopping techniques whenever you have an obsessive thought.

- Put a rubber band around your wrist. Any time you notice thoughts about your partner, snap the rubber band as a way to say to yourself, "Stop!"

- Tell yourself, "Stop," loudly and clearly. When you are alone, you can yell it for emphasis; when other people are around, you might want to "yell" it silently.

- Visualize a big red STOP sign.

- Use your right foot and put on the brakes as if you were in a car. Imagine that you are putting the brakes on the thought process.

- Use index cards to describe pleasant experiences or thoughts. For example, you might want to describe a vacation you would like to take. Any time you find yourself thinking about your partner, take out the index card and read about your vacation. Replace your obsessive thought with a pleasant one.

You may have to use these techniques hundreds of times to break the habit of thinking certain thoughts, but over time, this should reduce the number of times you think about your former partner. Keeping a log can help you realize that the number of thoughts about her is slowly reducing.

Case Study: Amanda

Amanda's partner, Jake, had recently left her. She couldn't stop thinking about him. She woke up in the morning wondering what he was doing. She couldn't call him; he had changed his number. She couldn't go see him; he wouldn't tell her where he was living. She wanted to see him, badly. Her whole day was taken up with thoughts of Jake. No matter what she did or how much she tried, Jake jumped back into her thoughts and then she would spend an hour or so daydreaming. Amanda's therapist suggested she make a STOP sign and keep it with her. Whenever she started thinking about Jake she took out the sign to remind herself to stop. It took a long time, but after a few weeks Amanda began to notice that she thought of Jake less and less, and when she did think about him, she was able to stop herself.

Again, it is important to find the reasons for your obsession. Simply reducing your obsession or replacing your obsession with another obsession (daydreaming about your next vacation can be an obsession if the thoughts stop you from getting anything accomplished) is not the end goal. You want to stop your obsession and understand it so you don't repeat the same mistake in your next relationship.

Self-Discovery

Your relationship took up a great deal of your time and thoughts. You aren't sure what you think or want anymore. As an obsessive lover, your thoughts center more around your partner—what she is doing, who she is with— than what you want out of life. As the partner of an obsessive lover, your thoughts have centered around how to keep your partner calm and happy. You have dismissed your own needs as unimportant and focused your life on fulfilling your partner's needs instead.

Who You Are

Now that you have made the decision to change your life, you need to figure out what will make you happy, what will make you feel fulfilled. This is a time of self-discovery. Below are some ways to find out what you think and believe.

Create a timeline of your life. What events have shaped who you are? Think about your accomplishments, your achievements, and the major events in your life. Include negative experiences because these have also had an impact on who you are, but don't dwell on the negative events. Creating a timeline helps you put situations and events into perspective. You realize that you become who you are based on all life experiences, not just one situation or event.

Focus on when you were happy. When were you happiest? What were you doing? Who were you with? This should give you some idea of what you like, and what type of people you should surround yourself with.

Find some time for solitude each day. Remove yourself from the expectations and beliefs of the people around you. What they want is not necessarily the same as what you want. Take time for yourself—whether you take a long walk, sit in a park, or lock yourself in your room—and use this time to focus on your thoughts without having them influenced by others.

Think about what you like. What movie would you choose? What books do you like to read? If you could pick any spot in the world to go on vacation, where would you go? Your partner has probably influenced many of your decisions and choices. Taking the time to think about what you enjoy will help you in your next relationship.

Make a list of five words that describe you. This is a list of your basic traits. Who are you? Your list might be: honest, loyal, loving, fun, optimistic. Sometimes we see negative traits; your list might include words like wimp or pushover. You can change these negative traits. The next section will focus on some exercises to start making positive changes in your life.

Taking the time to get to know yourself, to find who you are and to be comfortable with who you are, will help in your present and future relationships. You will be more apt to say, "This is what *I* want to do," rather than going along with whatever your partner wants.

We each have different spiritual beliefs that guide us in our actions and interactions with other people. For some these beliefs could be from an organized religion, for others there could be an inner spirituality that drives their actions. Your moral path may have been derailed during your tumultuous relationship. Use this time to redefine your moral guidelines.

Who You Want to Be

As you search for who you are now, you might find areas you want to change. Creating a strong self-image you are proud of and happy with will help you to be more confident in yourself and in future relationships. The following exercises help you explore what you want to do with your life, what you want to accomplish, and who you want to be.

Begin with a "fresh-start" mentality. There is no use feeling bad or feeling guilty about what you don't like about yourself. The exercises in finding out who you are right now were not meant to induce guilt. Remember that all experiences, good and bad, have created who you are right now. You have the ability to sort through and keep what you like about yourself, and change that which you don't.

Ask yourself questions. Instead of focusing on your past, think about what you want to do in the future. Use the following questions as a guideline and add your own:

- If money was not an issue, what would I do with my days?

- Where would I go on vacation if I could choose anywhere in the world?

- What is the one thing I would like to accomplish in my lifetime?

- What do I regret that I have not done?

Exploring the answers to these questions allows you to focus on what you want out of life. Write down your answers so you don't forget. Keep a notebook with you. When you take time each day to self-reflect, answer a question.

Choose one new thing to do each week. You have discovered who you are; now discover what you want. Writing down answers is one way, but trying new things will help you explore different options. Sign up for a class, join a gym. New experiences will open your mind to new opportunities and help you to expand what you want out of life.

Create a plan for your life. Make a list of specific actions you need to take to make your goals a reality. Have the courage to focus on those things you want but haven't had the guts to try.

Misc.

Finding Yourself

Dr. Rose Rothmeier at Austin College, Sherman, Texas, says finding yourself isn't about focusing on your weaknesses but, instead, is about building on your strengths. She says finding situations that utilize your strengths will help you succeed.

Finding yourself is a journey. Most people spend their lives searching for who they are and what they want and may reinvent their life several times. These exercises will hopefully help you to become comfortable and accepting of who you are, and to help you realize your goals and desires are important. Both obsessive lovers and their partners frequently give up goals in order to focus on the relationship. You could still be in a relationship and want to make some positive changes to improve yourself. Your relationship could have ended and you are having a hard time letting go. Spending time focusing on yourself helps.

Support Groups

No matter what situation you are in, having a network of people helps. You can talk through your fears. You can use your network to give you guidance and pull you back when your obsessiveness starts taking over your life. Having a network gives you a sense that you are not alone, that people care.

Support groups are made up of people who have been through, or are going through, the same situation as you. You might find groups for obsessive lovers or partners of obsessive lovers in your area, or you can take advantage of online support groups. The resource section at the end of the book provides some places to find support.

obsession Alert Finding a network of friends, joining a support group, and using self-help exercises are all part of the healing process for obsessive love. If you are not able to let go or if obsessive love behaviors are interfering with your life, you may need psychotherapy or counseling in addition to these strategies.

Meeting with others in your situation can help you …

- Decide whether to leave or stay.

- Make a plan to leave.

- Through the difficult first days after you leave.

- Stay away from future obsessive relationships.

Support groups can offer you the objectivity and honesty you need when deciding whether to stay and work on your relationship or to leave. Because those in your support group have not been emotionally involved in your relationship, they can offer their honest opinions and help you look at your relationship through different eyes.

If you have decided to leave, your support group, especially those that have already left an obsessive relationship, can help you make plans for leaving. They can help you be prepared for the loneliness or guilt you might feel after you have left. They can help with practical issues of where to live or how to create a budget. You can help yourself by helping others.

No matter how prepared you are or how certain you are that leaving is the right decision, it will be hard in the beginning. You are torn, guilty, ashamed, and lonely. Having a support group can give you the emotional support you need. As an obsessive lover, the first few days or weeks is hard. You can only think about how to get your partner back. A support group can help you focus on other parts of your life. Going to meetings can initially fill the time and space that you devoted to your relationship.

The obsessive relationship is an unhealthy love relationship. If you have chosen to leave it or your partner has left, you need to understand what went wrong. Support groups often have presentations and education about relationships, allowing you to analyze your relationship. Support groups do not take the place of psychotherapy, which can help sort through all of the reasons why you were attracted to an obsessive lover or why you became obsessive, but groups can teach you what a healthy love relationship should look and feel like.

Essential Takeaways

- Writing down your thoughts helps you to look at situations more objectively.
- You believe your own thoughts. Controlling how you talk to yourself can help change how you view yourself.
- Focusing on what you want out of life can help you overcome obsessiveness, or avoid being a partner of an obsessive lover in future relationships.
- A support group can give you the emotional support you need to overcome an obsessive relationship.

Part 5

When Obsessive Love Becomes Dangerous

Sometimes obsessive love relationships cross the line into a dangerous realm. Although most do not, some end with stalking or domestic violence. You need to know how to recognize the signs of abuse, whether physical, emotional, sexual, or economic. In this part we explain the different types of abuse and what the early warning signs are.

If your relationship has become dangerous, it is important to know how to protect yourself. You can improve the security in your home and be vigilant when out and about. We offer suggestions and tips for staying safe and protected, as well as where to find help and support.

Finally, some partners of obsessive lovers may need help from the law. We discuss what "orders of protection" are and give you some guidelines for talking with the police. We give ideas of what types of documentation you should have if you need to go to court to help you stay safe.

chapter 17

Stalking and Domestic Violence

Stalking in fantasy and previous relationships

Ways stalkers follow your life

Types of domestic abuse

How to know if you are in an abusive relationship

Obsessive love relationships are emotionally difficult for both partners but usually not dangerous. Sometimes, however, obsessive lovers cross the line, either stalking their partner or committing acts of violence, during the relationship or after it is over.

Stalking

Stalking is repeated, unwanted contact that incites fear or implies a threat against one person, by another person. Stalking normally occurs after a relationship has ended, when an obsessive lover can't accept that the relationship has ended. He wants and needs the relationship to keep going. Stalkers often believe that, given enough time, their partner will come around. He sees stalking as a way to show his love, not as a way to harass or annoy. They often don't think of it as stalking, "I just need to see her, I only want to talk to her." There is frequently little or no perception of the negative effect they are having upon the person they "love."

But stalking usually creates fear and intimidation; it is a type of emotional abuse. Partners who are being stalked may experience anger, anxiety, depression, or suicidal thoughts.

Some common stalking behaviors include:

- Following you

- Spying on you

- Repeatedly showing up at places you go

- Continuously calling you at home, work, or both

- Sending unwanted letters or e-mails

- Giving or sending unwanted gifts or flowers

- Vandalizing your property

- Making threats against you or someone you know

Most of these actions are legal on their own; however when combined, done repeatedly, and done to induce fear or cause injury, they become a criminal action.

Stalking in Obsessive Fantasy Relationships

Most often we hear about stranger stalkings when they involve a celebrity, but famous people are not the only victims of this crime. Stranger stalkings account for approximately 25 percent of the 3.4 million Americans stalked annually (U.S. Department of Justice, 2008 survey).

Stalkers may or may not be someone you know. A stalker can be someone you spoke with at the check-out line in the grocery store, someone you say hello to at work, or someone you met once, somewhere, anywhere. Your stalker could be someone you have never met. It could be someone who observed you jogging in the park or picking up your child at school. He may have watched you at the same time every day. Somehow, this person became attached to you, deciding you were the one and only love of his life.

In 1989, Rebecca Schaeffer, a popular actress from the television show *My Sister Sam*, was shot and killed outside her home. The investigation into the murder revealed that Robert Bardo, who was later convicted, had been stalking Ms. Schaeffer for the previous two years. At first he wrote a fan letter, and she wrote back, sending an autographed photo. Becoming obsessed, he built a shrine to her in his room. He tried to visit her on numerous occasions at Warner Brother's studio, but couldn't get in. His diary stated, "I don't lose." He hired a detective agency to find out her home address. In July 1989, he went to her apartment. When she answered the door, she sent him away. He knocked again. This time when she answered, he shot and killed her.

This case gained nationwide attention and was an impetus for creating the first antistalking division in the United States. Now, all 50 states and the federal government have laws against stalking, although the language in the laws varies.

Now you live in fear. You are afraid to answer your phone, you rush from your job to your car, avoid stopping at the store, and barely leave your home. You have become a prisoner of your stalker.

Stalkers of strangers often follow a pattern of behaviors:

- Infatuation

- Making contact

- Either experiencing or perceiving rejection

- Denial and delusion

- Anger and need for control

In some cases, as the need for control grows but doesn't result in a relationship, threats begin. Violence does not always follow, but is a possibility.

Did You Know?

One in every four women will experience domestic violence sometime in her life, according to the National Coalition Against Domestic Violence.

When a Previous Partner Is Stalking You

The most common type of stalking is a former spouse or significant other, according to a survey completed by the U.S. federal government in 2008. The survey results indicate women are stalked more often than men.

Rejection is frequently the catalyst for stalking. Divorce, separation, and breakups are the ultimate rejections. The obsessive partner ignores the rejection, believing if he can just talk with her, his former partner will change her mind and come back. As he is rejected again and again, anger builds and the need to control the situation intensifies.

As the partner of an obsessive lover, anytime you communicate with your former partner, even if it is to ask him to stop, you reinforce his stalking behavior. Any attention, even negative attention, gives the obsessive lover hope. Stalking becomes an obsession itself, phone calls come at all hours of the day and night or the stalker shows up unannounced, sure that this time their ex will listen; that secretly she wants him back.

The obsessive lover begins to make up excuses and constantly rationalizes why he should persist in his quest. If his ex is seeing someone else, it's just to make him jealous. If she doesn't speak with him when he calls her at work, she's just busy right now or is waiting for the right time, when they can be alone. For some people, the rejection is too hard to bear, so instead, they create an imaginary relationship that's still strong. This make-believe relationship gives him the right to continue to follow—to stalk—his former spouse or girlfriend.

MISC.

Stalking Statistics

According to the U.S. Department of Justice ...

- The most common types of stalking are unwanted phone calls, e-mails, or lies spread about the victim.
- Two thirds of stalking victims are women.
- Most victims of stalking are between ages 18 and 24.
- Approximately 75 percent of stalking victims knew or were acquainted with their stalker. Most stalkers were ex-spouses or former girlfriends or boyfriends.
- Only around 40 percent of stalking victims report it to the police.

Tools Stalkers Use

Stalkers are resourceful. They use a variety of tools to help gain control and leave the message: "I am here. I haven't forgotten you and I won't let you forget me."

Gifts, Notes, and Other Communication

In the early stages of stalking, when the obsessor is trying to win back or win over the victim, gifts can be romantic, such as flowers. For those in previous relationships with their stalkers, gifts could symbolize events from the past, for example, a souvenir from somewhere they visited as a couple. As the stalking progresses and the victim continues to reject the advances, gifts may become more threatening in nature—for example, a picture of the couple with an X over the victim's face, or dead roses in a box. These types of gifts show the obsessor's anger at being rejected and imply a threat.

Stalkers must make sure their victims know they are still around, and work hard to make sure the victim thinks about them every day. Phone calls are the most common form of communication. Your phone may ring at all times of the day and night. Stalkers have been known to call hundreds of times in a day. Your stalker will often not say anything, just call and hang up. It is enough to know that you know who was on the other end of the line and that you thought about him when the phone rang.

 obsession Alert Stalkers can use social networking sites to gain the trust and sympathy of friends of the victim in an attempt to isolate the victim, making her feel more vulnerable.

Notes can take the form of love poems, cards, or threatening letters. Today, modern technology gives stalkers even more avenues to harass their victims. Stalkers have been known to send a barrage of e-mails or send messages through social networking sites, such as Facebook. Stalkers also use these sites to harass victims by spreading lies in an effort to cause hurt and pain and leave the victim with nowhere to turn for help, except back to the stalker.

Vandalism

Vandalism happens when a stalker is trying to instill fear without inflicting personal injury, or acting out their anger toward you on your possessions. A stalker is making a stamp on your life by making his presence known. As with notes or gifts, vandalism serves the purpose of making you think about your stalker and drives the obsessor to continue.

Lisa was divorced. Her ex-husband was physically abusive. She had moved to a different town and had a Protection from Abuse order against him. Even so, he continued to stalk her. One morning a windshield wiper on her car was missing. Another morning one of the front lights had been smashed in. There was never any sign of her ex-husband and she could not prove it was him; the vandalism happened in the middle of the night and no one in her apartment complex ever saw anyone in the parking lot. It was enough for him to know that, when she found it in the morning, she would think about him; when she took her car to be repaired, she would think about him. That the thoughts were negative did not matter to him.

Surveillance

Spying on victims is common among stalkers. Knowing someone is watching your every move threatens your sense of security. Stalkers often want their victims to know they are watching them. They will leave tell-tale signs of their presence, for example, leaving cigarette butts on the front lawn. Many will cover their tracks so that you will not know how they know your whereabouts or what you did yesterday.

Technology offers new methods of surveillance. Stalkers can place digital tape recorders or cameras in convenient locations, hidden from view of the victim. They can use cameras with telephoto lenses from a distance, far enough away to not be seen by the victims.

Violence or Threats of Violence

Some stalkers like to create fear. They need to feel in control. Fear and intimidation are simple ways to control the situation. When a stalker threatens violence, it is imperative to immediately contact the local police.

We'll go into laws and additional ways to protect yourself in the next couple of chapters.

Cyberstalking

Surveillance also includes going through trash to find information on the victim, or surfing social networking sites, even signing up under false names to gather information.

Most people are aware of *cyberstalking* and the dangers, especially as it relates to young children and teens. Cyberstalking, however, can occur at any age and can involve strangers seeking new contacts online or can involve people you know harassing you electronically.

Definition

Cyberstalking is using threatening behavior or making unwanted advances to harass an individual or a group of individuals electronically, using e-mail, instant messaging, forums, and social networking sites.

Stranger stalking online often happens in chat rooms, on message boards, or on forums. Stalkers will seek out victims by pretending to befriend someone. Some will attempt to set up an offline meeting while others will be content stalking and harassing you online, through e-mails or inappropriate messages.

Some of the methods of online harassment include:

- Threatening or obscene e-mails
- Spamming
- Harassment in chat rooms
- Online verbal abuse
- Creating lies and damaging stories
- Inappropriate messages on message boards and forums
- Viruses
- Identity theft

With the popularity of social networking sites, online predators have the ability to find a great deal of personal information. Not only can they search through your information, but they can see who you are connected to. You (or your friends) may post information on where you shop, where you work, or what you like to eat. Stalkers can easily glean information from posts to narrow down where you live and easily move from online stalking to real-world stalking. Be careful posting on even your friends' pages. Stalkers can be quite creative in getting around privacy controls.

If you post a picture of where you are, anyone can find out where you are through geotagging. The website www.Icanstalku.com is dedicated to helping the public avoid inadvertent information sharing. A lot of smart phones encode the location of where pictures are taken. They can analyze your photos and figure out where you live, who you live with, where you go to lunch and with whom, and commuting and shopping patterns. Anyone who has a copy of the picture that was posted online can access the information regarding where the picture was taken. Go to this site to learn how to disable the geotagging on your smart phone if you are concerned about possible cyberstalking.

Either way, online stalking can be just as devastating as in-person stalking. Victims experience psychological trauma and are at risk for physical harm.

Domestic Violence

Domestic violence is about control. According to the U.S. Office on Violence Against Women, domestic violence doesn't happen just to women. It happens regardless of age, gender, race, sexual orientation, or religion. It can take the form of physical abuse, emotional or psychological abuse, sexual abuse, and economic abuse. The following sections outline some of the ways an obsessive lover uses abuse and power to control his partner.

MISC.

Case Study: Phyllis

Phyllis had been living with Sam for several years. Sam had always been jealous and possessive. One night, about two years into the relationship, Phyllis was late getting home from work. In a fit of jealousy, Sam pushed her. Phyllis couldn't believe Sam had done it and believed his apologies were proof that he wouldn't do it again. "It was pent-up worry," she thought. "I should have called and told him I was running late."

She tried to be more thoughtful, letting Sam know every time she was going to be late, but a few weeks later, it happened again. This time Sam grabbed her and threw her against the wall. Phyllis was stunned. She didn't know what to do. Sam's jealousy was getting worse, and now he was becoming physical. Phyllis talked to a friend and decided to separate from Sam.

Physical Abuse

Domestic violence is about controlling your partner to make sure she doesn't leave you. Obsessive lovers who are violent have a need to be in total control of their partners. Some believe they have a right to control every part of a relationship; some have such a fear of abandonment or rejection that they can only cope by having complete control of their partners and take away any possible means of leaving. Many abusers see themselves as the victims.

Some examples of this type of abuse include:

- Hitting, slapping, or punching
- Choking
- Pushing
- Denying medical care
- Denying basic and needed functions such as food, water, or sleep

obsession Alert

Research has shown a correlation between jealousy and aggression. According to the 2010 report, *The Relationship between Jealousy and Aggression*, published by the European Journal of Scientific Research, controlling and jealous spouses are more likely to act violently. This was true for both men and women.

Physical violence usually occurs between partners, but in some cases, physical violence may be directed toward children or pets as a way to cause distress to the partner.

Sexual Abuse

Sexual abuse is using force to make your partner participate in a sexual activity. Obsessive and abusive lovers will use sex to show their power in the relationship. They have little concern about whether the desire to have sex is mutual. As an obsessive lover, you might demand sex, feeling as if your partner must give you sex whenever you want. This sends the message, "You are mine, I can take you whenever I want." As the partner of an obsessive lover, you might not feel you have a choice. You can't say no, even if you are sick or are just not in the mood. You are too afraid of the consequences. Or perhaps you know they will nag you incessantly until you give them what they are demanding as a right. You can't take being hounded anymore.

Emotional or Psychological Abuse

Emotional abuse is often thought to be less harmful than physical abuse, but this is not true; it can be even more harmful—and long-lasting— than physical abuse. The scars from diminished self-esteem or loss of independence are hard to overcome. Emotional or psychological abuse is meant to demean, humiliate, or control the other partner. Here are some examples of emotional abuse:

- Isolating the partner from friends or family
- Humiliating the partner either in private or in public
- Constantly criticizing the partner
- Ignoring the partner
- Name-calling or yelling

Those who live with emotional abuse, as with other forms of abuse, can develop depression and have an increased risk of eating disorders, substance abuse, and suicide.

Economic Abuse

When the partner of an obsessive lover has money and resources, she has the ability to leave and start her own life without him. As an obsessive lover, it is important to block any opportunity to leave. Economic abuse is when an obsessive lover takes control of the finances.

As the partner of an obsessive lover, if your partner abuses you economically, you might experience …

- Not being allowed to have a credit card; your partner may have taken or shredded your credit cards.

- Being asked by your partner to account for every penny you spend, having him check receipts or getting only enough money to cover what you are going to buy.

- Getting a small allowance, and being forced to ask if you need more money.

- Having to stop going to school or take classes to improve your job.

- Being late for work or missing work entirely because your partner holds you up.

- Not having any say in any financial decisions or not having access to bank accounts.

- Being denied medical care or basic necessities such as food or clothes.

Economic abuse is meant to keep you completely dependent on your partner. If you have no financial resources, your ability to leave and start your own life is limited. But more than that, like all types of abuse, economic abuse takes away your feelings of confidence, independence, and self-worth. It is intended to make you feel worthless and that no one else would want you.

Early Warning Signs

Abusive relationships don't just happen overnight. Jealousy is common in many physically abusive relationships, but you should be aware of other warning signs. Check off the statements below that describe your relationship:

❏ My partner is jealous and possessive.

❏ I worry about pleasing my partner most of the time.

❏ My partner has a bad temper and has frequent outbursts or overreacts to small things.

❏ I will give up what I want to do if my partner doesn't want to do it with me, or if he doesn't want me to do it by myself.

❏ I keep in touch with my partner by phone or text at all times to let him know what I am doing and where I am.

❏ My partner calls or texts me constantly when I am not with him.

❏ My partner would prefer that I don't work.

❏ I frequently miss or am late for work because my partner stops me from going.

❏ My partner tells me how to dress or criticizes me when I wear something he doesn't like.

❏ My partner calls me names or teases me, even when I tell him it hurts my feelings.

❏ My partner tells me it is my fault when he is in a bad mood.

❏ My partner drives dangerously when I am in the car with him.

❏ My partner controls all the money in the household and does not include me in financial decisions.

❏ I am afraid to say no to sex with my partner, even when I don't want it.

❏ My partner uses violence to solve problems.

❏ My partner has rigid ideas about family and each person's role within the family.

Although this checklist is not definitive, if you have checked even a few of the previous statements, your partner might be showing signs of potential for future abuse. Abuse usually escalates, and even if your partner has not been physically abusive, you could be in danger. The following chapters outline steps you can take to protect yourself. No one deserves to be abused.

Essential Takeaways

- Stalking is repeated, unwanted contact with the goal of creating fear through intimidation. Frequently the stalker is a former spouse or significant other.

- The stalker often does not see his actions as stalking. He justifies his actions by thinking, "I just need to see her," or "I know she loves me; if I could be with her she would realize this."

- Domestic violence is a way to control your partner and prevent her from leaving. It is a way to eliminate her opportunities to start her own life.

- Research has shown a correlation between jealousy and aggression.

chapter 18

Protecting Yourself from Stalkers

Keeping yourself safe at home

Staying alert to changes or disturbances in your surroundings

Firmly letting someone know you aren't interested

Reaching out to resources and individuals who can help

Being stalked is frightening. As discussed in the previous chapter, stalkers use many different tools and resources to harass their victims. The one consistent thing about stalkers is their unpredictability. Because police cannot provide around-the-clock protection to everyone, much of your protection will be your responsibility. In this chapter, we will go over some of the ways you can protect yourself. Using the legal system, such as filing restraining orders, is covered in Chapter 20.

Whether you are being followed by your former partner or someone you just met has become attached to you and won't leave you alone, you need a secure and safe environment for yourself. The strategies in this chapter will help you at home and when you go out.

Reducing Your Risks at Home

Nothing is quite so disturbing as knowing you are being watched or having someone intrude into your sanctuary, your home. Stalkers may look in your windows, come to your door, or leave gifts at your front door. They may call your home or hide nearby and observe when you come and go. Some victims of stalkers feel so uncomfortable they are afraid to leave their homes.

Home Security

Protecting yourself begins at home. In order to reduce the chances of this happening, keep curtains and blinds shut. Installing motion-detection lights outside your home helps prevent a stalker from coming too close or hiding in your yard during nighttime hours. Make sure you keep your cell phone charged and with you at all times. Following are some more ideas to make your home more secure.

Get a dog. You don't need a watchdog or an attack dog. A dog that barks when someone approaches, comes to the door, or is walking outside will help to alert you to a possible threat—and intimidate whoever's out there. Dogs do not provide complete protection but can warn you and give you the chance to contact the police.

Install a security camera. A video camera placed outside your house gives you evidence of a stalker at your home or on your property. Video cameras come with a number of different features. Cameras can run all the time or have motion sensors, turning on only when someone walks into the camera's view. Cameras that run all the time use a great deal of video, so you will need to monitor and change the storage device regularly. Some cameras can capture clear video only during the day while others have night vision technology. Stationary video cameras have a limited area of vision but others will continually scan a preprogrammed area. You can use a camera hidden in a decorative accent or inside a protective case to limit the stalker's ability to disable the camera or put something over the camera to avoid being photographed.

Take Care of Yourself

If you are being stalked, you might feel overwhelmed, frustrated, angry, or depressed. You may lose your appetite or have frequent crying spells. You may develop symptoms of anxiety: nightmares, panic attacks, poor concentration, and jumpiness. These are all signs of stress. It is important to take care of yourself. Talking to a professional who is experienced with stalking victims can help. Your local crisis center or domestic violence center should be able to let you know what services are available in your area.

All of your doors should have locks in working order. Deadbolt locks provide the best protection. Check your windows to make sure the locking mechanism is working correctly. You also want to cut down any shrubs or trees that would allow a stalker to hide from view. Window coverings should block the view of the interior of your house when closed. If you are afraid of a stalker breaking into your home, replace your window glass with safety glass.

Get a home security system with sensors to sound alarms if someone enters, or tries to enter, through your doors or windows. The local police will be notified immediately when your alarm goes off. Security systems can be modified to fit your needs; you may elect to have video cameras installed and integrated with the security system.

Use lock boxes on any outside electric and phone boxes. Locking up electrical and phone lines makes it more difficult for a stalker to tamper with these lines from outside your home. Stalkers can make a phone call and have your electricity, phone, gas, or water turned off. Contact your utility companies, explain your situation, and ask that a flag be put on your account requiring a password for any changes to your services.

If your neighborhood has a town watch organization, notify them and provide a picture of your stalker, if you have one. If you live in an apartment complex, ask the manager to be on the lookout for any person who doesn't belong or is acting oddly. The same goes for neighbors: ask them to be aware of unfamiliar cars or people lurking in the area.

Don't Divulge Personal Information

The Internet is a large database of public information. Any information placed on the Internet, whether behind privacy settings or not, can appear in the public domain. Even an innocent post on Facebook about your weekend plans can be copied, pasted, and spread from one person to another.

Case Study: Casey

Casey had left her boyfriend, Stan, but three months later he was still calling her, and several times she had spotted his car going down her street. She didn't think much about it until he started showing up at the grocery store, or in restaurants when she met a friend for lunch. He seemed to know where she was going and when.

Casey didn't understand how Stan knew where she was going to be until one day she ran into Marcia, a friend from high school. Casey commented about being friends with Marcia on Facebook but Marcia looked surprised, saying she did not use any social networking sites. Casey checked her Facebook account when she got home and Marcia was listed as one of her friends. She remembered getting a friend request a couple months before from Marcia. But as she looked at Marcia's profile she realized there was very little information and what was there was vague. The profile picture wasn't of Marcia, but of a cat. Casey had assumed it was Marcia's pet.

Marcia realized that Stan had probably remembered Marcia's name and used it to become "friends" with her on Facebook. He could then read her updates, find out what she was doing, and dig for information from her other friends. Marcia immediately deleted her Facebook account and decided to go back to getting in touch with her friends the old-fashioned way, by calling them on the phone.

The best way to protect personal information online is not to post anything you don't want everyone to know or, if you're being stalked, to avoid posting on online social networks altogether. If you do choose to use social networking sites or other online resources, some safeguards include the following:

- Don't communicate with anyone if you are not 100 percent sure of their identity. It is easy for someone to pretend to be someone else in order to get you to divulge personal information about yourself.

- Take advantage of your computer's security settings, firewalls, and privacy settings. Check the privacy settings on social networking sites, such as Facebook, as well. The default security settings don't offer much privacy, but you can customize these settings for more security.

- Do not include your e-mail address, phone number, instant messenger names, or any other identifying information on your social networking profiles.

- Don't use public computers to access sites that contain personal information; someone could use the computer after you and gather password information or access your accounts. If you must use a public computer, be sure to delete cookies, temporary internet files, and user history before logging off the computer.

- Don't post any pictures on the Internet that can give a stalker any information about you, your home, or your friends.

When joining social networking sites, be selective about whom you choose as your friends. Don't be afraid to turn someone down if you aren't sure who they are.

Staying Safe When Out and About

The simple things in life—meeting a friend for lunch or driving to the store—become stressful events when you are being stalked. Friends and relatives, even though supportive, may not understand your constant fear. They may think you are overreacting to the situation. You may think so, too, which only contributes to your overall fear and uncertainty.

Be Aware of Your Surroundings

Stalkers want to catch you unaware. Being vigilant about where you are, what is around you, and what doesn't seem right, helps keep you protected. For example, when arriving home, look around for unfamiliar cars or things out of place. When going to the store, park in a well-lit location and look around for people who seem out of place or are not coming from or going to the store.

Did You Know?

According to a U.S. Department of Justice survey on stalking, 130,000 victims of stalking stated they had been fired or asked to leave their job because of the stalking.

Trust your instincts. Many times we will feel that something isn't right but ignore the feeling, believing we are being overly sensitive or anxious. Believe in yourself and your gut. Call the police or have a friend accompany you home and wait with you until you are sure your stalker is not lurking around.

Change Your Routine

Daily routines make it easier for a stalker to follow you. If you leave your house each day at the same time, drive the same route to work, visit the same restaurant for lunch each day and then stop at the same store after work, you are telling your stalker exactly where and when to find you. Vary your daily routine to make it more difficult for your stalker to know how to find you. When possible, ask a friend to accompany you. If you are used to doing things on your own, this might be difficult, but the less you are alone, the less you are a target.

Say No

Noreen had dated Shawn for a few weeks but didn't think they had much in common and told Shawn she didn't want to go out anymore. Shawn continued calling Noreen anyway and stopped by her house a few times. Noreen tried to be nice. It wasn't that she disliked Shawn, she just didn't think they clicked. She felt bad and it went against her personality to be mean. Instead she told Shawn she wasn't ready for a relationship and she needed time to think. Shawn didn't take it as an end to the relationship; he thought Noreen wanted a few weeks because she felt so strongly for him that it scared her. He continued to call Noreen for months to see if she was ready for a relationship. Shawn couldn't let go as long as Noreen couldn't say no.

Did You Know?

According to the organization End Stalking In America, Inc., one of the top 10 mistakes victims of stalkers make is trying to let someone down easy rather than saying no when not interested in a relationship.

When you are dealing with someone who has the potential to become obsessive, being nice leads to him hearing what he wants to hear, rather than the message you are giving. It is better to be honest and let the other person know, in no uncertain terms, that you are not interested.

Once you have said no to a stalker, you should cease all further communication. Resist the urge to reason with your stalker. An obsessive person won't be able to comprehend reason, he is too caught up in his own needs and wants. Your comfort, safety, or well-being is not his concern. It is better to avoid any further contact and use some of the strategies in this chapter to protect yourself.

Self-Defense Classes

Self-defense classes teach basic evasive strategies, martial arts training, awareness of your surroundings, and the use of firearms. These classes provide practical knowledge you can use in everyday life and are meant to be easy to employ if you are confronted by your stalker.

Finding Support

We discussed in Chapters 15 and 16 the importance of reaching out to family, friends, and support groups. In this section, we'll go into more detail on where to find organizations to help you overcome obsessive love that has turned dangerous.

Domestic Violence Shelters

Domestic violence shelters offer temporary housing for women and their children when protection is needed from an abusive partner. The services shelters offer are based on the specific organization running the shelter. Some of the services commonly offered are:

- **Temporary housing:** This is frequently a dorm-style shelter for women needing immediate assistance. Some shelters offer a room for each family, others may have a large room with bunk beds. This type of shelter is meant to be temporary, offering women the opportunity to stay for anywhere from one week to 30 days.

- **Transitional-living programs:** Some organizations have agency-owned apartments to house women and their families for an extended period of time. Cost for these programs is often on a sliding scale. There is frequently a waiting list for these types of programs.

- **Counseling:** Domestic violence programs include group and individual counseling for women. Some have educational and play-therapy groups for children. Some organizations also run counseling groups and workshops for men who are victims of abuse.

- **Case management:** Counselors at domestic-abuse shelters may help in completing paperwork for Protection from Abuse orders or refer clients to local legal networks and services to help in obtaining court orders for protection and custody. Some offer court advocates to accompany women to court.

- **Vocational services:** Women who have been abused may have been isolated or prevented from working outside the home. Some domestic violence centers provide job training and vocational counseling to help women get back on their feet.

Most domestic violence shelters have been created to help women and their families as women are more often victims of abuse. These shelters are rarely co-ed. Men, however, can also be victims of abuse. Some organizations will provide temporary shelter in a local hotel for a few nights for men when asked. In addition, centers might offer men's groups, or advocacy and case management for men.

These shelters are in secret places so that your partner cannot find them. To keep the location a secret, you may need to develop a relationship with the staff prior to requesting shelter. This helps protect you because female friends or relatives of partners have been known to call the shelter asking for help in order to get the address for the abuser. If you think you will need this service, call the shelter right away to start a relationship. Some shelters have a waiting list for counseling and shelter.

If you choose to leave an abusive partner, make sure you take time in advance to open a new e-mail account and change passwords for e-mail, banking, or other accounts. Your partner may know or be able to guess your old passwords.

Religious Institutions

Churches and other religious organizations offer a broad array of services to help individuals and families in need. If you are the victim of domestic abuse and need help, you can contact your church to find out what services are provided. If your church does not have any services, the church leader may be able to refer you to other religious institutions in your area that can help.

Churches may offer educational programs on relationships or parenting that can help you better understand your situation. Religious organizations also have any number of support services and groups. Check with your church and other area churches to see if they offer a domestic violence support group.

Many people feel more comfortable speaking with members of the clergy rather than a psychiatrist or someone in the mental health field. *Pastoral counseling* works with individuals, couples, or groups by combining theology and spirituality with psychotherapy. It is different from Christian counseling in that it is not necessarily Bible-based, and is also different from pastoral care, which provides emotional support and guidance to those in need. Clergy who practice pastoral counseling usually have additional training over and above their spiritual training. However, since training is not required, you might want to ask what training the counselor has had. Costs for pastoral counseling can be lower than private psychotherapists or may work on a sliding scale based on income.

Pastoral counseling is conducted by ministers, priests, rabbis, and other religious leaders. Although many states do not require licensing for clergy, many who perform pastoral care have received education in counseling or psychology and are licensed as well.

Essential Takeaways

- Stalkers can make you feel uncomfortable and unsafe in your own home. Taking the time to protect yourself will help you feel safe.

- Information you post on social networking sites can be copied or can get into the hands of your stalker. If you choose to use social networking sites, "friend" only those whom you are sure of their identity.

- Paying attention to your surroundings can help you to immediately notice if someone is following you or is trespassing at your home.

- If you are dealing with someone who might be obsessive, he may misinterpret your responses as interest. If you are not interested in someone, be clear and firm when saying no.

chapter 19

Building a Case

Has your stalker or former partner broken the law?

Talking to the police about your stalker

What to include in a police statement

Gathering evidence

Should you call the police? Should you press charges against your stalker or former partner? Are his actions criminal or simply annoying? Victims of stalking or domestic violence may suffer alone, needlessly, because they aren't sure if what their stalker or former partner has done is a crime or if it is a nuisance in their life they must deal with.

What Constitutes a Crime?

If your stalker calls you once a week, is it a crime? Or do the calls have to be more frequent? If your partner threatens to hurt you, can he be arrested? Or does he actually have to hit you before anything can be done? Before you can decide whether you should call the police or whether you should start building a case against your stalker or former partner, you need to understand the law. This section explains some of the major points of laws surrounding stalking, harassment, and domestic violence.

Stalking Laws

Each state has a specific definition for stalking. There are laws against stalking in every state. You can check with local police or your state attorney general's office for the exact legal definition in your state. Generally, however, stalking is unwanted contact that either contains a direct or implied threat or causes fear in the victim. This can include following someone, phone calls, e-mails, or any other type of repeated communication.

Did You Know?

Most crimes consist of one single act. Stalking, however, consists of a series of actions which are willful, repeated, and unwanted contact.

Usually, charges of stalking can be made in either the place where the communication was received or was made. If you live in San Diego and are receiving phone calls from your former partner in San Francisco, you can still file charges in San Diego. You do not have to travel to where your stalker lives to file the charges or contact the police.

The level of the crime can also vary from state to state. In Pennsylvania, a first offense would be considered a misdemeanor. If your stalker is convicted and continues to stalk you, the second offense would be considered a felony. The stalking would need to be against the same person, family, or household member in order for it to be a second offense.

What Is Harassment?

Harassment laws can also be used against stalkers. Like stalking laws, these vary from state to state, but there are generalities to all harassment laws. You can use the following to determine if you are being harassed:

- Actions that annoy, threaten, intimidate, or cause fear or alarm.

- Unwanted, unwelcome, and uninvited contact.

- Communication that demeans, threatens, or offends a person or creates a hostile environment, such as derogatory comments; racial, ethnic, or gender-based slurs; assault; not allowing someone to move or walk by blocking their path; touching in an offensive manner or touching that is unwanted and unwelcome.

- Following someone in a public place or acting in a way to create fear or intimidation.

- Repeated communication, either in person, by phone, or electronically, that causes annoyance or fear. The person committing harassment does not need to identify himself. Anonymous communications can be considered harassment.

Depending on the circumstances, harassment can be either a misdemeanor or a felony.

Laws for Domestic Violence

The definition of domestic violence or abuse is also different in each state. Some actions, such as hitting, pushing, or choking are obvious physical assaults, but other types of abuse, such as emotional or financial, are not so clear-cut. You can't call the police because your partner called you stupid, but you can call the police if your partner threatened to hurt you or hit you.

Traditionally, domestic violence must include some type of physical violence or threat of violence. Many states require the police to arrest someone if they have a strong belief that there has been physical violence, even when they have not seen the violence take place or if the victim denies abuse. In these states, if the police do not make an arrest, they must file a report explaining why no arrest was made.

In recent years, the definition of domestic violence has been expanded. More narrow views of this crime state that a spouse, current or former, is the only person who can be a victim of domestic violence. Many states, however, have expanded the law to include live-in partners, children, relatives, and intimate partners. Some states also include sexual, emotional, and financial exploitation or abuse in the law. Find out your state's legal definition of domestic violence by contacting your state attorney general or an advocacy group.

Case Study: Ryan

Ryan and Samantha had been married for 10 years. Although Ryan had always been jealous and possessive, it was not until the last few months that he had hit Samantha. She was completely surprised and knew she should leave, but he had never been violent before. One night Ryan was in a complete rage, he was screaming at Samantha and he hit her. Their neighbors heard the loud yelling, including Samantha yelling, "No!" "Stop!" and "Don't hit me." They called the police and reported what they had heard.

When the police showed up, the fight had ended. Samantha was scared and didn't want Ryan to go to jail. She was worried he would be even angrier when he got out. The police questioned both of them and saw Samantha's eyes, swollen from crying, and her puffy lip. They arrested Ryan even though Samantha continued to deny the violence. They left her with information on a women's shelter in the area. By the time Ryan arrived home the next day, Samantha was gone.

Contacting the Police

Whether you are receiving harassing phone calls, have been a victim of vandalism, think your stalker is following you, or have been a victim of domestic abuse, contact the police department. If you call 911, you will be asked if there is an emergency. If you are not in immediate danger, explain this and request that a police car come to your home or wherever you are. Some police departments prefer to complete a report over the phone. If possible, avoid this and let them know you want to speak with an officer in person. Stalking and domestic violence are crimes, and you want the police to take you seriously and treat it accordingly.

There is no magic number of phone calls that constitutes harassment. If you receive calls that include obscene language, threats, or heavy breathing, it is certainly harassment. If you tell someone you are not interested and ask him not to call you again, any further calls would be harassment.

If you are receiving harassing phone calls, you will need to keep a log, noting every phone call received. Your phone company should be able to help with documentation. (Some phone companies will require you to contact the police first.) Your phone company might have requirements as to the number or frequency of calls received.

Tiffany had left Joey several months ago and he was still calling her several times every day. One day he followed her home from work and she spotted his car outside her house several hours later. When Tiffany called the police, they seemed to brush off her concerns. The officer took her name and information quickly and told her there really wasn't anything they could do. Several days later Tiffany noticed Joey's car parked a few houses away. She called the police again, this time insisting an officer come to her home. When the police car pulled up, Joey quickly drove off. Tiffany gave the police officer her report. Talking in person, he seemed much more focused on her story and at the end, told her to call the police immediately if Joey returned.

By insisting on speaking to the officer in person, Tiffany was able to show she was serious about reporting Joey's behaviors. You can also go into the police department to file your report if they do not want to come to your house.

Filing a Report

When a police officer arrives, you will probably be asked to provide identification. In addition, the officer will ask you questions about what happened. You want to give as many details as possible. The following list gives an idea of what type of information is needed.

- Exactly what happened.

- A description of your stalker, if you have one, or the name and current address of your partner.

- Background information, if he was a previous partner, as well as address, phone number, and other details you may know.

- Type of car and other pertinent information to help the police locate the stalker or your partner.

You also want to ask how the police handle these situations. What do they do with the report?

- Do they handle as a report only?

- Is this considered a misdemeanor or a felony?

- Will the report be forwarded to the district attorney's office for review?

- How will the police department follow up?

In some jurisdictions, police departments will contact the other person and request that he not contact you again. Others may charge him with a crime. If you feel any of these actions will make the situation worse, tell the officer of your concerns and ask that this be included in the report. Ask him to notify you after contact has been made.

According to the National Center for Victims of Crime, stalking is a crime in all 50 states and the District of Columbia. In most cases, the first offense of stalking is a misdemeanor, and in more than half of the states, stalking is considered a felony for the second and subsequent offenses. Stalking could also be classified as a felony if the stalker has possession of a deadly weapon, the stalking violates a court order, the stalking is in violation of probation, or if the victim is under 16 years old.

Once the report is completed, ask the officer for the report number. In a few days, contact the police department and ask for a copy of the report. Depending on what happened, it can sometimes take a few reports to combine for a stalking charge. No matter how small you think the incident is, taking the time to report it will help you show a pattern of stalking.

Writing a Statement

Sometimes, the police will question you and complete all paperwork for your complaint. Other times, the police will ask you to write a statement about the incident or incidents. As you are writing your statement, make sure you include all pertinent information:

- Who was involved

- Where the incident took place

- Why the incident took place, including any prior incidents

- Any witnesses who saw the incident

Your statement should be thorough and include what you saw, heard, felt, and did. You should ask any witnesses to write a statement to include with your statement. If you are including new information not given to the police officer originally, you should explain why this information is now being given and why it was not included originally. You might also want to include photographs of property damage or injuries that were not taken at the time of the incident by the police officer.

Documents You Need

Documentation is the most important part of building a case against a stalker or abuser. You will share this information with the prosecutor once this office decides there is enough of a pattern to press charges against your stalker.

Some of the types of documentation you want to put together are:

- Copies of any messages you have received on your phone. If you are not able to save messages, keep a log of every phone call; the phone you received it on (home, work, cell); and the date, time, and what was said (transcribed word for word, if possible). If you have caller ID, document the incoming phone number.

- Copies of your cell phone records showing incoming calls.

- Copies of any police reports of harassment, stalking, or vandalism (even if you can't prove who it was).

- Pictures of any vandalism or signs of intruders, such as trampled flowers in the garden, trash left outside your house, your stalker's car parked near your home or work.

obsession Alert

If your phone number is included in Google's database, anyone can get not only your phone number but directions to your house. To protect yourself, do a Google search of your phone number (XXX-XXX-XXXX). If your phone number is listed, Google will provide a detailed listing including your name and address. You will also have the option to get a map to your location.

To remove your listing, click on the telephone icon on the upper left of the first entry. The page you are taken to will have a link to remove your phone number from the database.

If you are gathering evidence such as notes or gifts that were received, handle each with care, making sure not to smear possible fingerprints or handwriting. Place each one in a separate plastic or paper bag.

Keep a Log

If you are reporting either domestic violence or stalking, chances are, this is not the first incident that has happened. It is important to keep a log of everything that has happened to you. For stalking, it may take several incidents to show a pattern of behavior. If you are seeking a protection order, your log will help you explain why you think you need one. If you have to appear in court, your log will help you remember details and specific events. Your log should include …

- Phone calls—the date, time, what was said.

- Dates of any incidents that have occurred, along with a description of the incident and any photographs.

- Threats, including the date and what was said.

- The date the incident was reported to the police along with the officer's name and badge number, and the police report number.

- Names and contact information of any witnesses.

Your log could be presented in court as evidence. You do not want to include any information that would compromise your safety. For example, if your stalker or former partner does not know where you live, don't put your address in your log.

If you haven't kept a log and are worried that you are missing important information, take a few days to think back over past events. Keep a pad of paper or tape recorder with you so that when you think of something you can write it down. Talk to friends and relatives; some may be able to remind you of certain incidents. Don't worry that you don't have it in precise chronological order. Once you have a list, you can go back and try to put it in order and transfer to your log.

Some victims of stalking say they hadn't realized how much harassment and stalking was happening to them until they began to write it down.

Once they created the log and remembered more incidents, they were amazed that they had not seen what was going on sooner.

Mary thought the phone calls and e-mails she received were simply a nuisance. After her former boyfriend, Rob, threatened her, she contacted the police and started keeping a log. When she thought back over the past few months, she came up with over 100 separate times Rob had tried to contact her through e-mail, phone, or showing up at her job. And she knew this list was incomplete. This log helped both Mary and the police understand how much Rob was harassing her and led to charges being filed against him.

Save Gifts, Notes, or Other Communication

You should also save all communication that you have received from your former partner or your stalker.

- Printouts of any e-mails you received from your stalker
- Any mail or gifts you received from your stalker
- Messages left on your answering machine or cell phone
- Text messages

This type of information can help the police when looking for a pattern of harassment and help a judge determine whether you need a protection order. In many criminal cases, it is up to the victim to gather and protect any information or evidence that can be used in court. You should keep in touch with the police and let them know of all incidents, even after formal charges have been filed.

MISC.

Case Study: Phoebe

Phoebe had dated Seth for only about a month before breaking it off. But six months later, Seth still couldn't let it go. He called Phoebe several times a day and sent flowers to her at work, signing them, "Your boy-friend, Seth." Even though Phoebe had told Seth numerous times she wasn't interested, he kept calling. At first Phoebe was flattered, then she was annoyed.

Phoebe started getting worried when she spotted Seth at the grocery store, at the mall, and at the post office. She was suddenly running into him on a regular basis, even though he lived 30 minutes away. She wondered if he was following her.

When Phoebe contacted the police, they said they couldn't do anything. The officer did suggest she start keeping track of every phone call, and every time she saw Seth or received something from him. Since she had caller ID, Phoebe knew when Seth was calling most of the time and, in the first week, she logged over 25 calls from Seth. She wrote down several calls from numbers she didn't know, but wasn't sure if those calls were from Seth. Over the next month, Phoebe had written down more than 100 phone calls, 2 flower deliveries, and 7 times she saw Seth in various stores.

She went back to the police with the log. The officers were more open to filing charges based on the number of times Seth had contacted Phoebe. He was charged with harassment and was ordered by the court to stop all contact with Phoebe.

Finding Information

In 1990, the first antistalking law was passed in California. Since then every state has adopted a law and improved on those laws throughout the ensuing years. Every state has laws against harassment and domestic violence, and the police are much more sensitive and knowledgeable these days about stalking and domestic violence. Even so, police forces and local prosecutors don't have the time to investigate each phone call you receive or the background of your stalker or former partner. A lot of the leg work, such as completing a log, will be up to you. The tips that follow will help you dig a little deeper to provide law enforcement with as much information as possible to make their job—helping you—easier.

Track down anonymous gifts and flowers. Suppose you receive flowers. There either isn't a card, or it's signed, "With all my love," with no name. You believe you know who the flowers are from, but you can't prove it. Contact the store and ask for information on who placed the order. If they have a surveillance camera, ask for a copy of the video for the date and time the flowers were ordered. Ask the clerk for a description of the person who placed the order. Any information that points to your stalker should go into your log.

obsession Alert

If you don't know who your stalker is, keep a small tape recorder with you. If you should spot someone following you, record as much information as you can such as what the person looks like, what he is wearing, the license plate of the car, and where you saw him. Even though you may think you will remember this information later, it is more accurate if you record it immediately. Give any mail or gifts you have received to the police to have them tested for fingerprints.

Contact your phone company to find out what services are available in your area. Some companies have Call Trace or Last Call Return, which allows you to trace a call or get the phone number of the last call you received. Your local police can request the records from your phone company. Usually, three traces are needed before action can be taken.

Cellular phone bills list all incoming and outgoing calls along with the phone numbers. You may need to request detailed phone bills instead of summaries. Keep all cell phone bills with your documentation and highlight phone calls that came from your stalker or former partner.

Use online court sites. Many jurisdictions have placed information on previous and existing court cases online and anyone can access and search this information. Check to see if there are any previous or pending cases against your stalker or former partner. Some or all of this information may not pertain to your case but can be invaluable background information for the police or prosecutor and can show a pattern of behavior. You can call the police department where the case was and request a copy of the police report or contact the courts to ask for the final disposition of the case.

You can also hire a private investigator. This can be expensive, but if you need documentation to prove who your stalker is, it might be less expensive than having to change jobs, move, or install a complete security system in your home. A private investigator can provide documentation of who is stalking you.

When protecting yourself against a stalker or domestic violence, you, as the victim, need to take responsibility. There are laws to protect you and in the next chapter we will go over how the court system works on your behalf. However, these protections are only part of the solution. You must be vigilant in compiling information and taking steps, such as the ones discussed in Chapter 18, to keep you and your family safe.

Essential Takeaways

- Stalking, harassment, and domestic violence laws are different depending on where you live. Check with your state attorney's office to find out the wording of the laws in your area.

- Some police departments prefer to take reports about stalkers over the phone. If possible, request to have a police officer come and speak to you in person.

- When writing a statement for the police, be as accurate and complete as possible. Include what you did and what other incidents, if any, led up to this incident. Include what you saw, heard, and felt. Include the names of any witnesses.

- Building a case against your stalker often falls to the victim because you are the one who is involved and present during every incident. Keep records and logs of all contact, gifts, or communication you receive and share this information with the police.

chapter 20

Using the Law to Protect Yourself

How orders of protection help keep you safe

What happens if your former partner or stalker doesn't abide by a protection order

Civil complaints help victims receive monetary retribution

Ways to find an attorney

Some obsessive relationships go way beyond obsession and cross the line into criminal behaviors. In this situation, the partner of the obsessive lover needs protection from the law to stay safe. In the last chapter, we went over some of the specific laws surrounding stalking and domestic violence. In this chapter, we'll talk about how the court system works to help victims.

The Court System

The legal system has both criminal and civil divisions. Both stalking and domestic violence cases can have both civil and criminal court proceedings going on for the same action.

Orders of Protection

If you have experienced domestic violence, you can request a protection order issued by the court. This document might also be called a protection from abuse order or restraining order. A judge will order your stalker or former partner to stay away from you and not have any further contact with you. Because it can take several weeks for your case to get to court, you can request an emergency or temporary protection order, which would go into effect as soon as it is signed by a judge. If your stalker or former partner goes against the order, it is considered a crime and he can be arrested.

Even if you have not been the victim of domestic violence, you can still request a court document ordering your stalker to stay away from you. Unfortunately, according to the U.S. Department of Justice, 70 percent of stalkers violate these orders and continue to communicate with, follow, or harass their victims.

Although restraining orders do not guarantee protection, they do serve several purposes:

- Your stalker knows you are serious.

- The police may take further calls from you more seriously.

- Your stalker can be arrested for violating the order.

Stalking and Gender

Although the majority of stalking cases involve a man stalking a woman, according to the Stalking Resource Center, 1 in every 45 men will be stalked sometime in their life. Sixty-four percent of these men will be stalked by someone they know and 30 percent will be stalked by an intimate partner.

When requesting a restraining order, you need to complete the request as fully as possible. If your stalker does not know your address, do not fill this in and request it remain private. You also want to request no contact:

- In person

- By phone

- In writing

- By electronic communication

- By third party

In addition, you want to request the stalker not be able to come within a certain distance of you. This is commonly 100 feet.

Violating an Order of Protection

Restraining orders, or orders of protection, are not meant to punish your former partner. They are used as a tool to prevent further crimes and to keep you out of danger. If you have a restraining order in place, it is up to you to call the police if your former partner has violated the terms of the order. For example, suppose your order of protection states that your former partner is to have no contact with you. He calls you several times. This is a violation of the court order, but the police would have no way of knowing unless you call to report the phone calls.

obsession Alert

Besides the most common stalking behaviors—unwanted phone calls, gifts, or following someone—other stalking behaviors include:

- Manipulative behavior, for example, threatening suicide to elicit a response from you.

- Lying to others about the person being stalked, for example, claiming infidelity.

- Talking about or thinking about the person being stalked as an object, which allows the stalker to not feel empathy for the victim.

- Contacting and befriending your relatives and friends to gather information about you.

The order of protection may state exactly what will happen if your former partner violates the order. Depending on the circumstances, it may be a misdemeanor or a felony and can result in your former partner being taken into custody immediately. He may also need to pay a fine. Laws vary based on where you live. In California, for example, violation of an order of protection can result in jail time of up to one year and a fine of up to $1,000.00. However, if someone knowingly violates an order and the result is someone being physically injured, you face a mandatory jail sentence of at least 48 hours and fines are doubled to $2,000.00.

If you have a restraining order or order of protection, you should report all violations, no matter how small. For some victims, calling the police is very difficult. Chances are, if you are in danger, you have also been emotionally abused and may feel guilty about your previous partner possibly going to jail. Your previous partner might blame you for getting an order of protection just to hurt him. Your guilt can stop you from reporting the violation. Even so, it is important to contact the police for your own protection.

You should carry a copy of the order with you, have one on file at your local police department and the police department near where you work (you will need to bring the police department a copy of the order), give one to your employer, and keep one at home. Normally, once you report the violation, the prosecutor's office will decide whether to press criminal charges.

Civil Complaints

Although not often used, victims of stalkers can file civil complaints as well as criminal complaints. Civil complaints allow victims to collect monetary compensation for damages caused by the stalker or third parties who have contributed to the stalking. Civil complaints can be filed whether or not criminal charges have been filed. These types of complaints are not as rigid as criminal complaints on finding someone liable. In a criminal case, in order to be found guilty, a defendant must be found to be "guilty beyond a reasonable doubt." In civil cases, there must be a "preponderance of evidence."

For example, Marsha's previous boyfriend, Carl, is obsessed with her. She broke up with him several months ago but he won't let it go. He follows Marsha; she has seen him sitting in his car outside her workplace and her home. She has changed her phone number twice but he somehow manages to get it and continues to call her. One night he slashed her tires to prevent her from going out. Marsha has lost time from work, gone to therapy, and purchased a security system for her home. Even if Carl is found guilty of stalking and harassment, these expenses are Marsha's responsibility. Marsha could file a civil complaint against Carl, asking the court to find Carl liable for the expenses she incurred because of his stalking.

Civil vs. Criminal Cases

In a civil case, you are the person bringing charges against your stalker. In a criminal case, the prosecutor files charges. In civil cases, you do not usually need as much evidence as in a criminal case and you have the right to drop the case if you choose. If you file a civil complaint, you are not asking the court to put your stalker in jail but are asking for protection and restitution for any damages. However, if a stalker violates an order issued in civil court, he can still go to jail.

Some states have civil stalking statutes, allowing victims to use stalking as a cause, or legal basis, for filing a civil complaint for damages and expenses. In other states, these cases can be filed under common law. You might need to consult an attorney to find out how to file a civil complaint in your area. Based on your state laws you may be able to recover damages for property damage, emotional distress, loss of income, and other expenses incurred as a direct result of the harassment or stalking.

Do I Need an Attorney?

If you are an obsessive lover and have been charged with stalking or domestic violence, you need an attorney. But should the victim of stalking or domestic violence always hire a lawyer? In certain situations an attorney can help, such as …

- If you are filing for divorce.

- If there are children involved and you want to make sure the custody agreement considers your children's safety.

- If you are filing a civil complaint against your stalker or abuser.

It is not necessary to hire an attorney when getting a divorce. Some people manage to complete the entire process without the extra financial burden of using a lawyer. However, these cases are normally those where the partners are still amicable, don't have much property to divide, do not have children, or can agree on the major issues. Most obsessive relationships do not fall into this category. The obsessive partner rarely lets go easily. In many cases, the obsessive partner will try to hold on in any way possible, and that can mean trying to delay a divorce or continuing to cause controversy. In these cases, an attorney can help to protect your interests and save you from additional emotional or financial problems.

In Chapter 11 we talked about how children can, and often are, used as pawns in obsessive relationships. Obsessive partners may withhold child support, not abide by custody agreements by either not showing up or delaying bringing the children back, or use the children to gather information on what you are doing. Having a lawyer can help protect your children. Although an attorney cannot force your obsessive partner to act in a certain way or to show up on time, the attorney can work with you to include protections for you and your children in a divorce or custody agreement.

David consistently showed up late to pick up his two children on Saturday morning. Gina, his former partner, would end up wasting her morning waiting for him to show up. Her children, ages 5 and 7, would want to know where their father was. Sometimes, Gina thought David did this just to bother her. He seemed happy when she had to rearrange any plans she had made for the day. When they went to court to finalize child custody, her lawyer included that Gina needed to wait only 15 minutes for her former partner to show up; if he didn't arrive within that time, he forfeited seeing his children for that weekend. Gina made sure when the 15 minutes were up, she and the children went out. She only had to do this twice before David got the message and started showing up on time.

Did You Know?

Victims of stalkers or domestic violence can receive monetary damages if they win a civil complaint. Some of the reasons victims have filed civil complaints include:

- Reimbursement of moving expenses

- Counseling not covered by insurance

- Loss of income from either time away from work or losing their job

- Restitution from vandalism to personal property

- Tuition for self-defense classes

If you have suffered financially because of the actions of a stalker or former partner, keep your receipts and expenses and speak with an attorney about filing a civil complaint.

In civil cases, it is not necessary to have an attorney represent you, but in most cases it is advisable. An attorney understands the legal process and is familiar with the law. Civil cases, as explained in the previous section, can provide restitution when you have had to incur expenses or lose income because of your former partner's actions. An attorney can help you build your case and can represent you in court, explaining your argument to the judge.

If you still aren't sure if you need an attorney, ask for a free evaluation. Most good attorneys will be glad to meet with you to discuss your case prior to signing any agreements. You should be able to explain your situation and find out what benefit there is to hiring an attorney during this meeting. Once you decide, find out how much the attorney will cost and what additional fees you need to be aware of, such as court filing fees.

When You Cannot Afford an Attorney

If you have recently ended an obsessive relationship or marriage, you may not have enough money to hire an attorney. You might have difficulty making ends meet. Your obsessive partner may have controlled the finances and left you without any way to pay for your rent and necessities, let alone an attorney. The following are some tips to help you lower the cost of hiring a lawyer.

- Contact advocacy groups and your local bar association in your area to find out if there are attorneys who will work on a reduced rate or pro bono for stalking and domestic violence victims.

- Contact the legal aid department in your county to find out if you are eligible for a free or reduced cost attorney.

- Do as much of the legal work as you can. You can use the attorney to represent you in court, but you can file documents, complete research, and so on. The more you do yourself, the lower your bill will be.

- Compare the difference of hiring an attorney on a retainer basis (making an initial payment) and having the attorney control your case, or keeping control yourself and hiring the attorney on a consultant basis—only when you need expert advice. Keep close track of attorney hours; they add up quickly. Don't be afraid of asking for a detailed accounting.

Case Study: Casey

Casey was in a relationship with an abusive partner for over five years. When she finally left, she walked out with the clothes she was wearing and one small suitcase. Her partner, Eric, was furious. He wanted Casey to come back home. He closed all of their bank accounts and put the money into an account that was in his name alone. He changed the locks on the doors so she could not get back into the apartment. He thought if he took away Casey's options and resources, she would return.

Casey was determined to stay away. She temporarily moved in with her parents and spent each day looking for work so she could afford her own apartment. With no money and no job, Casey was sure she could not afford an attorney to help her recover the money Eric had taken out of the bank account, get some of the furniture and personal belongings in the house, or get a divorce.

When Casey contacted the local bar association, they gave her the name of two lawyers who represented victims of domestic violence pro bono. Casey was shocked. She was able to have a lawyer without paying anything. Her attorney immediately filed a civil complaint to request Casey be given one half of the money in the bank accounts on the day she left, one half of the furniture, and time for her to collect her personal belongings. He also started divorce proceedings. Casey had spent so long in a controlling, obsessive relationship, she had a hard time believing people were so caring and willing to help.

The cost of hiring an attorney is intimidating. It might seem impossible that you will ever have enough money to afford the legal fees. But the cost of not having an attorney can be high as well. If your former obsessive partner is refusing to allow you access to bank accounts, an attorney might be able to help. If your stalker is taking away your freedom, the cost of a lawyer may be well worth the budgeting.

Questions to Ask

As mentioned in the previous section, a good lawyer will give you a free initial consultation. Use this time to make sure the attorney is competent and is someone with whom you can work. The relationship between your lawyer and you is a partnership; you need to be able to trust that he has your best interests in mind and that you will be able to work closely with him to help prepare your case. You need to be able to work together rather than against each other.

During your initial evaluation, you want to find out about the attorney's past experience. You want to know his style; is he open to negotiating, does he use hardball techniques, or will he only talk with the "other side" in a courtroom. You also want to be sure you feel comfortable and can communicate with the lawyer. The following are some questions you can ask before deciding which attorney to hire.

- How many years experience does he have? How long has he been taking domestic violence, stalking, or divorce cases?

- How will he communicate with you and update you on your case? Will you receive phone calls? E-mails? How often will you be updated?

- How long does he expect the case to take?

- What are the possible outcomes? What outcome does he expect and why?

- What are his opinions on cases like yours? Does he have preconceived ideas about stalking, domestic violence, child custody, or divorce? Is he open minded enough to treat your case as unique? Is he willing to listen?

- How will you be billed? Will there be a set fee (for example, some attorneys charge a set fee to complete a divorce) or will you be billed by the hour? If you are being billed by the hour, will you receive regular updates on how many hours he is spending on your case and a breakdown of what he is doing?

- Is there work you can do, such as filing paperwork or doing research, to help reduce the bill? If paralegals or other assistants complete some of the work, is it billed at a lower rate?

- What other expenses, such as filing fees, should you expect?

- If you are being charged an hourly rate, is there an estimate of how much it will cost? Is the estimate done in writing?

Mixed Feelings

Be prepared to have mixed feelings about starting divorce proceedings. No matter how emotionally prepared you are to be divorced, a breakup is the end of your dreams of love everlasting. You believed, at least at one time, that you were going to spend your life with your partner. The finality of divorce forces you to accept the end of the relationship. Even people who are ending a bad relationship have mixed feelings, or sometimes feel anxious, sad, and confused. Accept these reactions as normal and they will lessen as time goes on. Believe in yourself and, if your relationship was unhealthy, know that your life will be better in the end.

Before meeting with a potential attorney, think about what you want to accomplish. You can't explain your case, or why you think you have a case, unless you know the outcome you're looking for. If you're thinking about a civil suit against a stalker, what type of settlement would you accept? If you are filing for divorce, are there financial assets you want to share or do you simply want to be done with a relationship? If you are filing for child custody, what is your idea of an ideal custody agreement? Although you may not end up with the exact outcome you want, it helps to have an idea of what you want before meeting with an attorney.

Places to Find a Lawyer

You can use the phone book or an Internet search to develop a list of potential attorneys. This will give you a lot of choices, but no way to narrow down the list without spending time calling and talking to each person. Here are some additional suggestions for locating the right attorney for your case.

- **Referrals:** Ask friends, relatives, and co-workers. If you are filing for divorce, chances are someone you know has also gone through a divorce. Who was their attorney? Did they like her? Why or why not? Asking people you know and trust can help you find a few attorneys to choose from.

- **Advocacy groups and nonprofit organizations:** Many *advocacy groups* offer referrals to local attorneys. Some may know of lawyers that will work on a reduced-fee schedule for victims of stalking or domestic violence. Talk to the group about your situation and find out whom they would recommend.

- **Bar association:** Your local bar association should be able to give you referrals to some attorneys who specialize in cases similar to yours.

- **Chamber of commerce:** If you have a chamber of commerce in your area, they can usually provide referrals. The attorneys they refer are normally members of the organization.

- **Lawyer referral services:** There are lawyer referral services through your local bar association or on a number of different websites. Some services prescreen attorneys based on their criteria or refer based on the attorney's specialty.

An **advocacy group** is a special-interest group that usually offers services to individuals such as support groups, referrals, and other resources. These groups also frequently work to help change public policy and educate the public about a specific cause.

No matter how you find an attorney, don't solely rely on the word of others; use the information from others as a way to narrow down your choices. Once you have three or four attorneys, call and have a brief conversation with each. Set up a time for a free evaluation. Once you have interviewed several attorneys, you should be able to choose one who best fits your needs.

Essential Takeaways

- An order of protection, or restraining order, can prohibit your former partner from contacting you and spell out what will happen if the order is violated.

- A victim of stalking or domestic violence can file a civil case to collect monetary compensation for damages incurred or time lost from work.

- Not everyone filing for divorce requires an attorney, but if your former partner can't let go of your relationship, is stopping you from accessing bank accounts, or is harassing you, it is probably best to hire a lawyer.

- There are many different ways to find an attorney. Take the time to interview several lawyers to find the one who best fits your situation.

Glossary

advocacy groups   A special interest group that works to change public policy, educate the public about a cause, and provide resources and support to those impacted by the cause.

affirmations   A declaration that something is true. They are often used to overcome negative thinking patterns.

civil complaint   A lawsuit brought about by one person against another person alleging damages and requesting monetary restitution for personal loss or property damage.

clinical depression   A medical illness that affects both the body and the mind. It is more than having the blues. Includes low mood, problems eating, and sleeping, which lasts at least two weeks. Typically treated with anti-depressants and psychotherapy.

codependency   When people are focused upon their partner's problems and neglect their own needs and do not focus upon their own problems. Codependents are attracted to partners struggling with a variety of problems, primarily addictions, or other mental health problems like those of obsessive lovers.

cognitive behavioral therapy (CBT)   Therapy based on the concept that how we think is related to how we act. CBT focuses on present behaviors rather than past events. The goal is to change the thought process behind the actions.

counseling   Sessions with a professional to provide guidance or advice when making a decision or choosing a course of action for your life.

couples counseling   Working with a counselor or therapist to recognize problems within a relationship and look for more effective ways to reconcile conflicts and improve communication.

criminal complaint   Charges filed by the prosecutor which can result in fines or jail time.

cyberstalking   Harassment using different electronic methods, such as e-mail, social networking sites, instant messaging, or posting messages on a web site.

domestic violence   Physical or emotional violence committed by one member of a household against another member. Also known as spousal abuse or intimate partner violence (IPV).

dysfunctional   Impairment in the ability to function. Dysfunctional relationships are those where conflict occurs regularly and the one partner acts in a way that is accommodating to the controlling partner.

electronic communication   Contact with another person via cell phone, text message, e-mail, or on the Internet through forums or social networking sites.

emotionally oppressed   To feel overwhelmed mentally or physically to the point of not being able to act.

enabling   Helping or giving the means for people to do something destructive to themselves.

financial abuse   Controlling behaviors that are meant to cause financial dependency of the abused on the abuser. This is sometimes listed under emotional abuse and can include not allowing the partner to work, withholding money, and restricting access to financial resources.

harassment   Using threatening behaviors to torment, annoy, or bother another person.

healthy love   A relationship built on mutual respect and open communication.

high-risk behaviors   Behaviors, actions, or activities done without regard for safety or health.

infatuation   An excessive passion, love, or admiration for another person which is usually short lived.

jealousy   The negative emotion felt when thinking of your partner being with someone else.

love addiction   An addiction to the feeling of being in love. A person with a love addiction will immediately seek to replace a lost relationship.

lust   An intense, highly charged physical attraction, combined with longing for an intimate sexual relationship.

manipulative behaviors   Behaviors used to try to get someone to do something your way or something you want to do. Behaviors differ depending on the person, for example, using guilt to get the other person to do what you want, pestering until you get your way, being nice just to get something in return, or using intimidation to get your way.

mediation   A way to reconcile differences using a neutral third party. The mediator works with both parties to find solutions and compromises to issues surrounding custody, property, or finances.

obsessions   An idea or thought that intrudes or continually occupies a person's mind.

obsessive compulsive disorder (OCD)   An anxiety disorder characterized by obsessive thoughts, ideas, or images followed by compulsive actions used to reduce the obsessions.

obsessive love   An all-consuming preoccupation with another person.

orders of protection   A document mandated by the courts limiting or prohibiting contact with another person.

pastoral counseling   Conducted by ministers, priests, rabbis, and other religious leaders, pastoral counseling combines theology and spirituality with psychotherapy. It is different from Christian counseling in that it is not necessarily Bible-based, and different from pastoral care, which provides emotional support and guidance to those in need. Although many states do not require licensing for clergy, many who perform pastoral counseling have received education in counseling or psychology and may be licensed as well.

personal accountability   Taking responsibility for your role in how your life has turned out.

personal boundaries   Guidelines, rules, or limits you set up within your relationships with other people to keep you safe. Some examples of personal boundaries are: you may not hit me, I will not fight with you if you are going to yell, don't call me after 11:00 at night, don't call me at work.

possessiveness   In relationships, a desire to own or dominate the partner.

psychotherapy   Using psychology to treat behavior disorders or mental illness. It is sometimes referred to as "talk therapy," but uses insight, suggestions, encouragement, and instruction to help you make positive changes in your life.

relational dependency   The unhealthy need to be in a relationship.

relationship log   A log containing information about your relationship in an effort to discern patterns of behavior.

restraining order   Sometimes called orders of protection, a legal document limiting or prohibiting contact with another person, often a previous partner.

romantic love   A term referring to feeling euphoric when being near or even thinking about your partner. It often is experienced early in relationships.

self-esteem   The opinion or feelings you have of yourself.

self-image   How we view ourselves. A self-image contains words we believe describe our individual traits. You might describe yourself as dependable, reliable, trustworthy, and outgoing. This is your self-image. Your self-image is created through personal interactions, achievements, and perceived failures. A self-image can be positive or negative.

self-punishment   Also known as self-harm or self-injury, it is intentional punishment or harm inflicted against yourself.

self-recrimination   Blaming and correcting yourself. It is associated with persistent blaming for current or past perceived failures.

self-talk   Internal communication where you give yourself feedback, both positive and negative on your thoughts and behaviors.

situational depression   A short-term period of depressive symptoms caused by life events.

social networking sites   Sites which allow people to interact with one another, mimicking offline relationships and networking.

social norms   Rules within a society or group that are used to determine acceptable and unacceptable behaviors. These rules may be unwritten but are understood within the group and are different depending on the individual culture of the group. Social norms define appropriate social interactions.

stalking   Unwanted, repeated contact in person or by following, through phone calls, electronic communication, notes and gifts, or third-party contacts.

support groups   A group of nonprofessionals who share a common problem or concern (sometimes the group is led by a professional) and provide emotional support through the sharing of experiences.

therapy   Treatment for a condition or help in resolving personal issues.

vandalism   The deliberate defacement, mutilation, or destruction of another person's property.

Resources

National Organizations

American Psychological Association
750 First Street N.E.
Washington, DC 20002
1-800-374-2721
www.apa.org

Break the Cycle
5200 W. Century Blvd., Suite 300
Los Angeles, CA 90045
310-286-3366
www.breakthecycle.org

Corporate Alliance to End Partner Violence
2416 East Washington Street, Suite E
Bloomington, IL 61704
309-664-0667
www.caepv.org

Emerge
2464 Massachusetts Avenue, Suite 101
Cambridge, MA 02140
617-547-9879
www.emergedv.com

Family Violence Prevention Fund
383 Rhode Island Street, Suite 304
San Francisco, CA 94103
415-252-8900
www.endabuse.org

National Center for Victims of Crimes
Stalking Resource Center
2000 M Street N.W.
Washington, DC 20036
202-457-8700
www.ncvc.org/SRC/Main.aspx

National Coalition Against Domestic Violence
1120 Lincoln Street, Suite 1603
Denver, CO 80203
303-839-1852
www.ncadv.org

National Domestic Violence Hotline
1-800-799-7233
www.ndvh.org

National Sexual Violence Resource Center
123 North Enola Drive
Enola, PA 17025
1-877-739-3895
www.nsvrc.org

Government Agencies and Information

National Institute of Justice
810 Seventh Street N.W.
Washington, DC 20531
www.ojp.usdoj.gov/nij

United States Department of Justice
950 Pennsylvania Avenue N.W.
Washington, DC 20530
202-514-2000
www.justice.gov

Advocacy Resources and Legal Information

American Coalition for Fathers and Children
1718 M. Street N.W. #187
Washington, DC 20036
1-800-978-3237
www.acfc.convio.net

Legal Resource Center on Violence Against Women
Takoma Park, MD
301-270-1550
www.lrcvaw.org

The National Center for Men
P.O. Box 531
Coram, NY 11727
631-476-2115
www.nationalcenterformen.org

Women's Law Project
55 Washington Street, Suite 614
Brooklyn, NY 11201
215-928-9801
www.womenslawproject.org

Psychologists, Therapists, and Counselors Professional Directories

American Psychological Association Find-A-Psychologist
www.locator.apa.org

AtHealth.com
www.athealth.com/Consumer/directory/

Find-a-Therapist
www.find-a-therapist.com/

GoodTherapy.org
www.goodtherapy.org/

Psychology.com

www.psychology.com/therapist/

Psychology Today

www.therapists.psychologytoday.com/rms/

Books

Bireda, Martha R. *Love Addiction: A Guide to Emotional Independence.* Oakland: New Harbinger, 1990.

Buss, David M. *The Dangerous Passion: Why Jealousy is as Necessary as Love and Sex.* New York: Free Press, 2000.

Forward, Susan. *Obsessive Love: When It Hurts Too Much to Let Go.* New York: Bantam, 2002.

———. *Obsessive Love: When Passion Holds You Prisoner.* New York: Bantam Books, 1991.

Hindy, Carl G. *If This is Love, Why Do I Feel so Insecure.* New York: Fawcett Crest, 1989.

Janov, Arthur. *The Biology of Love.* Amherst: Prometheus Books, 2000.

Johnson, Brad W. *Crazy Love: Dealing with Your Partner's Problem Personality.* Atascadero: Impact Publishers, 2007.

Mellody, Pia. *Facing Love Addiction: Giving Yourself the Power to Change the Way You Love.* San Francisco: HarperSanFrancisco, 1992.

Moore, John D. *Confusing Love with Obsession: When Being in Love Means Being in Control.* Center City: Hazelden Publishing, 2006.

Norwood, Robin. *Women Who Love Too Much: When You Keep Wishing and Hoping He'll Change.* New York: Gallery, 2008.

Orion, Doreen. *I Know You Really Love Me: A Psychiatrist's Account of Stalking and Obsession.* New York: Dell, 1998.

Peabody, Susan. *Addiction to Love: Overcoming Obsession and Dependency in Relationships.* Berkeley: Celestial Arts, 2005.

Schaeffer, Brenda. *Is It Love or Is It Addiction*. Center City: Hazelden, 2009.

Tallis, Frank. *Love Sick: Love as a Mental Illness*. New York: Thunder Mouth Press, 2005.

Websites and Blogs

American Bar Association Commission on Domestic Violence
740 15th Street, N.W., 9th Floor
Washington, DC 20005
www.abanet.org/domviol/home.html

DADs America
www.dadsamerica.org

HealthyPlace.com
Interview with Dr. Doreen Orion on Stalking and Obsessive Love
www.healthyplace.com/abuse/transcripts/stalking-and-obsessive-love/menu-id-52/

Lesbian Relationship Challenges Support Group
www.healingclub.com/

MentalHelp.net—Dating
www.mentalhelp.net/poc/view_doc.php?type=advice&id=391&at=1&cn=287

Our Family Wizard
www.ourfamilywizard.com/ofw/index.cfm

Paths to Empowerment—Melanie Tonia Evans
www.melanietoniaevans.com/articles/relationship-addiction.htm

Violence Against Women Online Resources
www.vaw.umn.edu

Women Against Domestic Violence
www.wadv.org

WomensLaw.org
www.womenslaw.org

Online Communities

CoDA Online
www.forums.onlinecoda.net

DailyStrength
www.dailystrenth.org

The Healing Club
www.healingclub.com

Obsessive Love on Facebook
www.facebook.com/pages/Obsessive-Love

oJar.com
www.ojar.com

Relationship Support Groups
www.relationship.supportgroups.com

StalkingVictims.com
www.stalkingvictims.com

Appendix C

References

American Bar Association. "Survey of Recent Statistics." *American Bar Association Commission on Domestic Violence*, date unknown. new.abanet.org/domesticviolence/Pages/Statistics.aspx.

Baram, Marcus. "How Do You Stop a Stalker From Killing You?" *ABC News*, April 5, 2007. abcnews.go.com/US/story?id=3007276&page=1.

Baum, Naomi. "A Therapist's Comments on Obsessive Love." *WholeFamily.com*, May 11, 2005. www.wholefamily.com/aboutteensnow/feelings/love/love_lost/therapist.html.

BBC News. "Falling in Love Drives You Mad." *BBC News*, July 29, 1999. news.bbc.co.uk/2/hi/science/nature/407125.stm.

Beattie, Melody. *Codependent No More: How to Stop Controlling Others and Start Caring for Yourself.* Harper/Hazelden 1987.

Berkeley Police Department. "Stalking." www.ci.berkeley.ca.us/police/department/sexcrimes/stalking.html.

Blue, Laura, "Recipe for Longevity: No Smoking, Lots of Friends," *Time Magazine*, July 28, 2010. www.time.com/time/health/article/0,8599,2006938,00.html.

California Criminal Defense Lawyers. "California Restraining Order Violation." *California Criminal Defense Lawyers*, 2010. www.mycaliforniadefenselawyer.com/criminal-charges/restraining-order-violation/.

California State University, Fresno. "Cyberstalking." *CSU, Fresno,* 2008. Women's Reource Center, California State University. www. csufresno.edu/vpp/stalking/cyberstalking.shtml.

Carey, Bjorn. "The Rules of Attraction in the Game of Love." Live Science, February 13, 2006. www.livescience.com/health/ 060213_attraction_rules.html.

CBS News. "1 Out of 100 Americans are Being Stalked." *CBS News,* January 13, 2009. cbs3.com/national/stalking.survey. americans.2.906842.html.

Chakraburtty, Amal, reviewer. "Mental Health and Psychotherapy." *WebMD,* February 9, 2009. www.webmd.com/anxiety-panic/guide/ mental-health-psychotherapy.

Davis, Jeanie Lerche. "Signs of a Codependent Relationship." *WebMD,* August 14, 2007. www.webmd.com/sex-relationships/features/ signs-of-a-codependent-relationship.

Dictionary.com, unabridged, s.v. "jealousy." dictionary.reference.com/ browse/jealousy.

Discovery Communications, Inc. "The Dawn of Stalking: The Murder of Rebecca Shaeffer." 2010. *Investigation Discovery,* 2010. investigation.discovery.com/investigation/hollywood-crimes/ schaeffer/rebecca-schaeffer.html.

Edelson, Stephen. "Understanding and Treating Self-Injurious Behavior." *Autism Research Insitute,* 2004.

Elliott, Roger Innes, and Mark Justin Tyrell. *Self Confidence Trainer: Train Yourself to Greater Self Confidence and Improved Self Esteem.* Oban, Scotland: Uncommon Knowledge, LTD, 2002.

End Stalking in America. "Filing a Police Report." *ESIA,* 2010. www.esia. net/Filing_a_report.htm.

———. "Top Ten Mistakes That Stalking Victims Make." *ESIA,* 2010. www.esia.net/Victim_Mistakes.htm. BIBLIOGRAPHY \l 1033 Fong, Tillie, "Body Identified as Suspect in Wheat Ridge

Shooting," *Rocky Mountain News,* February 20, 2009. www.
rockymountainnews.com/news/2009/feb/20/gunman-wanted-
killing-ex-wheat-ridge-believed-be-d/.

Fitzgerald, Matthew. "Are You In Love or Lust?" 2009. *AskMen.com,* 2009.
www.askmen.com/dating/curtsmith_100/110_dating_advice.html.

Ford, Elaine. "How to Deal with a Controlling Spouse, Boyfriend
or Girlfriend." *ControlingPartners.com,* 2008. www.
controllingpartners.com/.

Forwad, Susan, and Craig Buck. *Obsessive Love: When it Hurts too Much
to Let Go.* New York: Bantam Books, 1991.

Goldstein, Marianne. "Obsessive Love Ruins a Marriage." *CBS News,*
May 10, 2009. www.cbsnews.com/stories/2007/05/10/earlyshow/
leisure/celebspot/main2788142.shtml.

Grohol, John M. "Facebook Reinforces Relationship Jealousy."
PsychCentral.com, 2009. psychcentral.com/blog/
archives/2009/08/11/facebook-reinforces-relationship-jealousy/.

Halpern, Howard. *How to Break Your Addiction to a Person.* New York:
Bantam Books, 2004.

Hannig, Paul J. "Obsessive Love Disorder: A Profile."
PsychotherapyHELP, 2010. www.nvo.com/psych_help/
obsessivelovedisorder/.

Harper, Douglas. "stalk (v1.)." *Online Etymology Dictionary,* 2010. www.
etymonline.comindex.php?term=stalk.

Hechter, Michael, and Karl-Dieter Opp. *Social Norms.* New York: Russell
Sage Foundation Publications, 2001.

Hendrix, Harville. *Getting the Love You Want.* New York: Henry Holt, 1988.

Herkov, Michael. "What Causes Sexual Addiction." *PsychCentral,*
December, 2006. psychcentral.com/lib/2006/what-causes-sexual-
addiction/.

Hill, Amelia. "How to be Happy in Life: Let Out Your Anger." 1 Mar
2009. *Guardian.co.uk,* March 1, 2009. www.guardian.co.uk/
science/2009/mar/01/psychology-anger-business-workplace-study.

Jayne, Pamela. *Ditch That Jerk.* Alameda: Hunter House, 2000.

Jones, Amy, and Susan Schechter. *When Love Goes Wrong,* New York: HarperCollins, 1992.

Kingham, Michael, and Harvey Gordon. "Aspects of Morbid Jealousy." *Advances in Psychiatric Treatment,* 2004. apt.rcpsych.org/cgi/content/full/10/3/207.

Lee, John Alan. *The Colors of Love.* New York: Bantam Books, 1977.

Maack, L. H., and P. E. Mullen. "Jealousy, Pathological Jealousy and Aggression." Aggression and Dangerousness (1985): 103-126.

MedicineNet.com. "Sexual Addiction." www.medicinenet.com/sexual_addiction/article.htm.

Mental Health America. "Co-dependency." *MHA,* 2010. www.mentalhealthamerica.net/go/codependency.

Merrill, David B. "Alcoholism and Alcohol Abuse." *Medline Plus,* April 5, 2010. www.nlm.nih.gov/medlineplus/ency/article/000944.htm.

Mitchell, Kirk, "Stalking Murder Victim, Suspect Spoke of "Happy Reunion," *The Denver Post,* February 20, 2009. www.denverpost.com/news/ci_11744425.

Moore, John D. "Too Close for Comfort." *Mental-Health Matters,* February 3, 2009. www.mental-health-matters.com/index.php?option=com_content&view=article&id=178.

Mountain State Centers for Independent Living. "Positive Self Image and Self Esteem." www.mtstcil.org/skills/image-intro.html.

National Center for Victims of Crime. "Cyberstalking." *NCVC,* 2003. www.ncvc.org/ncvc/main.aspx?dbName=DocumentViewer&DocumentID=32458.

———. "Stalking Facts." *Stalking Resource Center,* 2010. www.ncvc.org/src/main.aspx?dbID=DB_statistics195.

National Institute of Mental Health. "Anxiety Disorders." *NIMH,* March 18, 2010. www.nimh.nih.gov/health/publications/depression/complete-index.shtml.

Nova Southeastern University. "Conflict Resolution Strategies, Resolving Roommate and Interpersonal Conflict." *NSU,* 2010. www.nova.edu/studentmediation/forms/conflict_resolution_strategies.pdf.

Nunes, Nalu de Araujo. "Marital Problems and Marital Satisfaction: An Examination of a Brazilian Sample." Master's thesis, Brigham Young University, December, 2008.

Oprah Online. "Begin to Set Personal Boundaries." *Oprah.com,* February 5, 2001. www.oprah.com/spirit/Begin-to-Set-Personal-Boundaries_1.

Orion, Doreen, guest speaker. "Stalking and Obsessive Love." Moderated by David Roberts. *HealthyPlace.com,* 2010. www.healthyplace.com/abuse/transcripts/stalking-and-obsessive-love/menu-id-52/.

Parr, Ben. "Study: Facebook Increases Jealousy in Relationships." *Mashable,* August 9, 2009. mashable.com/2009/08/09/facebook-relationship-jealous/.

Pathé, M., and P. E. Mullen. "The Impact of Stalkers on Their Victims." *The British Journal of Psychiatry,* 1997: 12-17.

Paymar, Michael. *Violent No More.* Alameda: Hunter House, 1993.

Pensel, Fred. "When People Become Obsessed with Other People." *WestSuffolk Psych,* March 2010. westsuffolkpsych.homestead.com/ObsessiveLove.html.

Perlman, Daniel, reviewer. "Sexual Addiction." 24 September 2007. *Cleveland Clinic Department of Psychiatry and Psyhology,* September 24, 2007. www.medicinenet.com/sexual_addiction/article.htm.

Proctor, Mike. *How to Stop a Stalker.* Amherst: Prometheus Books, 2003.

Sanchez, Jessica. "Healthy Relationships." *California Institute of Technology,* April, 2004. www.healtheducation.caltech.edu/healthy_relationships.html.

Schechter, Susan, and Ann Jones. *When Love Goes Wrong.* New York: Harper Paperbacks, 1993.

Seligman, Martin E. P. "The Effectiveness of Psychotherapy." *American Psychologist*, 1995. horan.asu.edu/cpy702readings/seligman/seligman.html.

Silva, J. A., et al. "The Dangerousness of Persons with Delusional Jealousy." *Psychiatry and the Law*, 1994: 30-33.

Sophia, et al. Pathological Love: Impulsivity, Personality, and Romantic Relationship. Study, Sao Paulo, Brazil, 2008, CNS Spectr. 2009 May. 14(5):268-74. http://www.ncbi.nlm.nih.gov/pubmed/19407726.

Smith, Melinda, and Ellen Jaffe-Gill. "Obsessive Compulsive Disorder." *HelpGuide.org*, May, 2010. www.helpguide.org/mental/obsessive_compulsive_disorder_ocd.htm.

Voo, Jocelyn. "Love Addiction—How to Break It." *CNN.com*, October 16, 2007. www.cnn.com/2007/LIVING/personal/10/09/end.relationship/index.html.

Yoder, Rachel. "Strung Out on Love and Checked In for Treatment." *New York Times*, June 11, 2006. www.nytimes.com/2006/06/11/fashion/sundaystyles/11love.html?pagewanted=1&_r=1.

Washington, D.C.: U.S. Department of Justice, 2008. "Stalking Victimization in the United States."

Womens Health: U.S. Department of Health and Human Services. "Stress and Your Health." www.womenshealth.gov/faq/stress-your-health.cfm.

WomensLaw.org. "Orders of Protection." *WomensLaw.org*, January 19, 2010. www.womenslaw.org/laws_state_type.php?id=561&state_code=NY.

———. "Overview of Civil vs. Criminal Law." *WomensLaw.org*, January 19, 2010. www.womenslaw.org/laws_state_type.php?id=560&state_code=NY.

Index

W-X-Y-Z

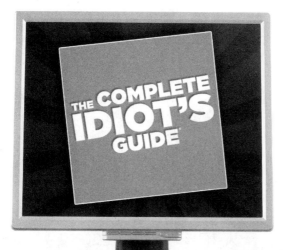

CHECK OUT THESE
BEST-SELLERS

More than 450 titles available at booksellers and online retailers everywhere!

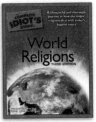

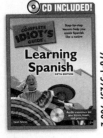

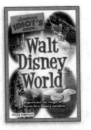